The Fuller Worthies' Library.

THE

WORKS

IN

VERSE AND PROSE COMPLETE

OF

THE RIGHT HONOURABLE

FULKE GREVILLE, LORD BROOKE:

FOR THE

FIRST TIME COLLECTED AND EDITED:

WITH

Memorial-Introduction: Essay, critical and elucidatory:

AND

NOTES AND FACSIMILES.

BY THE

REV. ALEXANDER B. GROSART,

ST. GEORGE'S, BLACKBURN, LANCASHIRE.

IN FOUR VOLUMES.

VOL. IV.

CONTAINING

THE PROSE:
LIFE OF SIR PHILIP SIDNEY WITH ADDITIONS AND
VARIOUS READINGS—
LETTER TO AN HONOURABLE LADY—
LETTER TO VARNEY IN FRANCE—
SPEECH FOR BACON—
ACCOUNT OF MSS. IN POSSESSION OF THE EARL OF WARWICK AND
BROOKE, WITH CORRECTIONS AND VARIOUS READINGS
FROM THEM—
INDICES.

PRINTED FOR PRIVATE CIRCULATION.

1870.

106 COPIES ONLY.   AMS PRESS, INC.
NEW YORK
1966

AMS PRESS, INC.
New York, N.Y. 10003
1966

Manufactured in the United States of America

1. From 'Excellencie of Monarchie' compared with 'Aristocracie' (st.588) shewing the Author's corrections of a Transcript

II. Signature from 'Dairy Account. December, 1601.

III. From "Of Religion" wholly in the Author's autograph (st. 1st)

What makes those manie lawes, these regnes of Power,
Wherewith mankind thus fettered is and bound!
These diverse worships which mens soules deflower,
Nature, and the God with noveltie confound!
Tis ignorance, sinne, infidelitie;
By which we fall from our Creation be.

IV. Lord Brookes corrections in old age (Cælica Sonnet, 77.)

Made slaves, not subiects, they to ~~[illegible]~~ Tyrants are.
the long stands

Contents.

		PAGE.
I.	Introductory Note	v—xii.
II.	Life of Sir Philip Sidney, with additions and corrections from the Cambridge MSS....................	1—224.
III.	Additions, as Appendix	225—229.
	A. One of the "Two Pastoralls made by Sir Philip Sidney ".	225—228.
	B. Pepys' account of buying the "Life".	228—229.
	C. Gamage's Epigram on Zutphen..	229.
IV.	Letter to an Honorable Lady [Lady Rich]	231—299.
V.	Letter to Varney ' residing in France' with various readings from an Oxford MS.	301—309.
VI.	Short Speech for Bacon : with Introduction containing additional Materials for a fuller ' Life'.	311—329.
VII.	Description of the MSS. at Warwick Castle, with various readings from them............................	331—337.
VIII.	Indices:	
	1. Things and Thoughts	387—410.
	2. Names : persons and places ..	411—428.
	3. Words : noticeable and rare ..	429—438.

*** Facsimiles of Lord Brooke's handwriting, to face title-pages of the present Volume (Vol. IV. large paper).

Introductory Note.

T HE Prose Writings of Lord Brooke consist of

(*a*). "The Life of the renowned S^r. Philip Sidney :"

(*b*). " A Letter to an Honorable Lady :"

(*c*). " A Letter to Greuill Varney," on his " Travells :"

(*d*). " Short Speech" for Bacon :

The whole of these are faithfully reproduced in the present closing volume of the Works. I have to submit a few remarks on each :

a. THE LIFE OF SIDNEY. LORD BROOKE himself never called this a " *Life* of Sidney ".[1] He intended it simply as an auto-biographic introduction to his own Poetry and Poem-Plays in vindication of the words in his general title-page " written in his Youth and familiar Exercises with SIR PHILIP

---

[1] The heading in the Cambridge MS. is simply " A Dedication to S^r. Philip Sidney ".

SIDNEY." Thus would he "eternize" their friendship and reveal the influences under which his own Writings were composed. Sir Philip cordially reciprocated Lord Brooke's pathetic boast. Witness, among many other proofs, his Verses in celebration of the triple-friendship between himself, GREVILLE and DYER. The well-worded Poem will be found in our Appendix. [A.]

The somewhat bombastic title-page of the original (posthumous) edition (1652) of the "Life", raised too high expectation, and since, has made readers feel disappointed. Taken for what its Author intended, viz., his contribution from personal knowledge, to an ultimate "Life" of Sidney, it will be pronounced most valuable by all competent to form an estimate, although the historical student must turn elsewhere for fuller details and larger discussions of the facts and principles of the short and lovely life. These have been amply though not exhaustively furnished in the various books and memoirs named and used by us : [Vol. I. pp XIX-xx, XXIV, *et alibi.*] It were to misunderstand my duty as an Editor to seek to so supplement this (mis-named) "Life" as to present in full and under recent lights and shadows the beautiful and imperishable story. But while disclaiming this, I have been enabled to furnish a text infinitely superior to the original one of 1652 and equally so to Sir Egerton Brydges' Lee Priory Press reprint—exceptionally slovenly and unworthy. By the great kindness and personal painstaking of my friend Mr. W. A. Wright, M.A. of Trinity College, Cambridge, I correct from the MS. under his care, well-nigh innumerable blunders, and supply not a few most interesting additions. One of the latter—a tribute hitherto suppressed, to Sir Francis Drake—is of supreme value. Our foot-notes shew *various readings* and every (minutest) addition or change. Let it be remembered that in the foot-notes P, is = the printed copy of 1652 : M = the Manuscript of Trinity College, Cambridge R. 7, 32, 33.

I have been favoured by John Harvey Esq of Ickwell Bury, Bedfordshire, with a most careful transcript of a strikingly interesting and touching Manuscript, viz, a long Narrative—extending to eleven closely written folios—of the illness and death of Sir Philip Sidney. It is headed, "The manner of Sr. Philip Sidney's Death. Written by the right hono^ble Foulke, Lord Brooke, 1586." Had this document been in the handwriting of our Worthy or had the signature at the close "Foulke Grevill" been his autograph, I should of course have had no difficulty in assigning it to him : and so must have included it among his

Works. But (*a*) It nowhere appears that our Fulke Greville was present with Sidney, whereas the Narrative is a kind of daily-diary by one who personally carried on the conversations placed on record : (*b*) The heading "by........Foulke, Lord Brooke" reveals that the transcript was made not earlier than 1620-1 when Sir Fulke was created Lord Brooke : (*c*) The Cotton MSS. contain an apparently contemporary transcript, if indeed it be not the original : and there seems no ground for disturbing the assignment of it by ZOUCH and all the Sidney-Biographers to the good and true REV. GEORGE GIFFORD, who attended at SIDNEY's death-bed, and is gratefully remembered in his Will. It is probable that SIR FULKE GREV-ILLE had himself made a copy of the Gifford MS. —attaching his name simply to attest its accuracy. In such case the Copyist of the Ickwell Bury MS. would naturally conclude from the name at the close that he was the Writer. Be this as it may the Cotton MS [Vitellius c. xvii. fo. 382] is now a mere fragment—having been injured by the great Fire, and indeed is described as 'fragmentary' by ZOUCH. Mr. Harvey's early transcript is of exceeding value. It presents a superior text, and is perfect. The after-biographers of Sidney would do well to consult it. I hope to give it

in integrity in my own Introduction to a contemp-
lated collection of Sidney's Poetry in the FULLER
WORTHIES. The Ickwell Bury Narrative is one
of the treasures brought to light by the Royal
Commission on Historical Manuscripts: and I owe
thanks to Mr. Harvey for the courtesy and
kindness with which he immediately responded
to my inquiries.

In the Appendix to Life of SIDNEY I add [B]
PEPYS' characteristic notices of the book, at a
later date, and [C] an Epigram on ZUTPHEN, where
SIDNEY fell—almost the one solitary grain out
of GAMAGE's sack of chaff.

b. A LETTER TO AN HONORABLE LADY. This
appeared in the folio of 1633 and fills pp, 257-
294. The whole facts and strain of this extraordinary Letter and its Writer's relation to the ' fair
friend-enemy' of SIDNEY, seem to determine that
the 'honourable lady' was the LADY RICH, when
she was contemplating a divorce for sake of
MOUNTJOY. The imperious lady I fear would
have been saucy rather than submissive over the
Letter: but as it is marked ' *Not finished* ', probably she never saw it. I have been enabled to
present some important corrections of the folio
from the MSS. at Warwick Castle.

c. A LETTER TO GREUILL VARNEY. This also

appeared in the folio of 1633, pp. 295-298. Our text exhibits various readings from an Oxford MS. as stated in its place.

d. SHORT SPEECH FOR BACON. We refer the Reader to our note *in loco* : prefixed are notices of Lord BROOKE's services and utterances in Parliament, from D'Ewes. As a fitting introduction to this Speech, I have gleaned from the 'Calendars' of State Papers in the Record Office and Lambeth and similar sources, additional references to his official life, pointing out materials that will be available for that larger and more adequate 'Life' of him to be counted on surely, when the Family-Papers yield their treasures. Meantime I am glad to be able to state that the present representative of this illustrious house—the Earl of Warwick and Brooke—has not only entrusted to me the very valuable MSS. noted below : but has also in the most generous manner possible promised an early examination of his Papers, and stated his hearty willinghood to make them available in the interests of Literature. Besides our Worthy himself, I fondly hope this examination will result in new letters, &c., of Bacon, and even of Shakespeare, as elsewhere expressed.

I have now to notice the remaining contents of the present Volume :

e. Description of the Manuscripts of Lord Brooke, at Warwick Castle, with various readings and notes from them. I refer the reader to this 'Description' for details : and I beg publicly to return my best thanks to Lord Warwick and Brooke for the use of these MSS.

f. The Facsimiles (*a*) A Scribe's copy of the 'Poems of Monarchy' (stanza 583) with corrections by the Author (*b*) Autograph to a Navy paper (*c*) From the holograph MS. of "Religion" (stanza 1st.) (*d.*) From "Cœlica" with handwriting in 'old-age. These fac-similes are prefixed to large paper copies only, in the present volume. (Vol. IVth.) See under the 'Description" *supra.* (*e*).

g. The Indices. It is anticipated that these will be found helpful, being most minutely distributed and done with care.

If the Warwick-Castle Manuscripts furnish the expected materials, I may also be tempted to collect into a volume the Works of Robert, Lord Brooke, the large-brained and high-hearted heir of our Fulke Greville : and therein give such new *data* as may result, on the Brookes and their associates.

I cannot close my work on Lord Brooke without expressing the satisfaction, if I may not say pride, with which I add this complete and worthy edition of our Worthy to the collections of our early and greatest Literature, and so actualize one of the visions and purposes of boyhood. As I write this, a pleasant letter reaches me from a well-known Book-lover: and I take the liberty to quote from it: "Lord Brooke is well worthy of all the pains you have bestowed upon him, and will now, I trust, be brought out into greater prominence. Of him I have been an admirer from very early days. I remember well that the last evening I spent with Charles Lamb—and it is now five and forty years ago—he descanted on the merits of this *Nobiliorum Poetarum nobilissimus,* as he called him, with the folio before him, reading his favourite passages with an interjectional commentary, and treating him with a sympathetic feeling and felicity of criticism which threw into the shade what he had written, good as it was, in his 'Specimens''. (James Crossley, Esq., Manchester).

ALEXANDER B. GROSART.

St. George's, Blackburn,
4th October, 1870.

The Works of Fulke Greville, Lord Brooke.

Prose.

VOL. IV.

Note.

The original title-page of the Life of SIDNEY is as follows :—

THE LIFE

Of the Renowned

Sr. PHILIP SIDNEY.

WITH

The true Interest of *England*

As it then stood in relation to all Forrain Princes : And particularly for suppressing the power of *Spain* Stated by Him.

His principall Actions, Counsels, Designes, and Death.

Together with a short Account of
the Maximes and Policies used by Queen
Elizabeth in her Government.

Written by Sir FULKE GREVIL
Knight, Lord BROOK, a Servant to Queen
Elizabeth, and his Companion
& Friend.

LONDON,
Printed for *Henry Seile*, over against St.
Dunstans Church in Fleet-street.
MDCLII. [12o.]

Collation—: title-page—Epistle Dedicatory 3 leaves
[unpaged] and pp 247 with several misprints of the
figures of pagination. See Introduction to the present
volume for account of a Manuscript of the Life of Sidney.
G.

Epistle Dedicatory.

MOST HUMBLY, TO THE RIGHT HON-
ORABLE THE COUNTESSE OF
SUNDERLAND.[1]

Since Madam,

BOTH your bloud and vertues do so strongly intitle you to this well-limb'd piece; it would be a stain upon the Publisher, to enshrine it to any other name but yours. Who can protect the story of a Sidney, but a Sidney's

---

[1] This Countess of Sunderland was Lady Dorothy Sydney, eldest daughter of Robert, 2nd earl of Leicester, by Dorothy Percy, daughter of Henry 9th earl of Northumberland. She was therefore sister to the renowned Algernon Sydney, beheaded at Tower Hill, 7th Decr. 1683. She was married at Penshurst 20th July 1639 to Henry, 3rd, Lord Spencer, who was created 8th. June 1643, earl of Sunderland. He was killed at the battle of Newbury, 20th. Septr. 1643. His widow was on'y 23 years of age: and remained in widowhood until the year of this Dedica-

A

name? Thus his matchless poem, seem'd providentially by him impatronag'd unto his peerless sister. And this—Madam—being another of his meaner monuments, disdains address to any other alliance but his own. Here at your feet—by no despicable pen—the History of our Nation's wonder lies; whose large spread fame, your noble meene improves, and convinces the world of this truth, That not only the endowments of Nature, but even the enoblements of the mind and genius, are many times inherent in the bloud and linage. Some Families are privileg'd from Heaven in excellencies, which now and then in particular branches, like new starrs, appear and beautifie the sphere they shine in. And doubtless if the departed into happiness, have any knowledge of our humane vicissitudes, his gallant soul looks down with contentment, to see the honour of his House continued in your unblemisht merit. Which, taking all, may excuse the presumption that I can be charged with, who not pretending to the

---

tion—8th July 1652, when she was married to a commoner of the universal name of Smythe, whom she also survived. She was buried beside her first husband at Brington 25th. Feby. 1683-4. She was the "Sacharissa" of Waller's praises.   G.

authorage, ave thought I could not doe more
right, either to him or the subject of the discourse,
than to inscribe it to her, who like day in this
eclipse of honour, enlightning our western orbe,
hath ambition'd me to make this offering from,

Madam,

the meanest of your

most obedient Servants,

P. B.[1]

---

[1] I can't fill up those initials · not likely to have been
Peter Butrech, Sidney's friend. G.

The Life of the Renowned Sᵣ. Philip Sidney.

CHAP. I.

THE difference which I have found between times, and consequently the
changes of life into which their naturall
vicissitudes doe violently carry men, as they have
made deep furrowes of impressions into my heart,
so the same heavy wheeles caused[1] me to retire my
thoughts from free traffique with the world, and
rather seek comfortable ease or imployment in the
safe memory of dead men, than disquiet in a
doubtfull conversation amongst the living Which
I ingenuously[2] confesse, to be one chief motive of
dedicating these exercises of my youth to that
Worthy, Sir Philip Sidney, so long since departed.[3] For had I grounded my ends upon active

---

[1] P, 'Cause.' G.

[2] M, 'ingeniously' G.

[3] The "Exercises" referred to are his Poems, to which
this "Life" was intended by him to be prefixed. G.

wisedomes of the present, or sought patronage out
of hope or fear in the future, who knowes not,
that there are some noble friends of mine, and
many honourable magistrates yet living, unto
whom my fortune and reputation were and are far
more subject? But besides this self-respect of
dedication, the debt I acknowledge to that gentleman is farre greater, as with whom I shall ever
account it honour to have been brought up : and
in whom the life it self of true worth—by way
of example—far exceed the pictures of it in any
moral precepts. So that—if my creation[1] had
been equal—it would have proved as easie for me
to have followed his patern, in the practice of reall
vertue, as to engage my self into this character-
isticall kind of Poesie : in defence whereof he hath
written so much, as I shall not need to say anything.[2] For that this representing of vertues,
vices, humours, counsells, and actions of men
in faigned[3] and unscandalous images, is an in-
abling of free-born spirits to the greatest affaires
of States : he himself hath left such an instance in
the too short scene of his life, as I fear many

---

[1] = creative faculty or genius. G.

[2] The immortal " Defence of Poesie " is alluded to. G.

[3] P, grossly misprints ' unfaigned '. G.

ages will not draw a line out of any other man's sphere to parallel with it.

For my own part, I observed, honoured, and loved him so much ; as with what caution soever I haue passed through my dayes hitherto as among the liuing, yet in him I challenge a kind of freed-ome even among the dead. So that although with Socrates,[1] I professe to know nothing for the present; yet with Nestor[2] I am delighted in repeating old newes of the ages past ; and will therefore stir up my drooping memory touching this man's worth, powers, wayes, and designes : to the end that in the tribute I owe him, our nation may see a sea-mark, rais'd upon their native coast, above the levell of any private Pharos abroad : and so by a right meridian-line of their own, learn to sayl through the straits of True Vertue, into a calm and spacious ocean of humane honour.

It is ordinary among men to observe the races of horses and breeds of other cattle. But few consider, that as divers humors mixt in[3] men's

---

[1] See Cicero, Acad. Quæst. II. 23 § 74 : [Socrates] 'Ex-cepit unum tantum, scire se, nihil se scire : nihil amplius.' Cf. also Plato, Apol. c. 6.　G.

[2] The Od. and Il. repeatedly : *e.g.* Od. iii. 245 : Il. i 250 : x. 18 : xi. 627.　G.

[3] M, ' into '.　G.

bodies make different complexions ; so every family
hath as it were, divers predominant qualities in
it ; which, as they are tempered together in
marriage, give a certain tincture[1] to all the
descent. In my time, I have observed it in many
houses, especially in this. Sir Henry Sidney his
father, was a man of excellent natural wit,[2] large
heart, sweet conversation : and such a governour,
as sought not to make an end of the State in himself, but to plant his own ends in the prosperity
of his Countrey. Witnes his sound establishments
both in Wales and Ireland, where his memory
is worthily grateful unto this day : how unequall
and bitter soever the censure of provincialls is usually against sincere monarchall governours ; especially such, as though in worth and place superior, are yet intheir own degrees of heraldry, inferior to them.

On the other side, his mother, as she was a
woman by descent of great nobility, so was she by
nature, of a large ingenuous[3] spirit. Whence,
as it were even racked[4] with native strengths, shee

---

[1] = lustre. See our Index of Words. G.
[2] =intellect, as before. G.
[3] M ' ingenious'. G.
[4] P, rancked .' : the small-pox is referred to. G.

chose rather to hide her self from the curious eyes of a delicate time, than come up on the stage of the world with any manner of disparagement : the mischance of sicknesse having cast such a kind of veile over her excellent beauty, as the modesty of that sex doth many times upon their native and heroicall spirits.

So that it may probably be gathered, that this clearnesse of his father's iudgement and ingenious sensiblenesse of his mother's, brought forth so happy a temper in this well-mixt ofspring of their's, as—without envy be it[1] spoken—Sir Philip deserves to be accompted amongst those eminent plants of our soyl, which blast[2] or bite not, but rather statuminate[3] and refresh the vines, corn, fruits, or whatsoever groweth under their shaddows. And as he was their first-born, so was he not the contraction, but the[4] extension of their strength, and the very acme,[5] and perfect type of it.

Of whose youth I will report no other wonder,

---

[1] M, 'it be ' G.

[2] M, 'whose shadowes blast'. G.

[3] = prop up. So Ben. Jonson in " New Inn " ii. 2. " I will *statuminate* and underprop thee ". G.

[4] M, 'the' dropped. G.

[5] P, ' aim ' an evident misprint. G.

but this; that though I lived with him and knew
him from a child, yet I never knew him other
than a man : with such staiednesse of mind, lovely,
and familiar gravity, as carried grace and reverence above greater years.   His talk ever of knowledge, and his very play tending to enrich his
mind : so as euen his teachers found something in
him to observe and learn, above that which they had
read or taught.   Which eminence, by nature and
industry, made his worthy father stile Sir Philip
in my hearing—though I unseen—*Lumen familiæ
suæ*.   But why doe I mention this relative harmony of worth between father and son ?   Did not
his Countrey soon after take knowledge of him as
a light or leading star to every degree within her?
Are not the arts and languages, which enabled him
to travail at fourteen years old, and in his travail
to win reverence amongst the chief learned men
abroad, witnesses[1] beyond exception, that there
was great inequality[2] of worth and goodnesse in
him.

Instance, that reverend Languet, mentioned for

---

[1] M, ' wittnesse '   G.

[2] = disproportion : the meaning being that he had far
beyond his share.   Cf. Shakespeare, (*Measure for Measure*
v. i) " do not banish reason for *inequality*."   G.

honour's sake in Sir Philip's Arcadia,—a Frenchman borne[1] learned *usque ad miraculum*; wise by the conjunction of practice in the world, with that well-grounded theory of books, and much valued at home; till his[2] great worth—even in a gentleman's fortune—being discovered for a dangerous instrument against Rome and Spain, by some sparkles,[3] got him[4] light enough, rather to seek employment elswhere, than to tarry and be driven out of his own Country with disparagement. In Franckford he settles; is entertained agent for the Duke of Saxony, and[5] underhand, Minister for his own king. Lodged he was in Wechel's house, the printer of Franckford, where Sir Philip in his trauell[6] chancing[7] likewise to become a guest, this ingenious old man's fulnesse of knowledge, travailing as much to be delivered from abundance by teaching, as Sir Philip's rich nature and industry thirsted to be taught and manured; this harmony of an humble hearer to an excellent teacher, so equally fitted them both,

---

[1] P, omits 'a Frenchman borne. G.
[2] P, 'this' another evident misprint. G.
[3] M, 'sparkes'. G.   [4] P, 'got light'. G.
[5] P, 'an under-hand.' G.   [6] P, 'in travail.' G.
[7] M, mis-writes 'changeing'. G.

as out of a naturall descent both in love and plenty, the elder grew taken with a net of his own thread, and the younger taught to lift up himself by a thread of the same spinning ; so as this reverend Languet, orderly sequestred from his severall functions under a mighty king, and Saxonie[1] the greatest prince of[2] Germany, became a nurse of knowledge to this hopefull young gentleman, and without any other hire or motive than this sympathy of affections, accompanyed him in the whole course of his three years travail. By which example the judicious reader may see, that worth in every Nation finds her Country, parents, neighbours, and friends, yea and often with more honour, dearnesse, and advancement in knowledges, than any pedigree of fleshly kindred, will, or[3] can at home raise or enlarge them unto. Nay to goe yet farther in this private instance : It may please the reader to observe, how the same parallel of worth, in what age or estate soever, as it hath power to win, so hath it likewise absolute power to keep. Far unlike those creations of chance, which hache[4] other birds'

---

[1] M, omits Saxonie.   G.   [2] M, 'in'.   G.
[3] M, omits ' will, or '.   G.
[4] P, ' hath ' : another evident mis-reading : ' hache ' = hatch.   G.

egges: and by advancing[1] men out of chance or
complement, lose them again as fast by neglect.
Contrary to which, even when diversity of years,
courses of life and fortunes, enforced these dear
friends to divide, there yet passed such a continuall
course of intelligence by letters from one of them
to another, as in their losse—if they be lost[2]—there
lye[3] buried many delicate images, and differences
betw een the reall and large complexions of those
active times and the narrow salves of this effeminate age : because in this excellent mould of their
friendship, the greatest businesses of Estate were
so mixed with the sweet remissions of ingenuous[4]
good will, as men might easily discern in them—
as unflattering glasses—that wisdome and love, in
good spirits have great affinity together. For a
farther demonstration, behold even the same Languet—after he was sixty-six years of age—
fashioning himself a journey into England, with
the Duke Cassimire, onely to see that excellent
plant of his own polishing. In which loving and
unexpected meeting, I dare confidently affirm,

---

[1] M, 'of men'.   G.

[2] Originally published at Frankfort in 1632 : reprinted
Lord Hailes in 1776, and since.   G.

[3] P, 'be'.   G.

[4] M, 'ingenious'   G.

neither side became loser.   At the Sea they
parted, end made many mutuall tears, omnious[1]
propheciers of their never meeting again.

These little sparks of two large natures I make
bold the longer to insist upon, because the youth,
life and fortune of this gentleman were indeed but
sparkles[2] of extraordinary greatnesse in him :
which for want of clear vent lay concealed and in
a maner[3] smothered up.   And again to bring the
children of favor and of chance,[4] into an equall
ballance of comparison with birth, worth, and
education : and therein abruptly to conclude, that
God creates those in His certain and eternall
mouldes, out of which He elects for Himself;
where kings choose creatures out of Pandora's tun,
and so raise up worth and no worth ; friends or
enemies, at adventure.   Therefore what marvail
can it be, if these Iacobs and Esaus strive am-
bitiously one with another, as well before as after
they come out of such erring and unperfect
wombes ?

[1] *S* : = ominous *i. e.* prophetic.   G.

[2] P, 'sparkes' : I adopt 'sparkles' from M, for uniformity with previous use of it.   G.

[3] M, 'in maner'.   G.

[4] P, 'and change : evident mis-reading.   G.

Now from these particular testimonies, to goe
on with Sir Philip's life : though he purposed no
monuments of books to the world, out of his[1] great
harvest of knowledge; yet doe not his Arcadian
Romantiæ[2] live after him, admired euen[3] by our
sower-eyed[4] criticks? who, howsoever their common end upon common arts be to affect reputation
by depraving censure; yet where Nature placeth
excellencie above envy, there—it seemeth—she
subjecteth these carping eyes to wonder,[5] and
shewes the judicious reader how he may be nourished in the delicacy of his own judgement.

For instance : may not the most refined spirits,
in the scope of these dead images—even as they
are now—finde, that when soveraign princes,
to play with their own visions, will put off publique actions,[6] which is the splendor of Majestie,
and unactively charge the managing of their
greatest affaires upon the second-hand[7] faith and

---

[1] P, 'this': repetition of a former misreading. G.

[2] P, 'Romanties'. G.

[3] P, 'admired by'. G.

[4] P, misprints 'foure-eyd.' G.

[5] P, misprints 'wander'. G.

[6] P, 'action'. G.

[7] P, puts comma after faith instead of after second-
hand. G.

diligence of deputies, may they not—I say—understand, that even then they bury themselves and their estates in a cloud of contempt, and under it both encourage and shaddow the conspiracies of ambitious subalternes to their false endes : I mean the ruine of States and princes ?

Again, where kingly parents will suffer, or rather force their wives and daughters, to descend from the inequality and reservednesse of princely education, into the contemptible familiarity and popular freedome of shepherds; may we not discern that even therein they give those royall birthes warrant or opportunity, to break over all circles of honor, safe-guards to the modesty of that sex ; and withall make them fraily apt to change the commanding manners of princely birth, into the degrading images of servile basenesse ? Lastly, where humour takes away this pomp and apparatus from king, crown, and scepter, to make Fear a counsellor, and Obscurity a wisdom; be that king at home what the current or credit of his former government, for a while, may keep him : yet he is[1] sure among forrain princes to be justly censured as a princely shepherd, or shepherdish king : which creatures of scorn seldome

---

[1] M, 'is he'. G.

fail to become fit sacrifices for home-born[1] discontentment or ambitious forrain spirits to undertake
and offer up.

Againe, who sees not the chanceable[2] arrivall of
Euarchus into Arcadia; his unexpected election
to the temporary soveraignty of that State; his
sitting in a cloudy seat of judgement, to give sentence—under a mask of shepherds—against his
son, nephew, neeces, the immediate successors to
that scepter; and all accused and condemned of
rape, paricide, adulteries, or treasons, by their
own lawes: I say who sees not, that these dark
webs of effeminate princes be dangerous forerun-
ners of innovation, even in a quiet and equally
tempered people? So that if Sir Phillipe[3] had
not made the integrity of this forrain king an
image of more constant, pure, and higher strain,
than nature makes those[4] ordinary mouldes,
wherein she fashioneth earthly princes, even this
opportunity and map of desolaon prepared for
Euarchus, wherein he saw all the successors of
this Province justly condemned under his own
sentence, would have raised up specious rights
and[5] pretences for new ambition in him; and upon

---

[1] M, omits 'home-born'. G.   [2] M, 'changable'. G.
[2] P, 'Philips': gross misprint. G.   [4] M, 'these'. G.
[5] P, 'or'. G.

the never-failing pillars of occasion, amasednes
of people, and sad offer of glorious novelties, have
tempted him to establish this election for a time,
successively, to him and his for ever ?

To be short, the like and finer moralities offer
themselves throughout that various and dainty
work of his, for sounder judgements to exercise
their spirits in ; so that if the infancie of these
ideas, determining in the first generation, yield
the ingenuous[1] reader such pleasant and profitable
diversity both of flowers and fruits, let him conceive, if this excellent image-maker had lived to
finish and bring to perfection this extraordinary
frame of his own Common-wealth : I meane, the
returne of Basilius, from his dreames of humour
to the honor of his former estate ; the marriages[2] of
the two sisters with two excellent princes ; their
issue ; the warres stirred up by Amphialus; his
marriage with Helena ; their successions ; together
with the incident magnificences, pompes of state,
providences of councells in treaties of peace or
aliance, summons of warres, and orderly execution[3]
of their disorders ; I say, what a large field an
active able spirit should have had to walk in, let

---

[1] M, 'ingenious'.   G.   [2] P, 'marriage'.   G.
[3] M, 'executions'.   G.

the advised reader conceive with griefe. Especially if he please to take knowledge, that in all
these creatures of his making, his intent and scope
was, to turn the barren philosophy precepts into
pregnant images of life ; and in them, first on the
monarch's part, lively to represent the growth,
state, and declination of princes, change of government and lawes : vicissitudes of sedition, faction,
succession, confederacies, plantations, with all
other errors or alterations in publique affaires.
Then again in the subjects case ; the state of favor,
disfavor, prosperitie, adversity, emulation, quarrell, undertaking, retiring, hospitality, travail,
and all other moodes of private fortunes, or misfortunes. In which traverses—I know—his
purpose was to limn out such exact pictures,
of every posture in the minde, that any man
being forced in the straines of this life, to pass
through any straights or latitudes of good or ill
fortune, might—as in a glasse—see how to set a
good countenance upon all the discountenances of
adversitie and a stay upon the exorbitant smilings[1]
of Chance.

Now, as I know this was the first project of
these workes, rich—like his youth—in the free-

---

[1] P, 'smiling'. G.

dome of affections, wit, learning, stile, form, and facilities, to please others : so must I again—as ingenuously[1]—confess, that when his body declined, and his piercing inward powers were lifted up to a purer horizon, he then discovered, not onely the imperfection but vanitie of these shaddowes, how daintily soever limned : as seeing that even beauty it self, in all earthly complexions, was more apt to allure men to evill, than to fashion any goodness in them. And from this ground, in that memorable testament of his, he bequeathed no other legacie, but the fire to his[2] unpolished embrio. From which fate it is onely reserved, until the world hath purged away all her more gross corruptions.

Again, they that knew him well, will truly confess, this Arcadia of his to be, both in form and matter, as much inferior to that unbounded spirit of his, as the industry and images of other men's works are many times raised above the writers' capacities : and besides acknowledge, that howsoever he could not but choose but give them many aspersions of spirit, and learning from the Father; yet that they were scribled rather as pamphlets, for

---

[1] M, ' ingeniously '.   G.   [2] P, ' this '.   G.

entertainment of time and friends, than any accompt of himself to the world. Because if his
purpose had been to leave his memory in books, I
am confident, in the right use of Logick, Philosophy, History, and Poësie, nay even in[1] the most
ingenuous[2] of mechanical arts, he would have
shewed such treits[3] of a searching and judicious
spirit, as the possessors of every faculty would
have striven no less for him, than the seaven
cities did to have Homer of their sept. But the
truth is : his end was not writing, even while he
wrote : nor his knowledge moulded for tables or
schooles ; but both his wit and understanding
bent upon his heart, to make himself and others,
not in words or opinion but in life and action,
good and great.

In which architectonical art he was such[4] a
master, with so commending and yet equall waies
amongst men, that whersoever he went, he was
beloved and obeyed : yea into what action soever he came last at the first, he became first at
the last : the whole managing of the business,

---

[1] M, omits 'in'.   G.
[2] M, 'ingenious'.   G.
[3] M, 'treits' = traits. P, grossly misprints 'tracts', G.
[4] M, omits 'such'   G.

not by usurpation or violence, but—as it were—by right and[1] acknowledgment, falling into his hands as into a naturall center.

By which onely commendable monopolie of alluring and improving men, looke how[2] the same drawes all windes after it in fair weather : so did the influence of this spirit draw men's affections and undertakings to depend upon him.

---

[1] M, 'an'.   G.

[2] P, omits by evident mistake 'looke'.   G.

CHAP. II.

HERE I am still enforced to bring pregnant evidence from the dead : amongst whom I have found far more liberall contribution to the honor of true worth, than amongst[1] those which now live; and in the markets[2] of selfnesse, traffique new interest by the discredit of old friends : that ancient wisdome of righting enemies, being utterly worn out of date in our modern discipline.

My first instance must come from that worthy Prince of Orange, William of Nassau,[3] with whom this young gentleman having long kept intelligence by word and letters, and in affairs of the highest nature that then passed currant upon the stages of England, France, Germany, Italy, the Low Countries, or Spaine, it seemes, I say,[5] that this young gentleman had, by

---

[1] P, 'among': I adopt 'amongst', as immediately before. G.

[2] P, 'market'. G.

[3] M, Wyllyam Nassau'. G.

[4] P, has not 'I say'. G.

this[1] mutuall freedome, so imprinted the extraordinary merit of his young yeares into the large wisdome and experience of that excellent prince,[2] as I passing out of Germany into England, and having the unexpected honor to finde this prince in the Towne of Delph,[3] cannot think it unwelcome to describe the clothes of this prince ; his positure[4] of body and minde, familiarity and reservedness, to the ingenuous reader, that he may see what divers characters princes please and govern cities, townes, and peoples.

His uppermost garment was a gown, yet such as—I dare confidently affirm—a mean-born student in our Innes of Court, would not have been well-pleased to walk the streets in. Unbuttoned his doublet[6] was, and of like precious matter and form to the other. His wast-coat—which showed it self under it—not unlike the best sort of those woollen knit ones, which our ordinary watermen row us in. His company about him, the burgesses of that beer-brewing town : and he so fellow-like encompassed with them, as—had I not

---

[1] P, 'by his'. G.   [2] P, misprints 'Ptince'. G.
[3] P, 'Town Delph'. G. [4] P, misprints 'posture'. G·
[5] P, misprints 'ths': M. has 'ingenious ', as usual. G.
[6] Misprinted 'doubled'. G.

known his face—no exterior signe of degree, or
reseruedness[1] could have discovered the inequality
of his worth or estate from that multitude. Notwithstanding I no sooner came to his presence,
but it pleased him to take knowledge of me. And
even upon that—as if it had been a signall to make
a change—his respect of a stranger instantly
begott[2] respect to himself in all about him : an
outward passage of inward greatness, which
in a popular estate I thought worth the
observing. Because there, no pedigree but worth
could possibly make a man prince, and no prince,
in a moment, at his own pleasure.

The businesses which he then vouchsafed to
impart with me were, the dangerous fate which
the crown of England, States of Germany, and
the Low Countries did stand threatned with, under
an ambitious and conquering monarch's hand.
The main instance, a short description of the
Spaniard's curious affecting to keep the Romans'
waies and ends, in all his actions. On the other
side the clear symptomes of the hectique feaver,
universally then reigning among the princes of

---

[1] P, misprints ' deservedness ', which spoils the sense.
G.

[2] P, 'begat'. G.

Christendome, ordain'd—as he thought—to behold this undermining disease without fear, till
it should prove dangerous, nay incurable to them.
This active King of Spain having put on a mask
of conscience, to cover an invisible conjunction
between the temporal and spiritual ambitions of
these two sometimes creeping, sometimes commanding Romish and Spanish conquerors. The particulars were many, both excellent and enlightning.

As first, the fatall neutrality of France, jealous
of the Spanish greatness, as already both wrong'd
and threatned by it : and yet their kings so full
of pleasures, and consequently so easily satisfied
with the complements of words, treaties, or alliances, and since the fall of the Sorbonists, their
own exempted Church so absolutely possest and
govern'd by the Jesuits ; as through the bewitching[1] liberties and bondages of auricular confession,
they were rather wrought to rest upon a vain
security of reputed strength, than really to hazzard loss, and help themselves by diversion or
assailing.

Againe, on the Queen's part, by the way of
question, he supposed a little neglect in her

---

[1] Misprinted 'bewithing'.   G.

princely mildness, while she did suffer a Protest-
ant party, rais'd by God in that great kingdome
of France, to be a ballance or counterpease to
that dangerous heptarchy of Spain—then scarce
visible, but since multiplyed by an unresistable
greatnesse—I say, for suffering this strong and
faithfull party—through want of imployment—
to sink into it self, and so unactively — like
a meteor—to vanish or smother out in vain
and idle apparitions. Withall reverently hee
demurr'd, whether it were an omission in that
excellent Ladie's government or no, by a remisse
looking on, whilst the Austrian aspiring family
framed occasion to gain by begging peace, or
buying war from the Grand Signior; and
both exceeding much to their own ends; in
respect that once in few years, this emperor made
himself general by it, over all the forces of Christendome; and thereby gained the fame of action;
trained up his owne instruments martially, and
got credit with his fellow-bordering princes,
through the common councell or participation of
fear. Besides that in the conclusions of peace,
he ever saved a mass of riches gather'd by Diets,
Contributions, Devotions and[1] Levies for common

---

[1] M, omits 'and'. G.

defence, which out of the ill-accompting hand of
War, became—in his Exchequer—treasure, to
terrifie even those Christian neighbours that did
contribute to it. And the more especially he
insisted upon this: because all those crafty pageants
of her enemies were disguisedly acted, even whilst[2]
her Majesty had an agent of extraordinary diligence, worth, and credit with that vast estate of
Turkie, into whose absolute and imperious spirit,
without any further charge than infusing the
ielowsie[3] of competition, these practises among
those Austrian usurpers, might easily have been
interrupted

Lastly, it pleased him to question yet a greater
over-sight in both these kingdoms, England and
France : because while their princes stood at gaze,
as upon things far off, they still gave way for the
Popish and Spanish invisible arts and counsels,
to undermine the greatness and freedom both of
secular and ecclesiasticall princes : a mortall sickness in that vast body of Germany, and by their
unsensible[1] fall, a raising up of the house of
Austria many steps towards her long affected

---

[1] M, ‘while’. G.   [2] P, ‘jealousies’. G.

[3] P, ‘insensible’ : ‘un’ is Lord Brooke’s usual form of
prefix in such words. G.

monarchy over the West. The ground of which
opinion was—as he thought—in respect that even
the Catholique princes and bishops themselues
—had their eyes bin well wakened—would never
have endured any cloud or colour of religion, to
haue[1] changed their princely soveraignties into
such a kind of low and chaplaine tenure : as since
they have sleepily[2] fallen into : but would rather
have stirred them with many hands, to binde[3]
this miter-superstition, with the reall cords of
Truth. And to that end perchance to[4] haue set Spain
on work with her new and ill digested conquests :
her dangerous enemy Fess :[5] her native Moors
and Iews—since craftily transported—and so
probably have troubled the usurpations both of the
Pope and Spain over that well-tempered, though
over-zealous and superstitiouse region of Italy.
These, and such other particulars, as I had in
charge, and did faithfully deliver from him to her
Majesty, are since performed, or perished with
time or occasion.

The last branch was his free expressing of himselfe in the honor of Sir Philip Sidney, after this

---

[1] P, misprints 'hape'.   G.

[2] M, 'sleepily haue'.   G.   [3] M, 'bound'.   G.

[4] P. omits 'to'.   G.   [5] Fez.   G.

[6] P, 'superstitions' : evident misprint.   G.

manner : That I would first commend his own
humble service, with those before-mentioned ideas
to the Queen ; and after crave leave of her freely
to open his knowledge and opinion of a fellow-
servant of his, that—as he heard—lived unim-
ployed under her.   With himselfe he began[1] *ab
ovo*, as having been of Charles the fift's privie
Counsell, before he was one and twenty years of
age : and since—as the world knew—either an
actor or at least acquainted with the greatest
actions and affairs of Europe ; and likewise with
her greatest men, and ministers of estate.   In all
which series of time, multitude of things and persons, he protested unto mee—and for her service—
that if he could judge, her Majesty had one of
the ripest and greatest councellors of estate in Sir
Philip Sidney, that at this day lived in Europe :
to the triall of which hee was pleased to leave his
owne credit engaged, untill[2] her Majesty might
please to employ this gentleman, either amongst
her friends or enemies.

At my return into England, I performed all his
other comandments ; this that concerned Sir
Philip Sidney[3]—thinking to make the fine-spun

---

[1] M 'begunne'.   G.   [2] M 'till'.   G.
[3] P, omits ' Sidney ' : M, spells ' Sr Phillip Sidney.'   So
also on a little where P again omits ' Sidney.   G.

threads of friendship more firm between them—I acquainted Sir Philip Sidney with : not as questioning, but fully resolved to do it. Unto which he at the first sight opposing, discharged my faith impawn'd to the Prince of Orange, for the delivery of it ; as an act only entending his good, and so to be perform'd or dispens'd with at his pleasure ; yet for my satisfaction freely added these words : first, that the Queene[1] had the life it self daily attending her : and if she either did not or could[2] not value it so high,[3] the commendation of that worthy prince could be no more— at the best— than a lively picture of that life, and so of far lesse credit and estimation with her. His next reason was, because princes love not that forrain Powers should have extraordinary interest[4] in their subjects ; much lesse to be taught by them how they should place their own : as arguments either upbraiding ignorance, or lack of large rewarding goodness in them.

---

[1] P, ' Qu.' G.   [2] P, ' would. ' G.

[3] P, ' highly.' G,

[4] P, omits ' interest ' : but the catchword at bottom of this page is ' in- ' shewing ' interest' was dropped inadvertently. G.

This narration I adventure of, to shew the clearness and readiness of this gentleman's judgement in all degrees and offices of life : with this further[1] testimony of him, that after mature deliberation being once resolved, he never brought any question of change to afflict himself with, or perplex the business; but left the success to His will that governs the blind prosperities and unprosperities of Chance ; and so works out His own ends by the erring frailties of humane reason and affection. Lastly, to manifest that these were not complements, self-ends, or use of each other, according to our modern fashion, but meer ingenuities of spirit, to which the ancient greatness of hearts ever frankly engaged their fortunes, let actions, the lawfully begotten children, equall in spirit, shape, and complexion to their parents, be testimonies ouer[3] sufficient.

My second instance comes from the Earle of Leicester, his unckle, who told me—after Sir Philip's, and not long before his owne[4] death—that when he undertook the government of the Low Countries, he carryed his nephew over with him, as one amongst the rest, not only despising his

---

[1] P, 'farther'. G.   [2] P 'the'.   G.
[3] P 'ever' G.   [4] M omits 'own'. G.

youth for a counsellor, but withall bearing a hand vpon[1] him as a forward young man. Notwithstanding, in short time he saw this sun so risen above his horizon, that both he and all his stars were glad to fetch light from him, and in the end acknowledge[2] that he held up the honor of his causuall[3] authority by him, whilst he lived, and found reason to withdraw himself from that burthen, after his death.

My third record[4] is Sir Francis Walsingham his father-in-law ; that wise and active Secretarie. This man—as the world knoweth[5] —upheld both Religion and State, by using a policy wisely mixt with reflexions of either. He had influence in all Countries and a hand upon all affairs ; yet even this man hath often confessed to my self, that his Philip did so far overshoot him in his own bow, as those friends which at first were Sir Philip's for this Secretarie's sake, within a while became so fully owned and possest by Sir Philip, as now he held them at the second hand, by his son-in-law's native courtesie.

This is that true remission of mind, whereof I

---

[1] P, ' over him '. G.   [2] P, ' And ....acknowledged.' G.
[3] P, ' casual '. G.   [4] M, omits 'record.' G.
[5] P, ' knows '. G.

C

would gladly[1] have the world take notice from these dead men's ashes : to the end that we might once again see that ingenuity amongst men, which by liberall bearing witnesse to the merits of others, shews they have some true worth of their own ; and are not meerly lovers of themselves, without rivals.

---

[1] M, omits ' gladly '.   G.

CHAP. III.

TO continue this passage a little further : I must lift him above the censure of subjects, and give you an account what respect and honour his worth wanne him amongst the most eminent monarchs of that time : as first with that chief and best of princes, his most excellent Majesty, then king of Scotland, to whom his service was affectionately devoted, and from whom he received many pledges of love and favour.

In like manner, with the late renowned Henry of France, then of Navarre, who having measured and mastered all the spirits in his own Nation, found out this master-spirit among us, and used him like an equall in nature, and so fit for friendship with a king.

Again, that gallant prince Don John of[1] Austria, vice-roy in the Low Countries for Spain, when this gentleman in his embassage to the emperor came to kiss his hand, though at the first, in his

---

[1] P, ' de '.   G.

Spanish hauture,[1] he gave him access as by descent, to a youth of grace as to a stranger, and in particular competition—as he conceived—to an enemy; yet after a while that he had taken his just altitude, he found himself so stricken with this[2] extraordinary planet, that the beholders wondered to see what ingenuous[3] tribute that brave and high-minded prince paid to his worth; giving more honour and respect to this hopefull young gentleman, than to the embassadors of mighty princes.

But to climb yet a degree higher: In what due estimation his extraordinary worth was, even amongst enemies, will appear by his death. When Mendoza, a secretary of many treasons amongst[4] us, acknowledged openly that howsoever he was glad king Philip his master had lost, in a private gentleman, a dangerous enemy to his estate; yet he could not but lament to see Christendome depriv'd of so rare a light in those[5] cloudy times; and bewail poor widdow England—so he term'd her—that having been many years in breeding one eminent spirit, was in a moment bereaved of him, by the hands of a villain.

---

[1] P, 'haughture' : both the transition-form of hauteur. G.

[2] M' misreads 'his'.   G.   [3] M, 'ingeniouse'.   G.

[4] P, 'against'.   G.   [5] P, 'these'.   G.

Indeed he was a true modell of worth; a man fit for Conquest, Plantation, Reformation, or what action soever is greatest and hardest amongst men: withall, such a lover of mankind and goodnesse, that whoever had any reall parts, in him found comfort, participation, and protection to the uttermost of his power: like Zephyrus he giving life where he blew. The Universities abroad and at home, accompted him a general Mecænas of learnning; dedicated their books to him; and communicated every invention, or improvement of knowledge with him. Souldiers honoured him, and were so honoured by him as no man thought he marched under the true banner of Mars, that had not obtained Sir Philip Sidney's approbation. Men of affairs in most parts of Christendome, entertained correspondency with him. But what speak I of these, with whom his own waies, and ends did concur? since—to descend —his heart and capacity were so large, that there was not a cunning Painter, a skilfull Engenier, an excellent Musician, or any other artificer of extraordinary fame, that made not himself known to this famous spirit, and found him his true friend without hire; and the common *Rende-vous* of Worth in his time.

Now let princes vouchsafe to consider, of what

importance it is to the honour of themselves and
their estates, to have one man of such eminence ;
not onely as a nourisher of vertue in their Courts
or service, but besides for a reformed standard, by
which even the most humorous persons could not
but have a reverend kinde of[1] ambition to be
tried, and approved currant.   This I doe the more
confidently affirm, because it will be confessed by
all men, that this one man's example and personall respect, did not onely encourage Learning and
Honour in the Schooles, but brought the affection
and true use thereof both into the Court and Camp.
Nay more, even many gentlemen excellently
learned amongst us, will not deny, but that
they affected to row and steer their course in
his wake. Besides which honour of unequal nature
and education, his very waies in the world,
did generally adde reputation to his prince and
Country, by restoring amongst us the ancient
majestie of noble and true dealing: as a
manly wisdome, that can no more be weighed
down by any effeminate craft, than Hercules could
be overcome by that contemptible army of dwarfs.
And this[2] was it which, I profess, I loved dearly
in him, and still shall be glad to honour in the

---

[1] P, omits 'kinde of'.   G.   [2] P, 'This'.   G.

great men of this time : I mean, that his heart
and tongue went both one way, and so with every
one that went with the Truth ; as knowing no
other kindred, partie, or end.

Above all, he made the Religion he professed,
the firm basis of his life : for this was his judgement—as he often told me—that our true-heart-
edness to the Reformed Religion in the beginning,
brought peace and safety[1] and freedome to us;
concluding, that the wisest and best way, was
that of the famous William Prince of Orange,
who never divided the consideration of Estate
from the consideration of Religion, nor gave that
sound party occasion to be jealous, or distracted,
npon any appearance of safety whatsoever; prud-
ently resolving, that to temporize with the enemies of our Faith, was but—as among sea-guls—-
a strife, not to keep upright, but aloft upon the top
of every billow : which false-heartednesse to God
and man, would in the end find it self forsaken of
both ; as Sir Philip conceived. For to this active
spirit of his, all depths of the devil proved but
shallow fords ; he piercing into men's counsels
and ends, not by their words, oathes, or complements, all barren in that age, but by fathoming

---

[1] P, omits 'and ', and spells 'safetie '. G.

their hearts and powers, by their deeds, and found
no wisedome where he found no courage, nor
courage without wisdome, nor either without
honesty and truth.   With which solid and active
reaches of his, I am perswaded, he would have
found, or made a way through all the traverses,
even of the most weak and irregular times.   But
it pleased God in this decrepit age of the world,
not to restore the image of her ancient vigour in
him, otherwise than as in a lightning before
death.

Neither am I—for my part—so much in love
with this life, nor believe so little in a better to
come, as to complain of God for taking him, and
such like exorbitant worthyness from us : fit—as
it were by an ostracisme—to be divided, and not
incorporated with our corruptions : yet for the
sincere affection I bear to my prince and country,
my prayer to God is, that his[1] woorth and way
may not fatally be buried with him ; in respect,
that before his time and since, experience hath
published the usuall discipline of greatnes to have
been tender of it self onely ; making honour a triumph, or rather trophy of desire, set up in the eyes
of mankind, either to be worshipped as idols, or else

---

[1] P, as before, misprints ' this ' and spells ' worth '.   G.

as rebels to perish under her glorious oppressions. Notwithstanding, when the pride of flesh, and power of favour shall cease in these by death or disgrace ; what then hath Time to register, or fame to publish, in these great men's names, that will not be offensive, and[1] infectious to others ? What pen without blotting can write the story of their deeds ? or what herald blaze their arms without a blemish ? And as for their counsels and projects, when they come once to light, shall not they[2] live as noysome and loathsomely above ground, as their authors' carkasses lie in the grave ? So that[3] the return of such greatnes to the world and themselves, can be but private reproach, publique ill example, and a fatall scorn to the government they live in. Sir Philip Sidney[5] is none of this number ; for the greatness which he affected was built upon true worth ; esteeming fame more than riches, and noble actions far above nobility it self.

---

[1] P, 'or'.   G.

[3] M, misreads ·liue'.   G.

[5] M, omits ' Sidney'.   G.

[2] P, 'shall they not'.   G.

[4] P, ' as'.   G.

CHAP. IV.

AND although he never was magistrate, nor possessed of any fit stage for eminence to act upon, whereby there is small latitude left for comparing him with those deceased Worthies, that to this day live unenvied in story; yet can I probably say that if any supreme magistracie or employment, might have shewed forth this gentleman's worth, the World should have found him neither a mixt Lysander, with unactive goodness to have corrupted indifferent citizens; nor yet like that gallant libertine Sylla, with a tyrannizing hand and ill example, to have ordered the dissolute people of Rome; much less with that unexperienced Themistocles, to have refused, in the scat[1] of Justice, to deale equally between friends and strangers. So that as we say, the abstract name of goodness is great and generally currant; her nature hard to imitate, and diversly worshipped, according to zones, complexions, or educations[2]; admired by her enemies, yet ill followed by her friends. So may we truely

---

[1] M, 'state'.   G.   [2] P, 'education'.   G.

say,[1] that this gentleman's large yet uniform disposition, was every where praised; greater in himself than in the world; yet greater there in fame and honour than many of his superiors; reverenced by forrain Nations in one form, of his own in another; easily censured, hardly imitated; and therefore no received standard at home, because his industry, judgement, and affections, perchance loomed[2] too great for the cautious wisdomes of little monarchies to be safe in. Notwithstanding, whosoever will be pleased but[3] indifferently to weigh his life, actions, intentions, and death, shall find he had so sweetly yoaked fame and conscience together in a large heart, as inequality of worth or place in him, could not have been other than humble obedience, even to a petty tyrant of Sicily. Besides, this ingenuitie of his nature did spread it self so freely abroad, as who lives that can say he ever did him harm; whereas there be many living that may thankfully acknowledge he did them good? Neither was this in him a private, but a publique affection; his chief ends being not friends, wife, children, or himself; but

[1] P, 'I may well'. G.
[2] P, 'seemed' : M, reads 'loomed to'. G.
[3] P, drops 'but'. G.

above all things the honour of his Maker, and service of his prince or Country.

Now though his short life, and private fortune, were—as I sayd—no proper stages to act any greatness of good or evill upon ; yet are there — even from these little centers of his —lines to be drawn, not astronomicall or imaginary, but reall lineaments, such[1] as infancy is of man's estate ; out of which Nature often sparkleth brighter rayes in some, than ordinarily appear in the ripeness of many others. For proof wherof, I will pass from the testimonie of brave men's words, to his own deeds. What lights of sounder wisdome can we ascribe to our greatest men of affairs than he shewed in his youth and first employment, when he was sent by the late Queen, of famous memory, to condole the death of Maximilian, and congratulate the succession of Rodolph to the Empire ? For under the shaddow of this complement between princes, which sorted better with his youth than his spirit, did he not, to improve that journey, and make it a reall service to his soveraign,[2] procure one[3] article to be added to his instructions, which

---

[1] Misprints 'but' here. G.

[2] In the original edition, the sentence is by misprint repeated : and in the repetition ' Empire ' substituted for ' soveraign.' G.

[3] P 'an.' G.

gave him scope—as he passed—to salute such German princes, as were interested in the cause of our Religion, or their own native liberty?

And though to negotiate with that long-breathed Nation proves commonly a work in steel, where many stroaks hardly leave any print; yet did this master Genius quickly stir up their cautious and slow judgements to be sensible of the danger which threatned them hourely, by this fatall conjunction of Rome's undermining superstitions with the commanding forces of Spain. And when he had once awaked that confident Nation to look up, he as easily made manifest unto them, that neither their inland seat, vast multitudes,[1] confused strength, wealth, nor hollow-sounding fame, could secure their dominions from the ambition of this brave aspiring empire; howsoever by the like helps they had formerly bounded the same Roman, and Austrian supremacies. The reasons he alleged were, because the manner of this[2] conjunction was not like the ancient undertakers, who made open war by proclamation; but craftily—from the infusion of Rome—to enter first by invisible traffique of souls; filling people's minds with apparitions

---

[1] P, 'multitude':   M, spells 'multituds'.   G.
[2] P, 'their'   G.

of holines, specious rites, saints, miracles, in-
stitutions of new orders, reformations of old,
blessings of Catholiques, cursings of heretiques,
thunder-bolts of excommunication under the
authority of their Mother-Church.   And when
by these shadows they had once[1] gotten possession of the weak, discouraged the strong,
divided the doubtful, and finally[2] lulled inferior
powers asleep ; as the ancient Romans were wont
to tame forrain nations with the name of[3] *Socij* ;
then to follow on with the Spanish, less spirituall,
but more forcible engines, viz., practice, confeder-
acy, faction, money, treaties, leagues of traffique,
alliance by marriages, charge of rebellion, war,
and all other acts of advantagious power.

Lastly he recalled to their memories, how by
this brotherhood in evill—like Simeon and Levi—
Rome and Spain had spilt so much bloud, as they
were justly become the terror of all governments ;
and could now be withstood or ballanced by no
other means, than a general league in Religion :
constantly and truely affirming, that to associate
by an uniform bond of conscience, for the protection—as I said—of Religion and Liberty, would

---

[1] P, omits ' once.' G.   [2] P, misreads ' finely '. G.
[3] P, omits ' of '. G.

prove a more solid union, and symbolize far better
against their tyrannies, than any factious combination in policy, league of State, or other traffique
of civil or martial humours possibly could do.

To this end did that undertaking spirit lay, or
at least revive the foundation of a league between
us, and the German[1] Princes, which continueth[2]
firme to this day: the defensive part whereof hath
hitherto helped to support the ruines of our
Church abroad, and diverted her enemies from the
ancient ways of hostility unto their Conclave and
modern undermining arts. So that if the offensive part thereof had been as well prosecuted in
that true path, which this young genius trod out
to us ; both the passage for other princes over the
the Alps, would have been by this time more
easie than Hanibal's was ; and besides, the first
sound of that drum might happily have reconciled
those[3] petty dividing schismes which reign amongst
us ; not as sprung from any difference of religious
faith, but misty opinion ; and accordingly moulded
first upon the desks of busie idle Lecturers, then
blown abroad to our disadvantage by a swarm of
Popish instruments, rather Jesuits than Chris-

---

[1] M, 'Germanie'. G.   [2] P, 'contines'. G.
[3] 'these'. G.

tians; and to their ends most dangerously over-
spreading the world, for want of a confident
moderator.   This—I say—was the first prince
which did enfranchise his[2] master spirit into the
mysteries of[3] affairs of State.

---

[1] P, grossly misprints 'prize'.   G.
[2] P, as before 'this'.   G.
[3] P, 'and'.   G.

CHAP. V.

THE next doubtfull stage hee had to act upon—howsoever it may seem private—was grounded upon a publique and specious proposition of marriage, between the late famous Queen, and the Duke of Aniou. With which current, although he saw the great and wise men of the time suddainly carryed down, and every one fishing to catch the Queen's humor in it; yet when he considered the difference of years, person, education, state, and religion between them; and then called to minde the success of our former alliances with the French : he found many reasons to make question whether it would prove poetical or reall on their part ? And if reall ; whether[1] the ballance swayed not unequally, by adding much to them, and little to his soveraign ? The Duke's greatness being onely name and possibility ; and both these either to wither, or to be maintained[2] at her cost. Her state again in hand;

---

[1] P, misreads 'yet' before 'whether'. G.

[2] M, reads 'to maintained' which would seem to indicate 'be' to have been dropped inadvertently, and 'to' in like manner by P. G.

and though royally sufficient to satisfie that
Queen's princely and moderate desires or ex-
penses, yet perchance inferior to bear out those
mixt designes into which his ambition or necessities might entice or draw her.

Besides, the marriage of Kinge Phillipe,[1] to Queen
Marie[2] her sister, was yet so fresh in memory,
with the many inconveniences of it, as by comparing and paralleling these together, he fouud credible instances to conclude, neither of those[3] forrain
alliances could prove safe for this Kingdom.   Because in her marriage with Spain, though both
princes continuing under the obedience of the
Roman Church, neither their consciences, nor
their peoples could suffer any fear of tumult, or
imputation by change of faith; yet was the winning of St. Quintin[4] with the loss of Calice, and
the carrying away of our money to forrain ends,
odious universally; the Spanish pride incompet-
ible ;[5] their advantagious delayes suspicious; and
their short reign here[6] felt to be a kinde of exhausting tax upon the whole Nation.

Besides, he discerned how this great monarch

---

[1] P, ‘K. Philip’.   G.   [2] P, ‘Q. Mary’   G.
[3] P, ‘these’.   G.   [4] P, ‘St. Quintins’.   G.
[5] P, ‘incompatible’   G.   [6] M, misreads ‘their’.   G.

countenanced with our forces by sea and land,
might and did use this addition of her strength to
transform his Low-Countrey dukedomes, fall'n to
him by descent, into the nature of a soveraign
conquest : and so by conjoyning their dominion
and forces by Sea, to his large empires and armies
upon the mayn, would probably enforce all absolute princes to acknowledge subjection to him
before their time.   And for our Kingdome, besides
that this king then meant to use it as a forge, to
fashion all his soveraign designes in, had he not—
except some bely him—a fore-running hand in the
change of Religion after king Edward's death ?
And had he not—even in that change—so mastered us in our own Church, by his chaplain and
Conclave of Rome, that both these carried all
their courses byaced to his ends, as to an elder
brother, who had more abundant degrees of wealth
and honour to return them ? so as every body—
that devoted Queen excepted—foresaw we must
suddenly have been compelled to wear his livery
and serve his ends ; or else to live like children
neglected or disfavoured by our holy mother.

Again, for our temporall government, was not
his influence—unless[1] report belie him—as well in

---

[1] P, misreads 'except'.   G.

passing many sharp lawes and heavy executions
of them with more strange councels ; as fashioning[1] our leagues both of peace and traffique, to his
conquering ends? All these, together with that
master prize of his[2] playing, when under colour of
piety, he stirred up in that wel-affected Queen
a purpose of restoring those temporalities to the
Church, which by the fall of abbies, were long
before dispersed among the nobility, gentry, and
people of this kingdome : all these—as he said—
did clearly shew, that this ambitious king had an
intent of moulding us to his use, even by distracting us amongst our selves.

Neverthelesse, to give him the honor of worldly
wisedom, I dare aver, he had no hope of bringing
these enuiouse[3] assumptions to pass ; but rather
did cast them out, as sounding lines, to fathome
the depths of peoples mindes ; and with particular
fear and distraction in the owners, to raise a generall distast in all men against the Government.
Now, if we may judge the future by what is past,
his scope in all these particulars could be no other,
but when our inward waters had been thoroughly[4]
troubled, then to possess this diversly discas'd

---

[1] M, 'and fashioninge'.   G.   [2] P, drops ·his'.   G.
[3] P, 'curious'.   G.   [4] P, 'throughly'.   G.

Estate with certain poeticall titles of his own, devised long before, and since published by Dolman,
to the end, that under the shadow of such clouds,
he might work upon the next heir; and so cast[1] a
chance for all[2] our goodes, lives, and liberties, with
little interruption.   These and such like, were
the groundes which moved Sir Philip to compare
the past and present consequence of our Marriage
with either of these crowns together.

   And though in danger of subjection he did
confesse our alliance with the French to be lesse
unequall ; yet even in that he foresaw, diversitie
of Religion would first give scandall to both ; and
in progress, prove fatall of necessity to one side.
Because the weaker sorte[3] here, being fortified by
strong parties abroad, and a husband's name at
home, must necessarily have brought the native
soveraign under a kinde of *covert baron*, and
thereby forced her[4] Maiesty, either to lose the
freedom and conscience of a good Christian, the
honor of an excellent prince, or the private reputation of an[5] obedient wife.   Neither could that
excellent lady—as he and that time conceived—

---

[1] M, misreads 'ast'. G.   [2] M, omits. G.
[3] P, grossly misreads 'sect'. G.
[4] M omits. G.   [5] P, omits 'an'. G.

with these, or any other cautions, have counter-
mined the mines[1] of practice, whereby—it is
probable—this prince would have endeavoured to
steal change of Religion into her Kingdom.

1. As first, by cavelling at the Authors, and
Fathers that upheld her Church.

2. Then by disgracing her most zealous ministers, through aspersions cast upon their persons,
and advancing indifferent spirits, whose God is
this world, the Court their heaven, and consequently their ends, to byace[2] God's immortall truth
to the fancies[3] of mortall princes.

3. By the subtile latitude of School-distinctions,
publiquely edging nearer the holy mother the[4]
Church ; and therein first waving then sounding
the people's mindes ; if not with abrupt and spirit-
fall'n tolleration, yet with that invisible web of
connivencie, which is a snare to entangle great or
little flies, at the will of Power.

4. By a princely licenciousness in behaviour and
conference, fashioning atheisme among her subjects : as knowing that in confusion of thoughts,
he might the more easilie raise up superstitious

---

[4] M, 'minds', an evident misreading.   G.

[2] P, spells 'biace   G.   [3] P, ' fantasies .   G.

[4] P omits ' the '.   G.

idolatry: which crafty image of his, with all the nice lineaments belonging to it, was the more credible, in respect the French have scornfully affirm'd one chief branch of our prince's preroga- tives to be, the carrying of their people's con- sciences which way they list. An absoluteness the more dangerous to their subjects' freedom, because they bring these changes to pass—as the French say—under the safe conduct of our earth- eyd[1] common law; and thereby make change legally safe, and constancie in the truth exceeding dangerous.

5. By a publique decrying of our ancient cus- tomes and statutes; and from that ground, giving Proclamations a royall vigor in moulding of pleas, pulpits, and Parliaments, after the pattern of their own, and some other forain Nations; which in our government is a confusion, almost as fatall as the confusion of tongues.

6. By employing no instruments among the people, but such as devise to sheer them with taxes, ransome them with fines, draw in bondage[2] under colour of obedience, and—like Frenchified Empsons and Dudlies—bring the English people to the

---

[1] P, misprints 'earth-cy'.   G.

[2] M, 'poundage'.   G.

povertie of the French peasants, onely to fill up a
Danaus[1] sive of prodigality, and thereby to secure
the old age of Tyranny[2] from that which is never
old : I mean, danger of popular inundations.

7. To lift up[3] monarchie above her ancient legall
circles, by banishing all free spirits and faithfull
patriots, with a kinde of shaddowed ostracisme,
till the ideas of native freedom should be utterly
forgotten ; and then—by the pattern of their own
Duke of Guise—so to encourage a multitude of
impoverishing impositions upon the people, as he
might become the head of all discontentedness :
and under the envy of that art, stir them up to
depose their naturall annointed soveraign.

8. When he had thus metamorphosed our moderate form of monarchie into a precipitate absoluteness ; and therein shaken all leagues offensive and
defensive between us, the kings of Denmark or
Sweden, the free princes of Germany,[5] the poor
oppressed soules of France, the steady subsisting
Hanses ; and lastly weakned that league of Reli-

---

[1] M, omits　G.

[2] M, omits ' of prodigality .... old age ' and reads
simply ' a sive of tyrrany '.　G.

[3] M, omits.　G.

[4] P. mis-spells ' Garmany '.　G.

gion and traffique,[2] which with prosperous success hath continued long between us and the Nether-landers; then—I say—must his next project have been, either abusively to entise, or through fear enforce this excellent lady, to countenance his overgrown party abroad, by suffering the same sect to multiply here at home, till she should too late discover a necessity, either of changing her faith, hazarding her crown, or at least holding it at the joint courtesie of that ambitious Roman Conclave, or encreasing Monarchie of Spain. A scepter and miter, whose conjunction bringes forth boundless freedom to themselves, and begets a narrow servitude upon all other nations, that by surprise of wit or power become subject to them.

9. Besides, in the practice of this marriage, he foresaw and prophesied, that the very first breach of God's ordinance, in matching herself with a prince of a diverse faith, would infallibly carry with it some piece of the rending destiny, which Solomon, and those other princes justly felt, for having ventured to weigh the immortall wisdom in even scales, with mortall conveniency or inconveniency.

10. The next step must infallibly have been— as he conceived—with our shipping to disturb or

---

[2] Misprinted 'suffique': M, as in text.　G.

beleaguer the Netherlanders by Sea, under colour,
or pretence of honor unseasonably taken, even
when the horse and foot of France should threaten
their subsistence by land; and therby—in this
period of extremity—constrain[1] that active people
to run headlong into one of these three desperate
courses, viz., either to fly for protection to the
flower-de-luce,[2] with whom they join in continent;
or precipitately submit their necks to the yoking
cittadells of Spain, against whose inquisitions and
usurpations upon their consciences and liberties,
so much men[3] and bloud had been shed and consum-
ed already; or else unnaturally to turn pirates,
and so become enemies to that trade, by which
they and their friends have reciprocally[4] gotten,
and given so much prosperity. The choice or
comparison of which mischiefes to them and us,
he briefly[5] laid before me, in this manner.

First, that if they should incorporate with
France, the Netherlands manufactures, industry,
trade, and shipping, would add much to that
monarchie, both in peace and war: the naturall

---

[1] P, 'constraind.'   G.

[2] M, 'flower de lyce'.   G.   [3] P, 'money'   G.

[4] M, omits.   G.

[5] M 'preiflie (*sic*): the word has been corrected but
not completely.   G.

riches of the French having been hitherto either kept barrain at home, or barrainly transported abroad, for lack of the true use of trade, shipping, exchange, and such other mysteries as[1] multiply native wealth; by improving their man-hood at home, and giving formes both to domestique and forrain materialls; which defects[2]—as he said— being now abundantly to be supplied, by this conjunction with the Netherlands, would in a little time, not onely puff up that active Common-wealth with unquiet pride, but awake the stirring French to feel this addition to their own strengths; and so make them become dangerous neighbours by incursion or[3] inuasion to the Baltique Sea; many waies prejudice to the mutuall traffique between Italy, the Germans, and England; and consequently a terror to all others, that by land or Sea confine[4] upon them, yea and apt enough once in a year, to try their fortune with that growing monarch of Spain, for his Indian treasure.

Second, on the other side, if any stricter league

---

[1] M, 'a'. G.   [2] P, 'defect'. G.

[3] P, 'in'. G.

[4] See Milton: Paradise Lost (ii. 977)

"What readiest paths leads where your gloomie bounds *Confine* with Heav'n". G.

should come to pass between those adventurous
French spirits, and the solid counsells of Spaine;
and so through fear, scorn, or any other desperate
apparances force the Netherlanders[3] into a precipitate but steady subjection of that Spanish
monarchie; then he willed me to observe,
how this fearfull union of Earth and Sea, having
escaped the petty monarches of Europe, would in
all probability, constrain them to play after-games
for their own estates.   Because these two potent
navies—his and the Netherland's—being thus
added to his invincible armies by land, would
soon—as he thought—compell that head of holy
mother Church, whose best use for many yeares
had been — by ballancing these two emperiall
greatnesses one with another—to secure inferior
princes : would—as I said—soon enforce that
sacred mother-head to shelter her self under the
wings of this emperiall eagle, and so absolutely
quit her miter-supremacie; or at least become
chaplain to this suppressing, or supporting conqueror.

Besides, in this fatall probability he discovered
the great difference between the wisdom of quiet
princes, in their moderate desires of subsistence,

---

from the large and hazardous counsells of under-taking monarches; whose ends are onely to make force the umpier of right, and by that inequality become soveraign lords—with-out any other title —over equalls and inferiors.

Third, now for this third point, of constraining this oppressed, yet active Netherland people to become pirates : he willed me in the examples of time past to observe, how much Scirpalus[1] did annoy[2] the Grecians; Sextus Pompeius the Ro-mans, even in their greatness ; and in the modern, Flushing, Dunkerk, Rochell and Algiers. Infer-ring withall, that this people, which had so long prospered upon the rich materialls of all nations, by the two large spreading armes of manufacture and traffique, could not possibly[3] be forced at once to leave this habit : but would rather desperately adventure to maintain these enriching strengthes of marriners, souldiers, and shipping of their own, with becoming *rende-vous* for the swarm of discon-tented subjects universally; inviting them with hope of spoil, and by that inheritance, to try

---

[1] Qy = Sarpedon of Iliad vi. 199 : ii. 876 : V, 479 &c. &c. G.

[2] P, misreads 'among'.

[3] M, misreads 'possible'. G.

whether the world were ready to examine her old foundations of freedom, in the specious and flattering regions of change, and Power's encroachments?

Lastly, besides this uneven ballance of State; the very reflexion of scorn between age and youth; her comeliness, his disadvantage that way; the excessive charge by the[1] continuall resort of the French hither; danger of change for the worse; her reall native States and riches made subject to forrain humors; little hope of succession, and if any, then France assured to become the seat, and England the province; children, or no children, misfortune or uncertainty: These—I say—and such like threatning probabilities made him joyn with the weaker party, and oppose this torrent; even while the French faction reigning had cast aspersions upon his uncle of Leicester, and made him, like a wise man—under colour of taking physick—voluntarily become prisoner in his chamber.

---

[1] P, omits 'the'. G.

CHAP. VI.

HUS stood the state of things then : and if any judicious reader shall ask, Whether it were not an error and a dangerous one, for Sir Philip being neither magistrate nor coun- sellor, to oppose himself against his soveraign's pleasure in things indifferent? I must answer, That his worth, truth, favour, and sincerity of heart, together with his reall manner of proceed- ing in it, were his privileges. Because this gent- leman's course in this great business was, not by murmur among equals, or inferiours, to detract from princes; or by a mutinous kind of bemoan- ing error, to stir up ill affections in their minds, whose best thoughts could do him no good; but by a due address of his humble reason to the Queen her self, to whom the appeal was proper. So that although he found a sweet stream of sove- raign humors in that well-tempered lady, to run against him, yet found he safety in her self, against that selfness which appeared to threaten him in her; for this happily born and bred princess was not—subject-like—apt to construe things reverently done, in the worst sense; but rather with the spirit of annointed greatness—as created

to reign equally over frail and strong—more desirous to find waies to fashion her people, than
colours or causes to punish them.

Lastly, to prove nothing can be wise, that is
not really honest; every man of that time, and
consequently of all times may know, that if he
should have used the same freedome among the
grandees of Court—their profession being not
commonly[1] to dispute princes purposes for truth's
sake, but second their humours to govern their
Kingdomes by them—he must infallibly have
found worth, justice, and duty lookt upon with
no other eyes but Lamia's[2]; and so have been
stained by that reigning faction, which in all
Courts allows no faith currant to a soveraign,
that hath not past the seal of their practising corporation.

Thus stood the Court at that time; and thus
stood this ingenuous spirit in it. If dangerously

---

[1] M, 'comonly being, not'. G.

[2] Lamiæ (from Lamia, a female phantom) were conceived as handsome ghostly women who by voluptuous artifices
attracted young men: very much what the legendary
vampires are   Earlier, in Gascoigne's Glasse of Governe-
ment, Lamia, a courtesan, is one of the characters
(Hazlitt's Gascoigne, Vol. II. 2 *et alibi*): later, Lamia
gives title to one of Keats's greater poems, viz Lamia or
the Eve of St. Agnes. G.

in men's opinions who are curious of the present, and in it rather to doe craftily, than well: yet, I say, that princely heart of hers was a sanctuary unto him; and as for the people, in whom many times the lasting images of Worth are preferred before the temporary visions of art or favour, he could not fear to suffer any thing there, which would not prove a kind of trophy to him. So that howsoever he seemed to stand alone, yet he stood upright; kept his access to her Majesty as before; a liberall conversation with the French, reverenced amongst the worthiest of them for himselfe, and bound[1] in too strong a fortification of nature for the less worthy to abbord[2], either with question, familiarity, or scorn.

In this freedome, even whilst the greatest spirits and estates seemed hood-winkt or blind; and the inferior sort of men made captive by hope, fear, ignorance; did he enjoy the freedome of his thoughts, with all recreations worthy of them.

And in this freedome of heart being one day at tennis, a peer of this realm, born great, greater by alliance, and superlative in the prince's favour, abruptly came into the Tennis-Court; and speaking out of these three paramount authorities, he

---

[1] P, 'born'. G.   [2] =accost. G.

forgot to entreat that, which he could not legally command. When by the encounter of a steady object, finding unrespectiveness in himself—though a great lord—not respected by this princely spirit, he grew to expostulate more roughly. The returns of which stile comming still from an understanding heart, that knew what was due to it self, and what it ought to others, seemed—through the mists of my lord's passion,[1] swoln with the windes of this[2] faction then reigning—to provoke in yeelding. Whereby, the lesse amazement or confusion of thoughts he stirred up in Sir Philip, the more shadowes this great lord's own mind was possessed with: till at last with rage—which is ever ill-disciplin'd—he commands them to depart the Court. To this Sir Philip temperately answers; that if his lordship had been pleased to express desire in milder characters, perchance he might have led out those, that he should now find would not be driven out with any scourge of fury. This answer—like a bellows—blowing up the sparks of excess already kindled, made my lord scornfully call Sir Philip by the name of "puppy". In which progress of heat, as the tempest grew more and more vehement within, so did their hearts

---

[1] P, 'passions'. G.   [2] P, 'winde of his' G.

breath out their perturbations in a more loud and shrill accent. The French Commissioners unfortunately had that day audience, in those private galleries, whose windows looked into the Tennis-Court. They instantly drew all to this tumult : every sort of quarrels sorting well with their humors, especially this. Which Sir Philip perceiving, and rising with an[1] inward strength by the prospect of a mighty faction against him ; asked my lord, with a loud voice, that which he heard clearly enough before. Who—like an echo, that still multiplies by reflexions—repeates[2] this epithet of 'Puppy' the second time. Sir Philip resolving in one answer to conclude[3] both the attentive hearers and passionate actor, gave my lord a lie, impossible—as he averred—to be retorted ; in respect all the world knows, puppies are gotten by dogs, and children by men.

Hereupon those glorious inequalities of fortune in his lordship were put to a kinde of pause, by a precious inequality of nature in this gentleman. So that they both stood silent a while, like a dumb shew in a Tragedy ; till Sir Philip sensible of his own wrong, the forrain and factious spirits that

---

[1] P, omits 'an'. G.   [2] P, 'repeated'. G.

[3] = include. G.

attended ; and yet, even in this question between him, and his superior, tender of[1] his Countrie's honour ; with some words of sharp accent, led the way abruptly out of the Tennis-Court, as if so unexpected an accident were not fit to be decided any farther in that place. Whereof the great lord making another sense, continues his play, without any advantage of reputation; as by the standard of humours in those times it was conceived.

A day Sr. Philip remaines in suspense, when hearing nothing of or from the lord, he sends a gentleman of worth, to awake him out of his trance ; wherein the French would assuredly think any pause, if not death, yet a lethargy of true honour in both. This stirred up[2] a resolution in his lordship to send Sir Philip a challenge. Notwithstanding, these thoughts in the great lord wandred so long between glory and[3] anger and inequality of state, as the lords of her Majestie's Counsell took notice of these[4] differences, commanded peace, and laboured a reconciliation between them. But needlessly in one respect, and bootlesly in another. The great lord being—as it should

---

[1] P, 'to'. G.   [2] P, omits 'up'. G.
[3] P, omits 'and'. G.   [4] P, 'the'. G.

seem—either not hasty to adventure many inequalities against one, or inwardly satisfied with
the progress of his own acts: Sir Philip, on the
other side confident, he neither had nor would lose,
or let fall any thing of his right. Which her
Majestie's Counsell quickly perceiving, recom-
mended this work to her self.

The Queen, who saw that by the loss or disgrace
of either, she could gain nothing, presently under-
takes Sir Philip; and—like an excellent Monarch
—lays before him the difference in degree[1] between
earls and gentlemen; the respect inferiors owd[2]
to their superiors; and the necessity in princes to
maintain their own creations, as degrees descending
between the people's licentiousness and the annoynted soveraignty of crowns : how the gentleman's neglect of the nobility taught the peasant to
insult upon both.

Whereunto Sir Philip, with such reverence as
became him, replyed : First, that place was never
intended for privilege to wrong : witness her self,
who how soveraign soever she were by throne,
birth, education, and nature ; yet was she content
to cast her own affections into the same moulds
her subjects did, and govern all her rights by
their laws. Again he besought her majesty to

---

[1] M, 'degrees'.   G.   [2] P, 'ought'.   G.

consider, that although he were a great lord by birth, alliance, and grace ; yet hee was no lord over him: and therefore the difference of degrees between free men, could not challenge any other homage than precedency. And by her father's act—to make a princely wisdom become the more familiar—he did instance the government of Kinge[1] Henry the Eighth, who gave the gentry free and safe appeal unto[2] his feet, against the oppressions of the grandees; and found it wisdome, by the stronger corporation in number, to keep down the greater in power: inferring else, that if they should unite, the over-grown might be tempted by still coveting more, to fall—as the angels did —by affecting equality with their Maker.

This constant tenor of truth he took upon him ; which as a chief duty in all creatures, both to themselves and the soveraignty above them, protected this gentleman—though he obeyed not —from the displeasure of his soveraign. Wherein he left an authentical president to after ages, that howsoever tyrants allow of no scope, stamp, or standard, but their own will; yet with princes there is a latitude for subjects to reserve native and legall freedom, by paying humble tribute in manner, though not in matter, to them.

---

[1] P, ' K—g '. G.   [2] P ' to '. G.   [3] P, ' oppression.' G.

CHAP. VII.

THE next step which he intended into the world, was an expedition of his own projecting; wherein he fashioned the whole body, with purpose to become head of it himself. I mean the last employment but one of Sir Francis Drake to the West Indies. Which journey, as the scope of it was mixt both of sea and land service; so had it accordingly distinct officers and commanders, chosen by Sir Philip out of the ablest governors of those martiall times. The project was contrived between them[1] in this manner; that both should equally be governours, when they had left the shore of England; but while things were a preparing[2] at home, Sir Francis[3], was to beare the name, and by the credit of Sir Philip[4] have all particulars abundantly supplyed.

The reason of which secret carriage was, the impossibility for Sir Philip to win the Queen or Government—out of the value which they rated

---

[1] P, 'themselves'. G.   [2] M, 'prepareing'. G.
[3] P, 'Fran'. G.   [4] P, 'Phil'. G.

his worth at—to dispense with an employment for him so remote, and of so hazardous a nature. Besides his credit and reputation with the State lay not that way. So as our provident magistrates expecting a prentiship more seriously in martial, then[1] in mechanical actions ; and therein measuring all men by one rule ; would—as Sir Philip thought—not easily believe his unexperience equall for a designe of so many divers and dangerous passages : howsoever wise men, even in the most active times have determined this art of government, to be rather a riches[2] of nature, than any proper fruit of industry or education. This—as I said—was one reason, why Sir Philip did cover that glorious enterprise with a cloud. Another was, because in the doing, while it past unknown, he knew it would pass without interruption ; and when it was done, presumed the success would put Envy and all her agents to silence.

On the other side Sir Francis found that Sir Philip's friends, with the influence of his excellent inward powers, would add both weight and fashion to his ambition ; and consequently either with or without Sir Philip's company, yeeld unexpected ease and honor to him in this voiage.

---

¹ P, 'than'. G.   ² M, 'richesse'. G.

Upon these two divers counsels they treat confidently together; the preparations go on with a large hand amongst our governors; nothing is denyed Sir Francis that both their propounding hearts could demand. To make which expedition of less difficulty, they keep the particular of this plot more[1] secret than it was possible for them to keep the generall preparations of so great a journey; hoping that while the Spaniard should be forced to arm every where against them, he could not anywhere be so royally provided to defend himself, but they might land without[2] any great impediment.

In these termes Sir Francis departs for[3] Plimouth with his ships; vowed and resolved that when he staid for nothing but[4] a wind, the watchword should come post for Sir Philip. The time of the year made haste away, and Sir Francis to follow it either made more haste than needed, or at least seemed to make more than really he did. Notwithstanding, as I dare aver that in his own element he was industrious;[5] so dare I not con-

---

[1] M, omits. G.

[2] M, misreads ' with '. G.

[3] P, stupidly reads 'from '. G.

[4] P, inserts 'for' after 'but '. G.

[5] P, 'industrous'. G.

demn his affections in this misprision of time. Howsoever a letter comes post for Sir Philip, as if the whole Fleet stayed onely for him, and the wind. In the mean-season the State hath intelligence that Don Antonio was at sea for England, and resolved to land at Plimouth. Sir Philip turning occasion into wisdome, puts himself into the imployment of conducting up this king; and under that veil leaves the Court without suspicion; overshoots his father-in-law then secretary of Estate in his own bow; comes to Plimmouth; was feasted the first night by Sir Francis, with a great deale of outward pomp and complement.

Yet I that had the honor as of being bred with him from his youth; so now—by his own choice of all England—to be his loving and beloved Achates in this journey, observing the countenance of this gallant mariner more exactly than Sir Philip's leisure served him to doe; after we were laid in bed, acquainted him with my observation of the discountenance and depression which appeared in Sir Francis; as if our coming were both beyond his expectation and desire. Neverthelesse that ingenuous[1] spirit of Sir Philip's, though apt to give me credit, yet not apt to discredit others,

---

[1] M, 'ingeniouse' as usual. G.

made him suspend his own, and labour to change, or qualifie my judgement; till within some few daies after, finding the shippes neither ready according to promise, nor possibly to be made ready in many daies; and withall observing some sparcks of false fire, breaking out unawares from his yoke-fellow daily; it pleased him—in the freedom of our friendship—to return me my own stock, with interest.

All this while[1] Don Antonio[2] landed not; the Fleet seemed to us—like the weary passengers Inn—still to goe farther[3] from our desires; letters came from the Court to hasten it away: bot it[4] may be the leaden feet and nimble thoughts of Sir Francis wrought in the day, and unwrought by night; while he watched an opportunity to discover us, without being discovered.

For within a[5] few daies after a post steales up to the Court, upon whose arrivall an alarum is presently taken: messengers sent away to stay us, or if we refused, to stay the whole Fleet. Notwithstanding this first Mercury, his[6] errand being partly advertised to Sir Philip beforehand, was

---

[1] P, misprints 'whlie'. G.   [2] P, 'landes'. G.
[3] P, 'further'. G.   [4] P, omits 'bot' = but. G.
[5] M, omits 'a'. G.   [6] P, misprints 'this'. G.

intercepted upon the way; his letters taken from him by two resolute souldiers in marriners' apparell; brought instantly to Sir Philip, opened, and read. The contents as welcome as bulls of excommunication to the superstitious Romanist, when they enjoyn him either to forsake his right, or his holy Mother-Church, yet did he fit[1] this first processe, without noise or answer.

The next was a more imperiall mandate, carefully conveyed and delivered to himself by a peer of this realm; carrying with it in the one hand grace, the other thunder. The grace was an offer of an instant imployment under his unckle, then going generall into the Low-Countries; against which as though[2] he would gladly have demurred; yet the confluence of reason, transcendencie of Power, fear of staying the whole Fleet, made him instantly sacrifice all these sealf[3] places to the duty of obedience.

Wherein how unwillingly soever he yeelded up his knowledge, affections, publique and private endes in that journey; yet did he act this force in a gallant fashion. Opens his reserved ends to the generall; encourageth the whole army with pro-

---

[1] Query—sit? G.

[2] P, grossly misprints 'although'. G.

[3] P, misreads 'false' for 'sealf' = self. G.

mise of his uttermost assistance ; saves Sir Francis Drake from blastings of Court, to keep up his reputation among those companies he was presently to command; cleareth the daseled eyes of that army, by shewing them, how even in that forrain imployment, which took himself from[1] them, the Queen had engaged herself more waies than one against the Spaniard's ambition : so as there was no probability of taking away her princely hand from such a well-ballanced work of her own.

Neverthelesse as the limmes of Venus' picture, how perfectly soever begunne,[2] and left by Apelles, yet after his death proved impossible to finish:. so that heroicall design of invading and possessing America, how exactly soever projected and digested in every minute by Sir Philip, did yet prove impossible to be well acted by any other man's spirit than his own ; how sufficient soever his associate were in all parts of navigation ; whereby the success of this journey fell out to be rather fortunate in wealth, than honor. Yet to deale trulie with the dead, he was a man not onely sufficient in the triuiall parts of Nauigation, but euen large beyond his profession in untertakinge [*sic*] that vast Empire of Spaine, a masse so farre

---

[1] M, 'for'. G.   [2] P, 'began'. G.

aboue him in councell, wealth, and disciplin'd
armies.[1]

Whereupon, when Sir Philip found this and
many other of his large and sincere resolutions
imprisoned within the pleights of their fortunes,
that mixed good and evill together unequally,
and withall discerned how the idle-censuring
faction at home had won ground of the active
adventures abroad; then did this double depression
both of things and men, lift up his active spirit
into an universall prospect of time, States, and
things: and in them made him consider what impossibility there was for him, that had no delight
to rest idlie[2] at home, of re-propounding some
other forrain enterprise, probable and fit to invite
that excellent princesse's mind and moderate government, to take hold of. The placing of his
thoughts upon which high pinnacle, layd the
present map of the Christian world underneath
him.

---

[1] The words from 'Yet to deale .... disciplin'd armies',
printed here for the first time from the MS.   G.

[2] P, 'idle'.   G.

CHAP. VIII.

N which view, Nature guiding his eyes, first to his native Country, he found greatness of worth and place, counterpoysed there by the arts of power and favour. The stirring spirits sent abroad as fewell, to keep the flame far off: and the effeminate made judges of danger which they fear, and honor which they understand not.

The people — by disposition of the clime — valiant and multiplying, apt indifferently to corrupt with peace, or refine with action; and therefore to be kept from rust or mutiny, by no means better than by forrain employments: his opinion being that Islanders[1] have the air and waters so diversely moving about them, as neither peace nor war, can long be welcome to their humors, which must therefore be govern'd in either[2] by the active and yet steady hand of Authority. Besides he observed the sea to have so naturall a sympathie, with the complexions of them she

---

[1] P, 'Ilanders'.   G.   [2] P, omits 'in either'.   G.

invirons, as be it traffique, piracie, or war, they
are indifferent to wander upon that element;
and for the most part apter to follow undertaking
Chance, than any setled endes in a marchant-
traffique.

Now for the blessed lady which then governed
over us : how equall soever she were in her happy
creation, for peace, or war, and her people—as I
have shewed—humble to follow her will in either,
yet because she resolved to keep within the decorum
of her sex,[1] shewed herself more ambitious of ballancing neighbor princes from invading one another,
than under any pretence of title or revenge, apt
to question or conquer upon forrain princes posses-
sions. And though this moderate course carried her
into a defensive war, which commonly falleth[2] out
rather to be an impoverishing of enemies, than any
meanes to enrich or discipline their Estates that
undertake it; yet could not all the rackes of loss,
injury, or terror, stir this excellent lady into any
further degree of offensive war, than onely the
keeping of her Navy abroad, to interrupt the safe-
comming home of his Indian Fleet, and hinder
the provision contracted for in all parts of Europe,
to furnish another invincible Navy, wherewith he

---

[1] P, has 'she' after 'sex'. G.   [2] P, 'falls'. G.

purpos ed to besiege the world, and therein—as his first step—her divided Kingdomes.

On the other side, in his[1] survay of forrain Nations, he observed a fatall passivenesse generally currant, by reason of strange inequalities between little humours and great fortunes in the present princes' reigning.

Amongst whom for the first object Henry the Third of France appeares to him in the likeness of a good master, rather than a great king ; buried in his pleasures, his crown demain exhausted, impositions multiplyed, the people light, the nobility proud[2] to move, and consequently his Country apt, through scorn of his effeminate vices, either to become a prey for the strongest undertaker, or else to be cantonized by self divi-sion. In both which possible disasters, their native wealth and variety of objects, perchance have made both king and people—howsoever con-fusedly erring—yet to live secured by the provi-dence of Chance.

Again, he saw the vast body of the Empire resting—as in a dream—upon an immoveable centre of self-greatness; and under his[3] false

---

[1] P, 'this', as before. G.   [2] P, 'prone'. G.
[3] P, 'this' as before. G.

F

assumpsit, to have laid the bridle on the neck of the emperor, to work them artificially,[1] with a gentle or steady hand, to his own will.

And to confirm and multiply this clowdy danger, he discerned how that creeping monarchie of Rome—by her arch-instruments the Iesuits—had already planted fine Schooles of serving humanity in diverse of their reformed cities : intending so to tempt this welbelieving people, with that old forbidden tree of knowledge, as they might sin desperately against their own estates, before they knew it.

The like craftie mist-raisers[2] intented[3]—as he thought—to cast over that well-united fabrick of the Hanses : whose endes being meerly wealth, and their seats invironed on every side with active and powerfull neighbors, would—in all probability—make them as jealous of absolute princes in prosperity, as zealous in distress to seek protection under them.   So that they being at this time grown mighty by combination, if they should be neglected, would prove apt and able to sway the ballance unequally to the endes of the stronger.

---

[1] = artfully or with skill.   G.

[2] P, ' The like mist these crafty-raisers'.   G.

[3] P, invented : intented = intended G.

Besides, he discerned yet a greater and more malignant aspect from that spreading monarchie of Spain; which resolutely[1] commanding the house of Austria, governing the Conclave, and having gotten or affected[2] to get a commanding intelligence over these cities ; would soon multiply unavoidable danger, both to themselves and us, by mixing the temporall and spirituall sword, to his[3] crafty conquering ends.

Nay more ; how upon the same foundation they had begunne yet a more dangerous party, even amongst the German princes themselves; by adding to the fatall opposition of Religion between them, the hopes, feares, jealousies,[4] temptations of reward, or loss, with all the unnaturall seeds of division; which make them, through these confused threatnings and exticements, to become an easie prey for the Spaniard's watchfull, unsatiable, and much promising ambition.

He likewise observed Battorie,[5] that gallant man, but dangerously aspiring king of Poland, to be

---

[1] P, ' absolutely ' G.   [2] P, 'affecting ' G.

[3] P 'their'. G.

[4] P 'jealousie': M spells with 'i'. G.

[5] = Stephen Batory, duke of Transylvania, king of Poland: 1575-1586. G.

happily poysed[1] by the ancient competition between him and his nobility, and as busie to encroch upon their marches, and add more to his own limited soveraignty, as they were to draw down those few prerogatives it had, into that well mixt and ballanced Aristocracie[2] of theirs.

Denmark, howsoever by the opportunity and narrowness of his Sound, restrained to the self-ness of profit; yet by discipline and seat, able to second an active undertaker with shipping, money, &c. But too wise, with these strengths to help any forrain prince to become emperor over himself, or otherwise to entangle his Estate offen-sively or defensively in common actions.

The Sweden environed, or rather imprisoned with great and dangerous neighbours and enemies : the Polack[3] pretending title to his Kingdom, and with a continuall claim by sword, inforceing him to a[4] perpetuall defensive charge. The King of Denmark being unsafe to him upon every occa-sion, by ill neighbourhood among active princes.[5]

---

[1] P 'peised' = poised, ballanced.   G.

[2] M, 'Aristocrate' G.   [3] P, 'Polæ'.   G.

[4] M, omits 'a'.   G.

[5] M omits the sentence
     ' The king.........princes'.   G.

And lastly, the barbarous Moscovite, onely kept[1] quiet through his own distresse and oppressions else-where. So as like a prince thus strictly invironed, the king of Sweden could not — among princes—stand as any pregnant place of exorbitant help or terror, otherwise than by money.

The Switzers swoln with equality; divided at home; enemies, yet servants to monarchies, most[2] easily oppressed, in the opinion of those times; nor able to doe any thing of note alone : and so a dangerous body for the soul of Spaine to infuse designes into.

The princes of Italy carefull to bind one another by common caution; restrained from the freedom of their own counsells, by feare[3] of stronger powers above them, and as busie in keeping down their people, to multiply profit out of them, as to entise the stranger thither, to gain moderately by him. Through which narrow kind of wisdom, they being become rather merchant than monarchall States, were confined from challenging their own or enlarging their dominions upon neighbors ; and lastly, in aspect to other princes rights conjured

---

[1] P, omits 'kept' by mistake. G.

[2] P, 'not'. G.

[3] P, 'force'. G.

within neutrall circles, by the mysticall practise of an abusing Conclave and aspiring monarch of Spain.

The Moscovite bridled by his barbarous neighbor the Tartar : and through natural ignorance and incivility, like a poor tenant upon a rich farm, unequall to his inferiors.

The Grand Signior asleep in his Saraglia[1] ; as having turned the ambition of that growing monarchy into idle lust; corrupted his martiall discipline ; prophaned his Alcoran, in making war against his own Church, and not in person, but by his Basha's ; consequently by all appearance, declining into his people by such but more precipitate degrees, as his active ancestors had climbed above them.

Now while all these princes lived thus fettered within the narrowness of their own estates or humors ; Spain managing the popedome by vices,[2] and pensions among the cardinals, and having the sword both by land and sea in his hand ; seemed likewise to have all those Western-parts of the world, laid as a *tabula rasa* before him, to write where he pleased ; *Yo ill Rey.*[3]   And that which

---

[1] Seraglio. G.   [2] P, 'voices'. G.
[3] P, 'el Re'. G.

made this fatall prospect the more probable, was his golden Indian mines; kept open, not only to feed, and carry his threatning Fleets and Armies, where he had will or right to goe; but to make way and pretence for more, where he list, by corrupting and terrifying the chief counsels both of Christian and heathen princes. Which tempting and undermining course had already given such reputation both to his civill and martiall actions; that he was even then grown as impossible to please, as dangerous to offend.

And[1] out of which fearful almanack this wakeful patriot, besides an universal terror upon all princes saw—as I said—that this immense power of Spain did cast a more particular aspect of danger upon his native Countrey: and such as was not like[2] to be prevented or secured by any other antidote, than a generall League among free princes, to undertake this undertaker at home. To make this course plausible, though he knew the Qu[een] of England had already engaged her fortunes into it, by protecting the States Generall, yet perceiving her governours—as I said—to sit at home in their soft chairs, playing fast and loose with them that ventured their lives abroad; he

---

[1] M, omits 'and'. G.   [2] P, 'likely'. G.

providently determined that while Spain had peace, a pope, money or credit; and the world men, necessity or humors; the war could hardly be determined upon this Low-Countrey stage,[1] because if the neighbour-hood of Flanders, with help of the suddain sea-passage, should tempt these united princes to fall upon that limb of the Spanish empire; it would prove—as he supposed —an assailing of him in the strongest seat of his war; where all exchanges, passages, and supplies were already setled to his best advantage: and so a force bent against him, even where himself would[2] wish it.

Flanders being a province replenished with offensive and defensive armies: and fortified with divers strong cities: of which the assailing armies must be constrained, either to leave many behind them, or else to hazard the loss of time and their gallantest troops in besieging of one.

Again he conceived that France it self was like enough to be tender, in seconding our designes with horse or foot there; our neighbour-hood upon the same Continent—out of old acquaintance — not being over-welcome to them as he presumed.

---

[1] P, has period after 'stage'.   G.
[2] P, 'could'.   G.

And for succours from other princes; they were to come far and pass through divers dominions with difficulty, distraction, loss of time, and perchance loose-handed discipline: and so like the manie passages of a medicine, loose a great part of their vertue, before they come to worke.[1]

Whereupon he[2] concludes, first, that it would be hard for us to become absolute masters of the field in Flanders, or to ground our assailing of him there upon any other argument, than that ever-betraying *fallax* of undervaluing our enemies, or setling undertaking counsels upon market-men's intelligence, as Cæsar saith the French in his time used to do. Which confident wayes, without any curious examination what power the adverse party had[3] prepared to encounter, by defense, invasion, or division, must probably make us losers, both in men, money, and reputation. And upon these and the like assumpsits he resolved, there were but two ways left to frustrate this ambitious monarch's designes. The one, that which diverted Hanibal, and by setting fire on his own house

---

[1] P, The words "and so......worke" printed here for first time from the MS. G.

[2] P, 'and so' concludes'. G.

[3] P, 'hath'. G.

made him draw in his spirits to comfort his heart; the other that of Iason by fetching away his golden fleece, and not suffering any one man quietly to enjoy that, which every man so much affected.[1]

---

[1] Note in preceding pages the use of the word '*ballancing*' : and see a query onward (page 102) relative to its use. G.

CHAP. IX.

TO carry war into the bowels of Spain, and by the assistance of the Netherlands, burn his shipping in euery haven[1] as they passed along; and in that passage surprize some well-chosen place for wealth, and strength : easie to be taken, and possible to be kept by us : he supposed to be the safest, most quick, and honourable counsell of diversion. Because the same strength of shipping which was offensively imployed to carry forces thither and by the way to[2] interrupt all martiall preparations and provisions of that griping State, might by the convenient distance between his coast and ours—if the Spaniard should affect to pay us with our own monies[3] —fitly be disposed both wayes : and so like two arms of a naturall body— with little addition of charge—defend and offend : spend and supply at one time.

Or, if we found our own stock or neighbours' contribution strong enough to follow good success

---

[1] P, 'all havens'.   G.   [2] M omits 'to'.   G.
[3] M, omits 'if the......own monies'.   G.

to greater designes; then whether our adventure once more, in stirring up spirit in the Portugall against the Castilians tyranny over them, were not to cast a chance for the best part of his wealth, reputation and strength, both of men and shipping in all his dominions.

Again, lest the pride of Spain should be secretly ordain'd to scourge it self, for having been a scourge to so many, and yet in this reall inquisition escape the audacity of undertaking princes; Sir Philip thought[1] fit to put the world in mind, that Sevill was a fair city; secure in a rich soyl and plentiful traffique; but an effeminate kind of people, guarded with a conquering name; and consequently a fair bait to the piercing eyes of ambitious generals, needy souldiers, and greedy mariners. In like sort hee mentioned Cales, as a strength, and key to her[2] traffiquefull and navigable river, not fit to be neglected in such a defensive and diverting enterprise, but at least to be examined.

Lastly, whether this audacity of undertaking the conqueror at home; would not, with any moderate success, raise up a new face of things in those parts and suddainly stir up many spirits, to

---

[1] M, misreads 'though'. G.   [2] M omits 'her'. G.

move against the same power, under which they long have layne[1] slavishly conjur'd, and by this affront, prove a deforming blemish in the nice fortune of a fearfull usurper?

Or if that shall be thought an undertaking too full of charge, hazard, or difficulty; then whether it wil not be just in the wisdome of Estate, managed among active princes; that as Queene[2] Elizabeth had ever been tender, in preserving her soveraignty upon the narrow seas; and wisely considered, how Nature, to maintain that birthright of hers, had made all wars by sea far more cheap, proper, and commodious to her, than any expedition upon land could possibly[3] be: I say, whether to continue this claim, would not prove honour to herself, advantage to her traffique, and reputation to her people; I mean,[4] if shee should please, in those cloudy humors and questions reigning between her self and other princes, to keep a strong successive fleet, all seasonable times of the year, upon this pretty sleeve[5] or Ocean of hers? I say, to keep them as provident surveyers

---

[1] P, 'bin'. G.   [2] P, 'Qu.' G.
[3] M, misreads 'possible'. G. [4] M, omits 'I mean'. G.
[5] = narrow channel of the sea, especially that between England and France. G.

[of] what did passe from one State to another, wherein the law of Nature or Nations had formerly given her interest to an offensive or defensive security. A regall inquisition, and worthy of a sea-soveraign, without wronging friends or neighbours, to have a perfect intelligence what they had, or wanted for delicacy, peace, or war in generall: and in particular a clear perspective glass into her enemies merchant or martiall traffique, enabling this queen so to ballance this ambitious Leviathan in either kind; as the little fishes, his fellow citizens, might travell, multiply and live quietly by him under the protection of Nature.

Again, let us consider, whether out of this, or the like audit, it will not be found a just tribute to opportunity, the rudder of all state wisedoms. That as Queene[1] Elizabeth was a soveraign, which rested with her sex at home, and yet moved all sexes abroad to their own good; whether—I say —as she from a devoted zeal to the Church, had by Sir Nicholas[2] Throgmorton, in the beginning of her reign, stirred up spirits in that over-mitred French kingdom, to become watchfull guardians of peace and religion there. I say, whether in the same Christian providence there might not,

---

[1] P, 'Qu.' G. [2] P, 'Nich.' G.

by the neglect or breach of many Treaties, an occasion be justly taken to reap a reasonable harvest out of that well-chosen seed time, by receiving Rochel, Brest, Bourdeaux, or any other place upon that Continent, distressed for Religion, into her absolute protection? Nevertheless, not with intent of reconquering any part of her ancient demeasnes,[1] lineally descended from many ancestors; howsoever those places so taken may seem seated like tempters of princes, to plead in the court of Mars such native, though discontinued[2] rights, as no time can prescribe against; but only to keep those humble religious souls free from oppression, in that super-Jesuited soveraignty.

In which religious designe to encourage the Queen[3] he advised us to examine if the diuisions[4] naturally rising amongst their unlimited French grandees, grown up *per saltum* with their kings, above laws, Parliaments, and People's freedom; would not in all probability cast up som light dust into their superiors eys, as tributes to their common idol Discorder; and so perchance either

---

[1] P, 'Domaines'. G.

[2] M, 'disconted'. G.

[3] P, 'Qu.' G.

[4] P, grossly misreads 'diversions'. G.

by treaty, or sight of the first army, stir up Bouil-
lon and Rohan for religion; other royteletes[1] w^th
hope to make safe their subaltern governments,
even through the ruines of that over-soring soveraignty ?

And is it[2] not as probable again[3] that even the
great[4] cities, raised and standing upon the like
waving encroachments of time and advantagious
power, would readily become jealous of the least
strict hand carried over them, by interruptinge[5]
of traffique, greediness of governors, pride of their
own wealth, or indefinite impositions; as Paris,
Bourdeaux, Marseilles,[6] Roan, or Lyons ? whereby
they might likewise be tempted, either to run
head-long with the stream, or at the least to stand
at gaze, and leave the heraldries[7] of princes to be
decided by the stronger party, as for the most
part, they hitherto have been.

Nay in this climax to come nearer yet ; is it
probable that even the Catholique princes and
provinces environing this vast Kingdome, would
—as now they doe—for want of vent, break their

---

[1] = kinglets, little kings. G.   [2] P, misdrops 'it'. G.

[3] M, omits 'again'. G.   [4] P, 'greatest'. G.

[5] P, 'interruption'. G.   [6] M, 'Marsiles'. G.

[7] P, 'Heraldry'. G.

hopes, and servilly run out upon the ground like water, and not rather when this new rent should appear, chuse to shake off a chargeable and servile yoke of mountebank holiness under Spanish Rome, and to that end presently mingle money, counsels, and forces with ours? As quickly resolved that this way of a ballancing union, amongst absolute princes, would prove quieter rests[1] for them, and sounder foundations for us, than our former parties did, when we conquered France, more by such factious and ambitious assistances, than by any odds of our bows or beef-eaters, as the French were then scornfully pleas'd to terme us: I say, even when in the pride of our conquests, we strove to gripe more than was possible for us to hold; as appears by our being forced to come away, and leave our ancestors bloud and bones behind, for monuments not of[2] enjoying, but of over-griping and expulsion.

So that the sum of all is; whether the taking or surprize of Cales, Rochel, Bourdeaux, or some such other good out or inlet upon the maine[3], offered into our protection,[4] would not prove

---

[1] P. 'rest'. G.   [2] M, omits 'of'. G.
[3] P, , that Mayn '. See Glossary-index *s.v.* G.
[4] The words " offered......protection " *not* in MS. G.

G

an[1] honour to us, as a brave earnest either to war
or peace ?   Beneficiall to the French king and
crown against their wills ; as manifesting to their
hot spirits, and young councels, that undertaking
is not all ?   And besides clearly shewing, in Mars,
his true glass, how that once wel-formed Monarchy had by little and little, let fal her ancient,
and reverend[2] pillars—I mean Parliaments, lawes
and customes—into the narrowness of proclamations
or imperiall mandates : by which, like bastard
children of Tyranny, she hath transformed her
gentry into peasants, her peasants into slaves,
magistracy into sale works and crowne-revenue[3]
into impositions.   And therein likewise published
the differences between monarchs and tyrants so
clearly to the world, as hereafter all estates, that
would take upon their necks the yoke of Tyranny,
must justly be reputed voluntary slaves in the
choice of that passive bondage.

Whereby, one question naturally begetting
another, the next—as I take it—must be what
this Austrian aspiring familie would doe, while
these two kingdomes should stand thus engaged ?

---

[1] P, omits ' an ' : M spells ' honor '.   G.

[2] M, spells ' reuerent '.   G.

[3] P, ' crown-revenue '.   G.

Whether invade the king of Denmark alone, hoping by his ruine to subdue the yet unsubdued[1] princes of Germany, to get the Sound, and Eastern Seas, with all their maritime riches[2] into his power : to bring the Hanse towns into some captivated subjections, and thereby become soveraign over all Eastern traffique by sea, and by land ? Or else by lulling France asleep with imperiall matches or promises, finde meanes to steal the flower-de-luce into the lyon's garland ; and in that currant of prosperity to citadellize the long oppressed Netherlands into a tenure of uttermost bondage ; and so build up his eagle's nest above the threatening of any inferior region.

But it many times pleaseth God by the breaking out of concealed flashes from these fatall cloudes of craft, or violence, to awake even the most superstitious princes out of their enchanted dreams ; and cause them to resolue[5] suddainly to make head against this devouring Sultan, with leagues offensive and defensive: and by an unexpected union to become such frontier neighbours to this crown-hunter, as

---

[1] P, grossly misprints 'subdued'.   G.

[2] M, spells oddly 'ritchesses'.   G.

[3] P, omits 'by'.   G.

[5] P, grossly misprints 'resist'   G.

he might with great reason doubt their treadinge[1] upon-his large cloven feet, who intended to have set them so heavily upon the heads of many more ancient States, peoples, and[2] scepters than his own. And lastly in the same press, by this one affront in the lion's face, publishing to the world that power is infinite no where but in God : so as the first blow well stricken, most commonly succeeds with honor and advantage to the judicious, able, and active undertakers.

Out of which divine providence, governing all second causes by the First, is it not probable that even the natural vicissitudes of war and peace, would bring forth some active propositions between these many waies allied kingdomes of England and France, to a[3] perfect reconciliation, and as many again of irreconciliable divisions between them and Spain ?   France being stirred up by a joint counsell and proposition of assistance, to the recovery of her long sleeping rights in Navarre or Naples; and England onely to distract this ambitious monarch from his late custom, in deposing kings and princes, as Navarre, Portugall, the Palatine, Brunswick, &c., and[4] as in a second

---

[1] P, in like manner misprints 'trading.'   G.
[2] P, 'or'.   G.   [3] M, omits 'a'.   G.
[4] P, misplaces &c. after 'and'.   G.

course of his devouring gluttony, interrupt him from future prosecution[1] of Denmark, and Germany it self, to the same end ;[2] with this[3] constant intent, to bring all the earth under one man's tyranny.

To prevent which deluge of boundless power, Sir Philip was of opinion, that more than charge, it could be no prejudice; if to the unvizarding of this masked triplicity between Spain, Rome and the soveraign Iesuits of France ; I say if the Queen, as defendress of the faith, for a main pledg of this new[4] offensive and defensive undertaken League,[5] would be pleased to assist the French king with the same forces by Sea or land, wherewith, till then, she had justly opposed against him. And consequently putting the Spaniard from an offensive, to a defensive war, manifestly publish and give credit to this unbelieved truth, viz : that this arch-conqueror never intended other favor to the Pope, emperor, or Iesuits, in all this conjunction, than Poliphemus promised to Vlysses,[6] which

---

[1] P, ' prosecutions '.   G.

[2] M, omits ' to the same end '.   G.

[3] P, misprints ' his '.   G.

[4] M, omits.   G.

[5] M, ' league undertaken '.   G.

[6] Homer : Od. ix. 369.   G.

was, that they should be the last whom[1] he
purposed to devour.

And further[2] to encourage these great princes
in this true balancing designe[3] with the chargeable and thorny passages proper to it; he providently saw the long threatned Dutchie of Savoy
would be in their view : with assurance that this
active prince would think it a safe diversion of
dangers from his domesticall Estate, and a fit
stage to act his forrain cobwebbs upon, if he might
have them shadowed under the wings of stronger
and every way more able princes ;[4] without which,
his weake[5] Estate must in all probability force
him to shift his outward garments perchance too
often.

The Venetians again, foreseeing with their
aristocraticall jealousie, that their Estate had
onely two pregnant dangers hanging over it; the
one Eastward from the grand Signior, who easily
moves not his encumpassing half moon ; the other
Westward from this Solyman of Spain, whose
unsatiable ambition, they knew, would rest upon

---

[1] M' 'which '.   G.   [2] P, ' farther '.   G.
[3] Have we here the source of the phrase ' *balance* of
power '.   G.
[4] P ' Powers '.   G.   [5] P, ' mean '.   G.

no centre, but creep along the Mediterranean Seas, till he might—contrary to the nature of those waters—over-flow all weake[1] or secure neighbor princes, without any other title or quarrell, than *stet pro ratione voluntas*. And foreseeing again in this suddain violence, that they could expect no estate to be.selfly engaged to[2] their succor ; but must resolve to stand or fall alone by that course.[3] Where, on the other side, if the Eastern half moon should but seem to move towards them, they were assured to have all the estates of Europe, engaged by their own interest, to joine with them. Upon this view there is no doubt, but that wise city would have resolved it to be a choice of the[4] lesse evill, to joine with these great princes, in diverting his Spanish gallies and galleons by Sea, and his inveterate armies by land from disturbing or subjecting the safety and traffique of all Christendom to his seven patch'd coated kingdomes, rather than for want of heart not[5] opportunity, to stand neuter—as they doe—and become treasurers both of money and munition for him, that already intends thus[6] to conquer them and enjoy it.

---

[1] P, 'weak'. G.   [2] P, 'in'. G.

[3] 'By that course' not in M.   G.

[4] P, omits 'the'. G.   [5] P, 'or'. G.

[6] M, omits. G.

Again, shall we—said Sir Philip—in these collections of particulars, forget the State of Italy it self? which excellent temper of spirits, earth, and aire, having long been smothered and mowed down by the differing tyrannies of Spain and Rome, shall we not be confident they would, upon the approaching of these armies, both stir up those benumbed soveraignties, which onely bear the name of free princes, to affect their own manumissions, and help to chase away those[1] succeeding and oppressing[2] garrisons, whose fore-fathers for many years since[3] had sold life, libertie, and lawes for eight pence the day?[4] and so resolutely oppose those Spanish-born, or Spanish[5]-sworn tyrannies, which have for divers ages lorded over that most equally tempered Nation and their natiue Princes.[6]

Or whether the winter in those seas, giving opportunity without suspition, might[7] not encourage an advantagiouse[8] claime of our old rights in the kingdome of Sicilie, more legall laid[9] than

---

[1] P, 'these'. G. [2] M, 'suppressing'. G.
[3] P, omits 'since'. G. [4] P, ; . G.
[5] P, omits the second Spanish.' G.
[6] P, omits ' and......princes'. G.
[7] P, 'may'. G. [9] P, omits 'laid'. G.
[8] P, omits 'advantagiouse'. G.

most of his Spanish intrusions ; and therein be welcome to the Grand Signior, the freedome of Algiers, nay euen[1] to Italy it self. And besides, if we prospered, yield abundance of wealth by spoil and trade : with such a seat for diversion or possession, as by many visible and invisible helps, might be kept, or put away with infinite advantage ?

Lastly, he made a quære, whether the Pope himself could[2] not—like a secular prophet —to keep his becoming chaplain a little[3] farther off ; either wink or at least delay his thundering curses, or supplies of Peter-pence against these qualifying armies, onely to moderate the over-greatnesse of this[4] Spanish monarchie ? whose infancie having been nourished under the miter's holy water, and sophistries of his practising Conclaves, dares now imperiously publish to the world a resolution, of taking all other distinctions from amongst men, saving that canonicall regiment[5] of wit and might, seeing the Pope thereby might preserve[6]

---

[1] P, omits ' nay ', and spells ' even '.   G.
[2] P, ' would '.   G.
[3] P, misinserts ' the ' after ' little '.   G.
[4] P, as before, misprints ' his '.   G.
[5] Government or rule.   G.
[6] P, has ' whereby he might so preserve '.   G.

his spirituall ambition entire, without any charge
or change of Religion, or soveraignties from one
hand to another, but like a holy father mediate
the restoring of Italy to her ancient freed,[1] and
distinct principalities. Whereby[2] now by this
moderate course, admit the Pope for his part,
should impair his temporall profits and subaltern
jurisdiction a while, yet shall he be sure—as I
said[3]—to multiply his spirituall honors and inlarge
that kingdom, by these works of supererogation.
And by joyning with his fellow-princes in a contribution, by way of accompt or countenance to
pay these great armies, be sure to sit rent-free
under his and their own vines, as absolute spirituall and temporall princes ought to doe?

From which—saith he—this conclusion will
probably follow ; that the undertaking of this
Antonie single, I mean France, would prove a
begetting of brave occasions jointly to disturb this
Spanish Augustus,[4] in all his waies of crafty, or
forcible conquests. Especially since Queen Elizabeth,[5] the standard of this conjunction, would
infallibly incline to unite with the better part,

---

[1] P, ' free '. G.   [2] M, omits. G.
[3] M, omits ' as I said '. G.   [4] P, ' Ottoman '. G.
[5] ' M, ' Elizab '. G.

and by a suddain changing of Mars his imperious ensignes into a well ballanced treaty of universall peace, restore and keep the world within her old equilibrium or bounds.[1]

And the rather, because her long custom in governing, would quickly have made her discern, that it had been impossible, by force or any human wisdom to have qualified those[2] overgrown combinations of Spain; but onely by a countermining of party with party, and a distracting of exorbitant desires, by casting a gray-headed cloud of fear over them; thereby manifesting the well-disguised yokes of bondage, under which our modern conquerors would craftily entice the nown-adjective-natured princes and subjects of this time, to submit their necks. A map—as it pleased her to say—of his secrets, in which she confessed herself to be the more ripe, because under the like false ensignes, though perchance better masked, she had seen Philip the second after the same measure, or with little difference, to Henry the third of France, a principall fellow[3]-member in that earthly founded, though heavenly seeming Church of Rome, when he redelivered Amiens,[4]

---

[1] M, ' bonds ' : see Glossary-index for ' equilibrium.' G.
[2] P. 'these'. G.
[3] M, omits. G.   [4] P misprints ' Amiens'. G.

Abbeville, &c., together with that souldier-like passage made by the Duke of Parma through France to the relief of Roan ;[1] yet whether this provident Philip did frame these specious charities of a conqueror, Augustus-like aspiring to live after death greater than his successor ; or provi- dently foreseeing that the divers humors in suc- ceeding princes, would prove unable to maintain such green usurpations, in the heart of a kingdom competitor with his seven-headed Hydra kept together onely by a constant and unnaturall wheel[2] of fortune, till some new child of hers, like Henry the fourth, should take his turn in restoring all unjust combinations or encroachments ; or lastly, whether like a true cutter of cumine seedes, he did not craftily lay those[3] hypocriticall sacrifices upon the altar of death, as peace-offerings from pride to the temple of fear, as smoaks of a dyeinge diseased conscience[4] choked up with innocent bloud : of all which perplexed pedigrees, I know not what to determine otherwise ; than that these tyrannicall enchrochments[5] doe carry the images of

---

[1] P, ' Paris '.   G.   [2] M, omits.   G.

[3] P, ' these '.   G.

[4] P. misreads ' dying of a diseased '.   G.

[5] M, spells without the first ' h '.   G.

Hell, and her thunder-workers, in their own breasts, as fortune doth misfortunes in that wind-blown, vast, and various womb of hers.

Or if this should seem of too high a nature, or of[1] too many chargeable parts : then whether to begin again where we left, and by the example of Drake, a mean born subject to the crown of England, to[2] invade, possess, and inhabite some well chosen havens in Peru,[3] Mexico, or both, were not to strike at the root, and assail him where he is weakest; and yet gathers his chiefest strength to make himself monarch over all these[4] Western climes? supplyes being as easie to us, as to him, we having both winds and seas indifferently open between us.

---

[1] P, omits ' of '. G.

[2] P, omits ' to '. G.

[3] M, ' Pera ' (sic). G.

[4] P, ' all the '. G.

CHAP. X.

UPON due consideration of which particulars, he fore-seeing that each of the former required greater resolution, union, and expense, than the neutralitie,[1] diffidence, and quiet complexion of the princes then reigning could well bear; and besides the freedome of choyce to be taken away, or at the least obstructed by fatall mists of ignorance or factious councells reigning among the ministers of kings : he resolved from the only[2] grounds of his former intended voiage with Sir Francis Drake, that the onely credible means left, was, to assail him by invasion or incursion—as occasion fell out—in some part of that rich and desert West-Indian Mayne.[3]

First, because it is an observation amongst[4] the wisest, that as no man is a prophet in his own Countrey; so all men may get honour much cheaper far off than at home, and at sea more easily than at land.

---

[1] P, grossly misprints 'naturality'. G.

[2] M, omits. G.

[3] P, grossly misprints 'Mine'. G.

[4] P, 'among', G.

Secondly, in respect he discovered the Spanish conquests in those remote parts, so much noised throughout the world, to be indeed like their Jesuits miracles; which coming far, were multiplied by fame and art, to keep other Nations in wonder and blind worship.

Thirdly, out of confident beliefe, that their inhumane cruelties had so dispeopled and displeased those countreys that, as he was sure to find no great power to withstand him·; so might he well hope the reliques of those oppressed Cinnons[1] would joyfully take arms with any forrainer to redeem their liberty and revenge their parents' bloud.

Fourthly, by reason the scale of distance between Spain and America was so great; as it infallibly assured Sir Philip, he should find leasure enough to land, fortifie, and become master of the field, before any succour could come thither to interrupt him.

Fiftly, the pride, delicacy, and security of the Spaniard, which made him live without discipline,

---

1 P, 'Cimenons'. The correct word as in text is = savages. It is Spanish, and *s. v.* the Dictionary of the Spanish Academy explains it as " an adjective which is applied in the Indies to men and animals uncivilized and dwelling in the mountains, and to wild plants." G.

and trust more to the greatness of his name abroad, than any strength, order, courage, or munition at home.

Sixtly, Sir Philip prophecying what[1] pedigrees of princes did warrant, I mean the happy commixion[2] of Scotland to these populous realms England and Ireland, foresaw, that if this multitude of people were not studiously husbanded and disposed of,[3] they would rather diminish, than add any[4] strength to this monarchy. Which danger—he conjectured—could only by this designe of forrain imploiment, or the peaceable harvest of manufactures at home, be safely prevented.

The seventh, and a chief motive indeed was, that no other action could be less subject to emulation of Court, less straining to the present humors of State, more concurring with expectation and voice of time; nor wherein there was greater possibility of improving merit, wealth, and friends.

Lastly, he did, as all undertakers must doe, believe that there is ever good intelligence between Chance and Hazard, and so left some things not summed up before hand by exact minutes. But

---

[1] P, mis-inserts ' the ' after ' what '.   G.
[2] P, ' conjunction '.   G.   [3] P, omits ' of '.   G.
[4] M, drops ' any '.   G.

rather thought good to venture upon the cast of
a Rubicon dy ; either to stop his springs of gold,
and so drie up that torrent which carried his sub-
duing armies every where ; or else by the wakefull providence of threatned neighbors, force him
to waft home that conquering metall with infinite
charge, and notwithstanding unwarranted, from
enriching those enemies whom he principally studied to suppress by it.

To confirm which opinion, he fore-saw how this
ouer[1] racked unitie[2] of the Spanish-government—
intending to work a change in the free course of
Nature—had interdicted all manufacture, traffick,
or vent by sea or land, between the natives of
America, and all nations else, Spain excepted.
And withall, to make the barrenness of Spain
more fertile, how he had improved that idle
Castilian, by imployments, in activeness, wealth,
and authority over those vanquished creatures ;
suffering the poor native Americans to be supprest
with heavy impositions, discouraging idleness,
bondage of laws, sheering of the humble sheep to
cloath the proud devouring wolves ; finally, under
these and such like quintessences of tyranny,

---

[1] P, omits ' ouer '.   G.
[2] P, grossly misprints ' vanity '.   G.

striving—as I said—even besides Nature, to make
barren Spain[1] the monarchy, and that every way
more[2] fertile America to be the province. All which
affectations[3] of power to be wiser and stronger
than the truth, this gentleman concluded would
in the[4] fulness of time make manifest; that the
heavy can no more be forced to ascend and be[5]
fixed there, than the light to goe downward, as to
their proper center.

Notwithstanding, the state of tyrants is so
sublime, and their errors founded upon such precipitate steps, as this growing Spaniard both did,
doth, and ever will travell—with his forefathers in
Paradise—to be equall, or above his Maker; and
so to imprison divine lawe[6] within the narrownes
of will, and humane wisdome, with the fettred
selfnesses[7] of cowardly or ouer[8] confident Tyranny.
In which preposterous courses, to prevent all
possibility of commotion[9], let the reader be pleased to observe, how out of those desperate councells

---

[1] M, omits 'Spain'. G.   [2] M, omits. G.

[3] P, 'affections'. G.   [4] P, omits 'the'. G.

[5] P, 'rest'. G.   [6] P, 'laws'. G.

[7] P, misprints 'selfsnesses'. G.

[8] P, grossly misprints 'other'. G.

[9] M, 'comiction'. G.

of oppression[1] he forceth his own subjects in[2] free
denized America, to fetch weapons of defence,
conquest, invasion ; as well as ornament, wealth,
necessity, and delicacy, out of Spain, meerly to
retain want, supply, price, weight, fashion, and
measure, still—contrary to Nature—in that barren
crown of Castile, with an absolute power resting
in himself to rack,[3] or ease both peoples, according
to the waving ends of an unsteddy and sharp
pointed pyramis of power.

Nay, to rise yet a step higher in this bloudy
pride, Sir Philip, our unbelieved Cassandra, observed this limitless ambition of the Spaniard to
have chosen that uttermost citadell of bondage, I
mean the Inquisition of Spain, for her instrument.
Not, as in former masks, to prune or govern ; but
in a confidence rising out of the old age of superstitious fantasms, utterly to root out all seeds of
humane freedom ; and—as Sr Philip conceived—
with fatall dissolution to it self. In respect that
these types of extremity would soon publish to
the world, what little difference tyrants strive to
leave between the creation, use and honor of men

---

[1] P, reads simply 'how that continually he forceth.' G.
[2] P, omits 'in'. G.
[3] P, grossly misprints 'rock'. G.

and beasts, valuing them indifferently but as counters, to sum up the divers, nay contrary uses and audits of sublime and wandring supremacy, which true glass would — in this gentleman's opinion—shew the most dull and cowardly eye. that tyrants be not nursing fathers, but step-fathers ; and so no anointed deputies of God, but rather lively images of the dark prince, that sole author of dis-creation and disorder, who ever ruines his ends with over-building.

Lastly, where his reason ended, there many divine precepts and examples did assure him, that the vengeance of God must necessarily hang over those hypocritical cruelties, which under colour of converting souls to Him. sent millions of better than their own, they cared not whither : and in stead of spreading Christian religion by good life, committed such terrible inhumanities, as gave those that lived under nature, manifest occasion to abhor the liuelie[1] characts[2] of so tyranical a deity.

Now though this justice of the Almighty be many times slow, and therefore neglected here on

---

[1] P, oddly misreads 'devily'.   G.

[2] P, 'characters': M, is 'chararts', a slip for 'char-acts', on which see Glossary-Index.   G.

Earth; yet—I say—under the only conduct of this star, did Sir Philip intend to revive this hazardous enterprize of planting upon the main of America: projected, nay undertaken long before, —as I shewed you—but ill executed in the absence of Sir Philip; with a designe to possess *Nombre de Dios*, or some other haven near unto it, as places, in respect of the little distance between the two seas, esteemed the fittest *rendez-vouz* for supply or retreat of an army upon all occasions. And besides resolued to circle[1] in his wealth and freedome, with a joynt fore-running fleet in the South sea;[2] to the end, that if the fortune of conquest prospered with them, yet he should infallibly pay the charge of both Navies, with infinite losses[3] and disreputation to the Spaniard.

And in this project Sir Philip proceeded so far with the United Provinces, as they yeelded to assist and second the ships of his soveraign, under his charge, with a Fleet of their own. Which, besides a present addition of strength, he knew would lead in others by example.

Again, for supply of these armies, he had—out

---

[1] P, 'besides, by that means to circle'. G.

[2] P, omits 'in the South Sea'. G.

[3] P, 'losse'. G.

of that naturall tribute, which all free spirits acknowledge to superior worth—won thirty gentlemen of great bloud and state here in England, every man to sell one hundred pounds land, to second and countenance this first Fleet with a stronger.

Now when these beginnings were by his own credit and industrie thus well settled : then to give an excellent form to a reall work, hee contrived this new intended Plantation, not like an assylum for fugitives, a *Bellum Piraticum* for banditi, or any such base ramas[1] of people : but as an emporium for the confluence of all nations that love or profess any kind of vertue or commerce.

Wherein to incite those that tarried at home to adventure, he propounded the hope of a sure and rich return. To martiall men he opened the wide doore[2] of sea and land, for fame and conquest. To the nobly ambitious the fayre[3] stage of America, to win honour in. To the religious divines, besides a new apostolicall calling of the last heathen to the Christian faith, a large field of reducing poor Christians, mis-led by the idolatry of

---

[1] (French) = a heap, mass, medley.   G.

[2] P, ' wide the door '.   G.   [3] P, misprints ' for '.   G.

Rome, to their mother[1] primitive Church. To
the ingenuously[2] industrious, variety of natural
richesses, for new mysteries and manufactures to
work upon. To the merchant, with a simple
people, a fertile and unexhausted earth. To the
fortune-bound, liberty. To the curious, a fruitfull
womb of innovation. Generally, the word gold
was an attractive adamant,[3] to make men venture
that which they have, in hope to grow rich by
that which they have not.

What the expectation of this voyage was,[4] time
past can best witness; but what the success should
have been—till it be revived by some such generous undertaker[5]—lies hidden[6] in God's secret
judgements, who did at once cut off this gentleman's life, and so much of our hope.

Upon these enterprises of his, I have presumed
to stand the longer, because from the ashes of this
first propounded voyage to America, that fatall
Low Country action sprang up, in which this
worthy gentleman lost his life. Besides, I do
ingenuously[7] confess, that it delights me to keep

---

[1] M, omits. G. [2] M, 'ingeniouslie'. G.
[3] = loadstone. G.
[4] P, inserts 'the' after 'was'. G.
[5] P, 'undertakers'. G [6] P, 'hid'. G
[7] M, as before 'ingeniouslie'. G.

company with him, even after death ; esteeming
his actions, words, and conversation, the daintiest
treasure my mind could then lay up ; or can at
this day impart[5] with our posteritie.

---

[1] = communicate.   G.

CHAP. XI.

HEREFORE to come at the last to that diverting[1] imployment promised[2] him under his uncle in the Low-Countries : he was, upon his return to the Court, instantly made for garrison, governor of Flushing, and for the field, general of the horse ; in both which charges, his carriage testified to the world, wisdome and valour, with addition of honour to his Country by them.

For instance ; how like a souldier did he behave himself, first in contriving, then in executing the suprise of Axil ? where he revived that ancient, and seuere[3] discipline of order and silence in their march ; and after their entrance into the town, placed a band of choice souldiers to make a stand in the market-place, for securitie to the rest, that were forced to wander up and down by direction of commanders ; and when the service

---

[1] = turning aside.   G.

[2] P, inserts ' to ' after ' promised '.   G.

[3] P, ' secure '.   G.

was done, rewarded that obedience of discipline in every one, liberally, out of his own purse.

How providently again did he preserve the lives[1] and honor of our English army, at that enterprise of Gravelin[2], where though he was guided by directions from the State, and found all accidents concurringe with the directions giuen him ;[3] yet whether out of arguments drawn from the person of La Motte, commander of that town, who had a generall reputation of too much worth, either Sinon[4]-like to deceive, or easily to be deceived ; or out of the strength and importance of that place, precious to the owner in many respects, the least of which would redouble loss to the growing ambition of a conqueror; or whether upon caution given by intelligence; or whatsoever light of diversion else ; he—I say—was resolute not to hazzard so many principall gentlemen, with such gallant troops and commanders as[5] accompanied him, in that flattering expedition.   Yet

---

[1] P, misreads 'loues'.   G.

[2] M, ' Grauelinge '.   G.

[3] P, omits ' from the State . . . . with the'.   G.

[4] P, Simon : Sinon.   See Virgil Aen. ii.   The crafty Greek who persuaded the Trojans to admit the wooden horse.   G.

[5] P, 'which'.   G,

because he kept this steady counsel in his own
bosome, there was labouring on every side to
obtain the honour of that service. To all which
gallant kind of competition, he made this answer,
that his own comming thither was to the same
end, wherein they were now become his rivalls ;
and therefore assured them, that he would not
yeeld any thing to any man, which by right of
his place was both due to himself, and consequently disgrace for him to execute by others : again,
that by the same rule, he would never consent to
hazard them that were his friends, and in divers
respects his equalls, where he found reason to
make many doubts, and so little reason to venture
himself.

Yet as a commander, concluding something fit
to be done, equally for obedience and triall, he
made the inferior sort of captains try their fortune by dice upon a drum's head : the lot fell
upon Sir William Brown his own lieutenant, who
with a choice company presently departed, receiving this[1] provisionall caution from Sir Philip, that
if he found practise,[2] and not faith, he should

---

[1] M, mis-reads ' his '. G.

[2] So Bacon. See Mr. W. A. Wright's edition of the
" Essayes " as before, s. v. G.

streight throw down his arms, and yeeld himself prisoner; protesting that if they took him, he should be ransomed; if they broke quarter, his death most severely revenged.

On these forlorn companies go with this leader, and before they came into the town, found all outward signals exactly performed; when they were entred, every street safe and quiet, according to promise, till they were past any easie recovery of the gate; then instantly out of the cellars under ground, they were charged by horse and foot. The leader, following his generall's commandement, discovers the treason, throws down his arms, and is taken prisoner. The rest of the company retire, or rather fly towards their ships, but stil wounded and cut off by pursuit of their enemies; till at length a serjeant of a band, with fifteen more, all Sidney's men—I mean such as could die to win honour, and do service to their country—made a halt, and being fortunately mixt of pikes, halberds, and muskets, resolved to be slain with their backs to their friends and their faces, to their enemies. They moved or staied with occasion: and were in both continnually charged with foot and horse, till in the end, eight were slain, and eight left alive. With these the

serjeant wounded in[1] the side by[2] a square die out
of a field piece, made this brave retreat within
view, and at last protection of their own Navy ;
bringing home even in the wounds, nay ruins of
himself and company, reputation of courage, and
martiall discipline to his Country.

Moreover, in those private accidents of discontentment and quarrell, which naturally accompany
great spirits in the best governed camps, how dis-
creetly did Sir Philip ballance that brave Count[3]
Hollocke, made head of a party against his uncle ?
When putting himself between indignities offered
to his soveraign, through the Earl of Leicester's
person ; and yet not fit for a supreme governor's
place to ground a duel upon ; he brought those
passionate charges which the Count Hollock ad-
dressed upwards to the Earl, down by degrees
unto himself. Where that brave Count Hollock
found Sir Philip so fortified with wisdom, courage,
and truth ; besides the strong partie of former
friendship standing for him in the Count's noble
nature; as though sense of honour, and many
things else equal and unequal between them, were

---

[1] P, 'at' G.   [2] P, 'with'.   G.
[3] P, omits 'Count'.   G.

in appearance prouoked[1] beyond possibilitie of peecing; yet this one inequality of right on Sir Philip's side, made the propounder calm; and by coming to terms of expostulation, did not only reconcile those two worthy spirits one vnto[2] another, more firmly than before; but withall wrought[3] through himself if not a kind of unitie between the Earl of Leicester and the Count Hollock, at least a final surcease of all violent jealousies or factious expostulations.

These particulars I only point out, leaving the rest for them, that may, perchance, write larger stories of that time. To be short; not in complements and art[4], but reall proofe given of his sufficience above others, in very little time his reputation and authority among that active people grew so fast, as it had been no hard matter for him, with the disadvantage[5] of his uncle and distraction of our affairs in those parts, to have raised himself a fortune there. But in the whole course of his life, he did so constantly ballance ambition with the safe precepts of divine and moral duty,

---

[1] P, omits. G.   [2] P, 'to'. G.

[3] P, places 'wrought' after 'himself'. G.

[4] M, omits 'and art'. G.

[5] Qu. advantage? G.

as no pretence whatsoever could have entised that
gentleman, to break through the circles[1] of a good
patriot.

---

[1] P, 'circle'. G.

CHAP. XII.

THUS shall it suffice me to have trod out some steps of this BRITANE[1] SCIPIO, thereby to give the learned a scantling,[2] for drawing out the rest of his dimensions by proportion. And to the end the abruptness of this treatise may suit more equally with his fortune, I will cut off his actions, as God did his life, in the midst ; and so conclude with his death.

In which passage, though the pride of flesh, and glory of mankind be commonly so alayed[3] as the beholders seldome see any thing else in it, but objects of horror and pittie ; yet had the fall of this man such natural degrees, that the wound whereof he died, made rather an addition, than diminution of[4] his spirits. So that he shewed the world, in a short progress to a long home, passing fair and wel-drawn lines ; by the guide of which, all pilgrims of this life may conduct themselves humbly into the haven of everlasting rest.

---

[1] See Glossary to our Phineas Fletcher *s. v.*   G.

[2] *Ibid.*   G.

[3] P, 'allyed'.   G.   [4] P, 'to'.   G.

When that unfortunate stand was to be made before Zutphen, to stop the issuing out of the Spanish Army from a streict; with what alacrity soever he went to actions of honor, yet remembring that upon just grounds the ancient sages describe the worthiest persons to be ever best armed, he had compleatly put on his; but meeting the marshall of the Camp lightly armed — whose honour in that art would not suffer this unenvious Themistocles to sleep — the unspotted emulation of his heart, to venture without any inequalitie, made him cast off his cuisses; and so, by the secret influence of destinie, to disarm that part, where God — it seems — had resolved[1] to strike him. Thus they go on, every man in the head of his own troop; and the weather being misty, fell unawares upon the enemie, who had made a strong stand to receive them, near to the very walls of Zutphen; by reason of which accident their troops fell, not only unexpectedly to be engaged within the levell of the great shot, that played from the rampiers, but more fatally within shot of their muskets, which were laid in ambush within their own trenches.

Now whether this were a desperate cure in our

---

[1] M, omits.　G.

I

leaders, for a desperate disease ; or whether misprision, neglect, audacity, or what else induced it, it is no part of my office to determine, but only to make the narration clear, and deliver rumor, as it passed then, without any[1] stain or en-ammel.

Howsoever, by this stand, an unfortunate hand out of those fore-spoken trenches, brake the bone of Sir Philip's thigh with a musket-shot. The horse he rode upon, was rather furiouslie cholleric, than bravely proud, and so forced him to forsake the field, but not his back, as the noblest and fittest biere to carry a martiall commander to his grave. In which sad progress, passing along by the rest of the army, where his uncle the generall was, and being thirstie with excess of bleeding, he called for drink, which was presently brought him ; but as he was putting the bottle to his mouth, he saw a poor souldier carryed along, who had eaten his last at the same feast, gastly casting up his eyes at the bottle. Which Sir Philip perceiving, took it from his head, before he drank, and delivered it to the poor man, with these words, " Thy necessity is yet greater than mine." And when he had pledged this poor souldier, he was

---

[1] M, omits.   G.

presently carried to Arnheim. Where the principal
chirurgions of the Camp attended for him ; some
mercinarily out of gain, others for[1] honour to
their art, but the most of them with a true
zeal—compounded of love and reverence—to doe
him good, and — as they thought—many Nations in him. When they began to dress his
wound, he both by way of charge and advice,
told them, that while his strength was yet
entire, his body free from feaver, and his mind
able to endure, they might frooly use their art,
cut, and search to the bottome. For besides his
hope of health, he would make this farther profit
of the pains which he must suffer, that they should
bear witness, they had indeed a sensible natured
man under their hands, yet one to whom a stronger
Spirit had given power above himself, either to
do or suffer. But if they should now neglect
their art, and renew torments in the declination
of nature, their ignorance or over-tenderness would
prove a kind of tyranny to their friend, and consequently a blemish to their reverend science.

With love and care well mixt, they began the
cure, and continued it some sixteen days, not with
hope, but rather such confidence of his recovery,

---

[1] P, ' out of '.   G.

as the joy of their hearts over-flowed their dis-
creation, and made them spread the intelligence
of it to the Queen, and all his noble friends here
in England, where it was received, not as private,
but as publique good news.

Onely there was one owle among all the birds,
which though looking with no less zealous eyes
than the rest, yet saw, and presaged more despair:
I mean an excellent chirurgion of the Count
Hollock's, who although the Count himself lay
at that[1] instant hurt in the throat with a musket
shot, yet did he neglect his own extremitie to
save his friend, and to that end had sent him to
Sir Philip. This chirurgion notwithstanding—
out of love to his master—returning one day to
dress his wound, the Count cheerfully asked him
how Sir Philip did? And being answered with
a heavy countenance, that he was not well; at
these unexpected[2] words, the worthy prince—as
having more sense of his friend's wounds, than his
own—in a distracted passion cryes out,[3] 'Away villain, never see my face again, till thou bring

---

[1] P, 'the same instant.'   G.
[2] P, omits 'unexpected': M spells 'theis'.   G.
[3] P, has not 'in a........passion'.   G.

better news of that man's recovery; for whose redemption many such as I were happily lost.'

This honourable act I relate, to give the world one modern example; first, that greatness of heart is not dead every where; and then, that War is both a fitter mould to fashion it, and stage to act it on, than Peace can be; and lastly, that the reconciliation of enemies may prove safe and honourable, where the ciment on either side, is worth. So as this Florentine precept concerning reconciled enemies,[1] deserves worthily to be buried with worthines,[2] the author of it, or at least the practise[3] it cryed down and banished, to reign amongst[4] barbarous heathen spirits, who while they think life the uttermost of all things, hold it safe in no body that their own errors make doubtfull to them. And such seems every man that moves any passion but pleasure, in those intricate natures.

Now after the sixteenth day was past, and the very shoulder-bones of this delicate patient worn through his skin, with constant and obedient post-

---

[1] An Italian proverb says 'Amicizia riconciliata piaga mal saldata.' G.

[2] P, 'unworthines'. G. [3] P, 'practise'. G.

[4] P, 'among'. G.

uring[1] his body to their art; he judiciously
observing the pangs his wound stunge[2] him with
by fits, together with many other symptoms of
decay, few or none of recovery, began rather to
submit his body to these artists, than any further[3]
to believe in them. During which suspense, he
one morning lifting up the clothes for change and
ease of his body, smelt some extraordinary noisom
savor about him, differing from oyls and salvs,
as he conceived; and either out of naturall delicacy, or at least care not to offend others, grew a
little troubled with it; which they that sate by
perceiving, besought him to let them know
what suddain indisposition he felt? Sir Philip
ingenuously[4] told it, and desired them as ingenuously to confess, whether they felt any such
noisom thing or no? They all protested against
it upon their credits. Whence Sir Philip presently[6] gave this severe doom upon himself; that
it was inward mortification, and a welcome messenger of death.

Shortly after, when the chirurgions came to

---

[1] P, inserts 'of' after 'posturing'. G.
[2] P, 'stang'. G.   [3] P, 'farther'. G.
[4] M, 'ingeniously'. Ð.   [5] *Ibid.* G.
[6] M, omits. G.

dress him, he acquainted them with these piercing intelligences[1] between him and his mortality. Which though they opened by authority of books, paralleling of accidents and other artificiall prob- abilities; yet moved they no alteration in this man, who judged too truly of his[2] estate, and from more certain grounds than the vanity of opinion in erring artistes[3] could possibly pierce into. So that afterward,[4] how freely soever he left his body subject to their practise, and con- tinued a patient beyond exception; yet did he not change his minde; but as having utterly[5] cast off all hope or desire of recoverie, made and divided that little span of life which was left him in this manner.

---

[1] M, ' intelligences'. G.   [2] P, ' own ' after ' his '.   G.
[3] P, ' artifices '.   G.   [4] P, ' afterwards'.   G.
[5] M, omits.   G

CHAP, XIII.

IRST, he called the Ministers unto[1] him ; who were all excellent men, of divers Nations, and before them made such a confession of Christian faith, as no book but the heart can truly and feelingly deliver. Then desired them to accompany him in prayer, wherein hee besought leave to lead the assembly, in respect,—as he said—that the secret sins of his own heart were best known to himself, and out of that true sense, he more properly instructed to apply the eternall Sacrifice of our Saviour's Passion and Merits to him.[2] His religious zeal prevailed with this humbly devout, and afflicted company; in which wel chosen progress of his, howsoever they were all moved, and those sweet motions witnessed by sighes and tears, even interrupting their common devotion ; yet could no man judge in himself, much less in others, whether this racke[3] of heavenly agony, whereupon they all stood, was[4] forced by reason of[5] sorrow for him, or ad-

---

[1] P, 'to'. G.   [2] M, 'them'. G.
[3] P, 'rake'. G.   [4] P, 'were'. G.
[5] P, omits 'reason of'. G.

miration of him ; the fire of this phenix being hardly[1] able out of any ashes to produce his equall, as they conceived.

Here this first mover stayed the motions in every man, by staying himself. Whether to give rest to that frail wounded flesh, of his unable to bear the bent of eternity so much affected, any longer ; or whether to abstract that spirit more inwardly, and by chewing as it were the cudd of meditation, to imprint these excellent images in his soul ; who can judge but God ? Notwithstanding, in this change—it would seem—there was little or no change in the object. For instantly after prayer, he entreated[2] his quire of divine philosophers about him, to deliver the opinion of the ancient heathen, touching the immortality of the soul : First, to see what true knowledge she retains of her own essence, out of the light of her self ; then to parallel with it the most pregnant authorities of the Old, and New Testament, as supernatural revelations, sealed up from our flesh, for the divine light of faith to reveal and work by. Not that he wanted instruction or assurance ; but because this fixing of a lover's thoughts upon those eternall[3] beauties, was not only a cheering up of

---

[1] P, 'hardly being'. G.   [2] P, 'this' G.

[3] P, very grossly misreads 'externall.' G.

his decaying spirits, but as it were a taking possession of that immortall inheritance, which was
given unto him by his brother-hood in Christ.

The next change used, was the calling for his
Will; which though at first sight it may seem a
descent from heaven to earth again; yet he that
observes the distinction of those offices, which he
practised in bestowing his own, shall discern, that
as the soul of man is all in all and all in every
part ; so was the goodnes of his nature equally
dispersed, into the greatest and least actions of his
too short life.   Which Will of his, will ever
remain for a witness to the world, that those sweet
and large, even dying affections in him, could no
more be contracted with the narrowness of pain,
grief, and[1] sickness, than any sparkle of our
immortality can bee priuatiuely[2] buried in the
shadow of death.

Here again this restless soul of his—changing
only the aire, and not the cords of her harmony—
cals for musick ; especially that song which himself had intitled, *La cuisse rompue :* partly—as I
conceive by the name—to shew that the glory of
mortal flesh was shaken in him : and by the[3]

---

[1] P, 'or'   G.   [2] P, 'privately'.   G.
[3] P, ' that' : but M here is miswritten ' and by the and
by the musicke ' (*sic*).   G.

musick it self, to fashion and enfranchise his heavenly soul into that everlasting harmony of angels, whereof these concords were a kinde of terrestriall echo : and in this supreme, or middle orb of contemplation,[1] he blessedly went on, within a circular motion, to the end of all flesh.

The last scene of this tragedy, was the parting of[2] the two brothers : the weaker shewing infinite strength in suppressing sorrow, and the stronger infinite weakness in expressing[3] it. So far did vnvaluable[4] worthinesse, in the dying brother enforce the living to descend beneath his owne worth, and by abundance of childish tears, bewail the publique, in his particular loss. Yea so far was his true remission of minde transformed into ejulation,[5] that Sir Philip—in whom all earthly passion did even as it were flash, like lights ready to burn out—recals those spirits together with a strong vertue, but weake voice ; mildly blaming him for relaxing the frail strengths left to support him ; in this[6] finale combate of

---

[1] M, spells 'contemplacōn ': P, 'contemplations'. G.

[2] P, 'between'. G.   [3] P. 'of it'. G.

[4] P, 'invaluable'. G.

[5] = lamentation, wailing. G.   [6] P, 'his'. G.

separation at hand.   And to stop this naturall
torrent of affection in both, took his leave, in
theis[1] admonishing words :

"Love my memorie, cherish my friends ; their
faith to me may assure you they are honest.   But
above all, govern your will and affections, by the
will and Word of your Creator; in me, beholding
the end of this world, with all her vanities."

And with this farewell, desired the company to
lead him away.   Here the[2] noble gentleman
ended the too short line of[3] his life ; in which
path, whosoever is not confident that he walked
the next way to eternall rest, will be found to
judge uncharitably.

Thus you see how it pleased God to shew
forth, and then suddainly withdraw this precious
light of our skie ; and in some sort adopted patriot
of the States-Generall.   Between whom and him,
there was such a sympathie of affections ; as
they honoured that exorbitant worth in Sir Philip,
by which time and occasion had been like enough
to metamorphose[4] this new aristocracy of theirs
into their ancient, and much-honoured forme of

---

[3] P, 'with these'.   G.   [1] P, 'this'.   G.

[2] P, 'short scene his'.   G.   [3] M, 'metamorphise'.   G.

dukedome. And he again applauded that universall ingenuitie and prosperous undertakings of
theirs; over which perchance he felt something in
his own nature, possible in time to become[1] an
elect commander. So usuall is it for all mortall
constitutions, to affect that, which insensibly often
works change in them to better or worse.

Now though I am not of their faith who affirme
wise men may[2] governe the starres; yet do I
beleeve no star-gazers can so well prognosticate
the good or ill of all governments, as the providence of men trained up in publique affaires may
doe. Whereby they differ from prophets only
in this; that prophets by inspiration, and these by
consequence, judge of things to come.

Amongst which kind of prophets, give me leave
to reckon this gentleman; who first having, out
of the credible almanach of History, registred the
growth, health, disease, and periods of government:[3] that is to say, when monarchies grow
ready for change, by over-relaxing or contracting,
when the states of few or many continue or forsake to be the same:[4] and in the constant course

---

[1] P, 'come'. G.   [2] P, 'can'. G.
[3] P, 'governments'. G.
[4] M, misreads 'forsake to the same'. G.

of those[1] vicissitudes, having[2] foreseen the easie
satietie of mankinde with Religion and Government, their naturall[3] discontentment with the
present, and aptnesse to welcome alteration; and
againe, in the descent of each particular forme to
her owne centre, having observed how euen[4] these
United Provinces had already changed from their
ancient dukedoms to popularitie : and yet in that
popularitie, been forced to seek protection among
the monarchs[5] then raigning; and to make perfect
this judgment of his, had summ'd up the League
offensive and defensive between us and them;
even then he grew doubtfull, least[6] this advantage
would in time leave latitude for envy and compet-
encie[7] to work some kind of rent in our Union.

But when in the progress of this prospect, he
fell into a more particular consideration of their
traffique and ours : they without any native commodities—art, and diligence excepted—making
themselves masters of wealth in all Nations :
we againe by exporting our substantiall riches,

---

[1] P, 'these'.   G.   [2] M, omits.   G.

[3] M, omits.   G.   [4] P, omits.   G.

[5] P, 'monarchies'   G.

[6] M, 'least, whether ', as is alternate words not decided
on.   G.

[7] = competition, strife.   G.

to import a superfluous masse of trifles, to the
vaine exhausting of our home-borne staple commodities ; he certainly concluded, that this true
philosopher's stone of traffique, which not only
turned base mettals into gold, but made profit
by Wars in their owne bosomes, would infallibly
stir up emulation in such lookers on, as were far
from striving otherwise to imitate them.

And out of these and[1] the like grounds, hath
many times told me, that this active people—
which held them[2] constantly to their Religion
and Freedome—would at length grow from an
adjective to a substantive and prosperous subsistence. Whereas we on the other side, dividing
our selves, and waving in both, should first become jealous, then strange to our friends, and in
the end—by reconciliation with our common
enemie — moderate that zeale, wherein excesse
only is the meane; and so be forced to cast our
fortunes into their armes for support, who are
most interessed[3] in our dishonour and ruine.
These with many other dangers—which he pro-
visionally feared—howsoever the wisdome of our
government may perchance have put off by pre-

---

[1] P, 'or'. G.   [2] P, 'themselves'. G.
[3] P, 'interested'. G.

vention, yet were more then conjecturall in the aspectes[1] of superior, inferior, forraigne, and domestique princes then raigning.

But suppose we could not by this Kalender comprehend the change of aspects and policies in severall kingdomes ; yet we may at least therein discerne, both the judgment of this Prometheus concerning our selves, and the tender affection he carried to that oppressed Nation.   Which respect of his they againe so well understood, as after his death the States of Zealand became suitors to her majesty, and his noble friends, that they might have the honour of burying his body at the publique expence of their government.   A memorable wisdome of thankfulnesse, by well handling the dead, to encourage and multiply faith in the living.

Which request had it been granted, the reader may please to consider, what trophies it is likely they would have erected over him, for posterity to admire, and what inscriptions would have been devised for eternizing his memory.   Indeed fitter for a great and brave Nation to enlarge, then the capacitie or good will[2] of a private and inferior

---

[1] P, ' aspect '.   G.

[2] M, omits ' or good will '.   G.

friend. For my own[1] part I confesse, in all I have here set downe of his worth and goodnesse, I find my self still short of that honour he deserved, and I desired to doe him.

I must therefore content my selfe with this poor demonstration of homage; and so proceed to say somewhat of the toyes[2] and pamphletes,[3] which I inscribe to his memory, as monuments of true affection between us; whereof—you see—death hath no power.

---

[1] M, omits.   G.   [2] Trifles.   G.

[3] Γ, 'or pamphlets'.   G.

CHAP.[1] XIV.

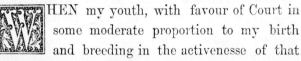HEN my youth, with favour of Court in some moderate proportion to my birth and breeding in the activenesse of that time, gave mee opportunity of most businesse: then did my yet undiscouraged genius most affect to finde or make work for it self. And out of that freedom, having many times offered my fortune to the course of forraigne employments, as the properest[2] forges to fashion a subject for the reall services of his soveraign; I found the returnes of those mis-placed endeavours to prove, both a vaine charge to my selfe, and an offensive undertaking to that excellent governesse over all her subjects' duties and affections.

For instance, how mild soever those mixtures of favours and corrections were in that princely lady: yet to shew that they fell heavy in crossing a young man's ends; I will onely choose, and alleage foure out of many, some with leave, some without.

---

[1] Printed 'Cap'.   G.
[2] P, grossly misprints 'propriest'.   G.

First, when those two mighty armies of Don
Iohn[1], and the Duke Casimires, were to meet in
the Low Countries ; my horses, with all other
preparations being shipped at Dover, with leave
under her bill assigned : even then was I stayed
by a princely mandate, the messenger Sir Edward
Dier[2].　Wherein whatsoever I felt, yet I appeale
to the judicious reader, whether there be latitude
left—more than humble obedience—in these nice
cases between duty and selfenesse, in a soveraigne's
service?

After this, when Mr. Secretary Walsingham
was sent ambassador, to treate with those two
princes in a businesse so much concerning Christian blood and Christian empires : then did the
same irregular motion—which seldome rests, but
steales where it cannot trade—perswade me, that
whosoever would venture to go without leave,
was sure never to bee taxed.[3]　Upon which false
axiome—trusting the rest to chance—I went over
with Mr. Secretary, unknown : but at my return
was forbidden her presence for many moneths.

---

[1] P, ' Iohns '.　G.

[2] See Sidney's poem on the three friends—himself,
Brooke, and Dyer, in Appendix to this Life.　G.

[3] P, ' stayed '.　G.

Againe, when my Lord of Leicester was sent
generall of her Majestie's Forces into the Low
Countries, and had given me the command of an
hundred horse; then I giving my humors over
to good order, yet found, that neither the earnest
intercession of this grandee, seconded with my[2]
own humble sute, and many other honourable
friends of mine, could prevaile against the constant course of this excellent lady with her servants.   So as I was forced to tarry behind; and
for this importunity of mine to change my course,
and seem to preferre anything[2] before my service
about her: This princesse of government, as well
of government[3] as of kingdomes, made me live in
her Court, a spectacle of disfavour, too long as I
conceived.

Lastly, the universall fame of a battle to be
fought between the prime forces of Henry the
Third and the religious ones of Henry the Fourth,
then king of Navarre; lifting me yet once more
above this humble earth of clay, made me resolve
to see the difference between kings present and
absent in their martiall expeditions.   So that
without acquainting any creature, the Earle of

---

[1] P, 'mine'.   G.   [2] P, 'nothing'.   G.
[3] P, omits ' of government' and ' of'.   G.

Essex excepted, I shipped myselfe over : and at
my returne, was kept from her presence full six
moneths, and then received after a strange manner.
For this absolute princesse[1] to sever ill examples[2]
from grace, averrs my going over to bee a secret
imployment of hers: and all these other petty
exiles, a making good of that cloud or figure
which she was pleased to cast over my absence.
Protecting me to the world with the[3] honour of
her imployment, rather then she would, for example's sake, be forced either[4] to punish mee
further,[5] or too easily forgive a contempt or neglect,
in a servant so near about her, as she was pleased
to conceive it.

By which many warnings, I finding the specious
fires of youth to prove far more scorching then
glorious, called my second thoughts to counsell,
and in that map cleerly discerning action and
honor, to fly with more wings then one : and that
it was sufficient for the plant to grow where his[6]
soveraigne's hand had placed[7] it ; I found reason
to contract my thoughts from theis[8] larger, but

---

[1] P, blunders, and reads ' prince '. G.

[2] P, 'example'. G.   [3] M, omits. G.

[4] M, omits. G.   [5] P, ' farther '. G.

[6] M, the ', and spells ' soueraign's '. G.

[7] P, ' planted '. G.   [8] P, ' those '. G.

wandring horizons, of the world abroad, and to[1] bound my prospect within the safe limits of duty, in such home-services, as were acceptable to my soveraigne.

In which retired view, Sir Philip Sidney, that exact image of quiet and action, happily united in him, and seldome well divided in any; being ever in my[2] eyes, made me thinke it no small degree of honour to imitate, or tread in the steps of such a leader. So that to saile by his compasse, was shortly—as I said—one of the principall reasons I can alleage, which perswaded me to steale minutes of time from my daily services, and employ them in theis kind of writeings.[3]

Since my declining age, it is true that I had— for some yeeres—more leasure to discover their imperfections, then care, or industry to amend them : finding in my selfe, what all men complaine of in the world, that it is more easie to find fault, excuse, or tolerate, then to examine and reforme.

The workes—as you see—are Tragedies, with some Treatises annexed. The Treatises—to speake truly of them—were first intended to be for every act a chorus : and though[4] not borne out of the

---

[1] P, omits. G.   [2] P, 'mine'. G.
[3] P, 'this kind of writing.' G.
[4] M, 'that'. G.

present matter acted, yet being the largest subject,[1]
I could then think upon, and no such strangers
to the scope of the Tragedies, but that a favourable
reader might easily find some consanguinitie be-
ween them ; I preferring this generall scope of
profit, before the self[2]-reputacon[3] of being an exact
artisan in that poeticall mystery, conceived that[4]
a perspective into vice, and the unprosperities of
it, would prove more acceptable to every good
reader's ends, then any bare murmur of disconten-
ted spirits against the[5] present government, or
horrible periods of exorbitant passions among
equals.

Which with humble sayles after I had ventured
once[6] upon this spreading ocean of images, my
apprehensive youth, for lack of a well touched
compasse, did easily wander beyond proportion.
And in my old age againe, looking back upon[7] them
with a father's eye : when I considered first, how
poorly the inward natures of those glorious names
were expressed : then how much easier it was to
excuse deformities then[8] cure them ; though I

---

[1] M, is contraction-form for 'subject'. G.

[2] M, 'safe'. G.   [3] P, 'reputation'. G

[4] M, omits. G.   [5] P, 'their'. G.

[6] P, 'once ventured'. G.

[7] P, 'on'. G.   [8] P, 'to cure'. G.

found some reason to change their places, yet I
could not find in my heart to bestow cost or care
in altering their light and limited apparell in
verse.

From hence to come particularly to thàt Treatise
intitled, the Declination of Monarchy : let me
beg leave of the favourable reader, to bestow a few
lines more in the story of this changling, then I
have done in the rest ; and yet to use no other[1]
serious authority then the rule of Diogenes, which
is[2], to hang the posie where there is most need.

The first birth of that phantasme was divided
into three parts, with intention of the Author, to
be disposed amongst their fellows, into three
diverse acts of the Tragedies. But—as I said
before—when upon a second review, they and
the rest were all ordain'd to change their places,
then did I—like an old[3] fond parent, unlike to get
any more children—take pains rather to cover the
dandled deformities of these creatures with a coat
of many seames, then carelessly to drive them
away, as birds doe their young ones.

Yet againe, when I had in mine own case well
weigh'd the tendernesse of that great subject, and

---

[1] P, 'more'. G   [2] P, 'was'. G.
[3] P, 'and'. G.

consequently, the nice path I was to walke in between two extreames;[1] but especially the danger,
by treading aside, to cast scandall upon the sacred
foundations of Monarchy; together with the fate
of many metaphoricall[2] Phormio's[3] before me, who
had lost themselves in teaching]kings and princes,
how to governe their people : then did this new
prospect dazzle mine eyes, and suspend my traveli
for a time.

But the familiar self-love, which is more or
lesse born in every man, to live and dye with
him, presently moved me to take vp this bear-
whelpe[4] againe and licke it. Wherein I, rowsing
my spirittes[5] under the banner of this flattery,
went about—as a fond mother—to put on richer
garments, in hope to adorne them. But while
these clothes were in making, I perceived that
cost would but draw more curious eyes to observe
deformities. So that from these checks a new

---

[1] P, 'extremities'. G.   [2] P, 'metaphysicall'. G.

[3] From Phomion, the Peripatetic philosopher of Ephe-
sus, of whom it is told that he lectured for many hours on
the art and duties of a general to Hanibal, to the intense
scorn of his illustrious auditor. (Cicero, de Orat. ii.,
18) G.

[4] P, ·this bear-whelp up'. G.

[5] P, 'my selfe'. G.

counsell rose up in me, to take away all opinion
of seriousnesse from these perplexed pedegrees;
and to this end carelessly cast them into that
hypocriticall figure Ironia, wherein commonly
men[1]—to keep above their workes—seeme to
make toies of the uttermost[2] they can doe.

And yet againe, in that confusing mist, when
I beheld this grave subject—which should draw
reverence and attention—to bee over-spangled
with lightnesse, I forced in examples of the
Roman gravity and greatnesse, the harsh severity
of the Lacedemonian government; the riches of
the Athenian learning, wit, and industry; and
like a man that plaies divers parts upon severall
hints, left all the indigested crudities, equally
applied to kings, or tyrants : whereas in every
cleere judgement, the right line had beene sufficient
enough to discouer the crooked : if the image of it
could have proved credible to men.

Now for the severall branches or discourses[3]
following; they are all members of one and the
same imperfect body, so as I let them take their
fortunes—like Essayes—onely to tempt and stir
up some more free genius, to fashion the whole

---

[1] P, 'men commonly'.   G.   [2] P, 'utmost'.   G.
[3] M, omits 'or discourses'.   G.

frame into finer moulds[1] for the world's use. The
first limme of theis[2] Treatises[3]—I mean that
fabrick of a superstitious Church—having by her
masterfull ambition over emperours, kings, princes,
free States, and Councels, with her Conclave
deceits, strengths, and unthankfulnesse, spred so
far beyond my horizon, as I at once gave over her
and all her deriuatiues[4] to Gamaliel's infallible
censure; leaving lawes, nobility, War, Peace, and
the rest,—as glorious trophies of our old Pope,
the sin—to change, reforme, or become deformed,
according as vanity, that limitlesse mother of
those[5] idolatries—should either winne of the Truth,
or the Truth of them.

Lastly, concerning the Tragedies themselves, :
they were in their first creation three; Whereof
Antonie and Cleopatra, according to their irregular
passions, in forsaking empire to follow sensuality,
were sacrificed in[6] the fire. The executioner, the
author himselfe. Not that he conceived it to be
a contemptible younger brother to the rest: but
lest while he seemed to looke over-much upward,
hee might stumble into the astronomer's pit.

---

[1] P, 'mould'. G.   [2] P, 'those' G.
[3] P, 'treaties'. G.   [4] P. 'derivations'. G.
[5] P, 'these'. G.   [6] P, misreads 'to'. G.

Many members in that creature—by the opinion
of those few eyes, which saw it—having some
childish wantonnesse in them, apt enough to be
construed or strained to a personating of vices in
the present governors and government.

From which cautious prospect, I bringing into
my minde the ancient poet's metamorphosing of[1]
man's reasonable nature into the sensitive of
beasts, or vegetative of plants; and knowing these
all—in their true morall—to bee but images of
the unequall ballance between humors and times,
nature, and place. And again in the practice of
the world, seeing the like instance not poetically
but really fashioned in the Earle of Essex then
falling; and even till then worthily beloved, both
of Queen and people : this sudden descent of a[2]
greatnesse, together with the quality of the actors
in every scene, stir'd up the Author's second
thoughts, to bee carefull—in his owne case—of
leaving faire weather behind him. Hee having,
in the Earle's precipitate fortune, curiously observed. First, how long that[3] nobleman's birth,
worth, and favour had beeu flattered, tempted,
and stung by a swarm of sect-animals, whose prop-
erty was to wound and fly away : and so, by

---

[1] P, omits. G.   [2] P, 'such'. G.   [3] P, 'this'. G.

a continuall affliction probably enforce great hearts to turne and tosse for ease; and in those passive postures, perchance to tumble sometimes upon their soveraigne's circles.

Into which pitfall of theirs, when they had once discerned this Earle to be fallen: straight, under the reverend stile of *Læsæ Majestatis*[1] all inferiour ministers of Justice—they knew—would be justly let loose to work upon him. And accordingly, under the same cloud, his enemies took audacity to cast libels abroad in his name against the State, made by themselves: set papers upon posts, to bring his innocent friends in question. His power, by the Jesuiticall craft of rumour, they made infinite; and his ambition more then equall to it. His letters to private men were read openly, by the[2] piercing eyes of an Atturnie's office, which warrantes[3] the construction of every line[4] in the worst sense against the writer.

Myselfe, his kinsman, and while I remained about the queen, a kind of *Remora*, staying the

---

[1] P, 'Læsa Maiestas'. G.

[2] P, misprints 'the' twice. G.

[3] P, 'warranteth'. G.

[4] P, 'time'. G.

violent course of that fatall ship, and those[1] winde-
watching passengers — at least, as his enemies
imagined — abruptly sent away to guard a figura-
tive Fleet, in danger of nothing but these *pros-
opopeia's* of invisible rancor; and kept — as it
were[2] in a free prison — at Rochester, till his
head was off.

Before which sudden journey, casting mine eyes
upon the catching Court-ayres, which[3] I was to
part from; I discerned my gracious soveraigne to
bee every way so invironed with these, not Jupiter's, but Pluto's thunder-workers; as it was impossible for her to see any light, that might tend[4]
to grace, or mercy: but many encouraging meteors
of severity, as against an unthankfull favourite
and traiterous subject; hee standing, by the law
of England, condemned for such.

So that let his heart bee — as in my conscience
it was — free from this unnaturall crime, yet these
unreturning steps seemed well worth the observing. Especially in the case of such a favorite, as
never put his soveraigne to stand between her
people and his errors; but here and abroad, placed

---

[1] P, 'these'.   G.   [2] P, omits 'it were'.   G.
[3] M, omits.   G.   [4] P, 'lead'.   G.

his body in the forefront, against all that threatned or assaulted her.

And being no admirall, nor yet a creator of admiralls, whereby feare or hope might have kept those temporary Neptunes in a kinde of subjection to him ; yet he freely ventured himselfe in all sea-actions of that tyme, as[1] if he would war the greatnesse of place, enuy,[2] and power, with the greatnesse of worth, and incomparable industry. Neverthelesse hee wanted not judgement to dis-cerne, that whether they went with him or tarried behind, they must probably prove unequall yoke-fellowes in the one; or in the other, passing curi-ous and carping judges over all his publike actions.[3]

Againe, this gallant young Earle, created—as it seemes—for action, before he was martiall, first as a private gentleman, and after as a lieu-tenant by commission, went in the head of all our land troops, that marched in his time ; and besides experience, still wan ground, even through compe-tency, envy, and confused mixtures of equality or

---

[1] P, ' of his time. As '. G.
[2] P, ' envy, place '. F.
[3] M, ' accōns publicke '. G.

inequality amongst the English factions[1] all inferior to[2] his owne active worth and merit.

Lastly, he was so far from affecting the absolute power of Henry the Third's favourites, I meane under a king to become equall at least with him, in creating and deposing chancelors, treasurers, and secretaries of State, to raise a strong party for himselfe ; as he left both place and persons entire in their supreme jurisdictions, or magistracies under his soveraigne, as shee granted them. And though he foresaw a necessary diminution of their peaceful predicaments by his carrying up the standard of Mars so high, and withal knew they —like wise men—must as certainly discern, that the rising of his, or the[3] falling of their scales, depended upon the prosperity or unprosperity of his undertakings : yet—I say—that active heart of his freely chose to hazard himselfe upon their censures, without any other provisionall rampier against the envious and suppressing crafts of[4] party, then his owne hope and resolution to deserve well.

Neither did he—like the French favorites of that time—serve his own humors or necessities,

---

[1] P, 'factious English'.   G.   [2] P, ' in '.   G.

[3] P, omits.   G.   [4] P, ' of that '.   G.

by filling[1] seats of Justice, Nobility, or orders of honor, till they became, *Colliers pour toute beste*, to the disparagement of treating power, and discourageing of the subjects' hope or industry, in attaining to advancement or profit : but suffered England to stand alone, in her ancient degrees of freedomes and integrities, and so reserved that absolute power of creation sacred in his soveraigne, without any mercenary staine or allay.

---

[1] P, misreads, 'selling'. G.

CHAP.[1] XV.

NOW after this humble and harmlesse
desire of a meane subject, expressed in
qualifying a great subject's errors, by
the circumstance of such instruments, as naturally
—like bats—both flye and prey in the darke: let
the reader pardon me, if I presume yet againe to
multiply digression upon digression, in honour of
her to whom I owe my selfe, I meane Queen
Elizabeth: and in her name clearly to avow,[2] that
though I lament the fall of this great man in
Israel, neverthelesse the truth forceth[3] me to confesse, that howsoever these kinds of high justice
may sometimes—like the uttermost of the[4] Law—
fall heavy upon one brave spirit; yet prove they[5]
mercy to many by example: and therefore as
legall,[6] and royall wisdomes, ought to be honoured
equally in all the differing soveraignities through
the world, of one, few, or many.

---

[1] Printed, as before, Cap.   G.

[2] P, 'know'.   G.   [3] P, 'enforceth'.   G.

[4] M, omits.   G.   [5] M, misreads 'the '.   G.

[6] P, grossly misreads 'regall'.   G.

And if this assumpsit must be granted universally; then how much more in the case of such a princesse, as—even while she was a[1] subject—left patterns that might instruct all subjects, rather to undergoe the indignation of soveraignes with the birthright of duty, then the muteines[2] of over-sensible and rebellious affections; which ever—like diseased pulses—beat faster or slower then they should, to shew all to be infected about them ?[3]   Whereas this lady, in the like straines, by an humble, and a[4] constant temper, had already with true obedience[5] triumphed over the curious examination[6] of ascending flattery or descending tyranny, even in the tendernesse of princes' successions.

And to make this manifest to bee choice and not chance : even when her stepmother Misfortune grew ripe for delivery, then was she neither born crying, as children be: nor yet by the sudden change from a prison to a throne, came she upon that

---

[1] P, omits. G.

[2] P, 'then with the mutiny '. G.

[3] M, omits ' to shew.... them '. G.

[4] P, omits. G.

[5] M, omits ' with true obedience '. G.

[6] M, spells ' examinacon ', P, ' examinations '. G.

stage confusedly barking after all that had offended : but like one borne to behold true light, instantly fixeth her thoughts upon larger notions
then revenge or favour. And in the infancy of
her raigne, cals for Benefield[1] her hard-hearted
gaoler; bids him enjoy not a deserved, but a[2] free
given peace under his narrow vine : with this
assurance, that whensoever she desired to have
prisoners over severely intreated, she would not
forget to commit the custody of them to his
charge.

Againe, for the next object, looking backward
upon her sister's raigne, she observes Religion to
have been changed ; persecution, like an ill weed,
suddenly grown up to the highest ; the mercy of
the infinite perscribed[3], by abridgment of time,
in[4] adding torments to the death of his creatures :
salvation published in many more creeds then she
was taught to beleeve : a double supremacy in
one kingdome ; Rome become emperor of the clergy,
and by betwitching the better halfe of man—I
meane the soule challenging both over clergy,

---

[1] = Sir Henry Bedingfield, Constable of the Tower when
Elizabeth was imprisoned there after Wyat's rebellion. G.

[2] P, omits '. G,   [3] Prescribed. G

[4] P, ' and '. G.

and laity, the stile of the great God : *Rex Regum,
Dominus Dominantium*.

This view brought forth in her a vow, like
that of the holy kings in the Old Testament ; viz :
that she would neither hope, nor seeke for rest
in the mortall traffique of this world, till she had
repaired the precipitate ruines of our Saviour's
militant Church, through all her dominions ; and
as she hoped, in the rest of the World, by her
example. Upon which princely[1] resolution, this
she-David of our's ventured to under-take the
great Goliath[2] amongst[3] the Philistins abroad, I
mean Spain and the Pope ; despiseth their multitudes, not of men, but of hosts ; scornfully rejectes[4]
that holy Father's wind-blowne superstitions,
and takes the—almost solitary—truth, for her
leading-star.

Yet tears she not the lyon's jawes in sunder at
once, but moderately begins with her own chang-
lings ; gives the bishops a proper motion, but
bounded : the nobility time to reforme themselves,
with inward and outward councell ; revives her
brother's lawes for establishing of the Churche's
doctrine and discipline, but moderates their sever-

---

[1] P, 'princelike.' G.   [2] M, 'Goliah'. G.
[3] P, 'among'. G.   [4] P, 'rejecteth'. G.

ity of proceeding ; giues frailty and sect, time to
reform at home : and in the mean season supplyes
the prince of Conde with men and money, as chief
among the Protestants in France ; gathers, and
releiues[1] the scattered hosts of Israel at the worst :
takes New-Haven, perchance with hopes of redeem-
ing Callice, to the end her axle-trees might once
againe lie upon both shores, as her right did :
refuseth marriage, reformes and redeemes Queen
Marie's vanities, who first glorying in the Spanish
seed, published that she was with childe, and
instantly offers up that royall supposed issue of
her's, together with the absolute government of all
her natives, to the mixt tyrannie of Rome and
Castile.

In which endlesse path of servitude, the noune-
adjective nature of this superstitious princesse,
proceedes[2] yet a degree farther ;[3] striving to confirme that double bondage of people and posterity,
by act of Parliament. Where on the other side, the
Spanish king, beholding these remisse homages of
frailty, with the unthankfull and unsatiable[4] eyes
of ambition, apprehends these petty sacrifices, as
fit strawes, sticks, or feathers, to be pull'd out of

---

[1] P, 'revives'.   G.   [2] P, 'proceeded'.   G.
[3] P, 'further'.   G.   [4] P, 'insatiable'.   G.

faint wings, for the building up and adorning of[1] a conqueror's nest. And under this tyrannicall crisis, takes freedome to exhaust her treasure to his own ends, breakes our league with France, and in that breach shakes the sacred foundation of the rest, winnes St. Quintins, while we lost Callice.

Contrary to all which thought-bound councels of her sister Mary,[2] Queen Elizabeth—as I said—not yet out of danger of her Romish subjects at home; threatned with their mighty faction at home[3] and party abroad; pester'd besides with want of money, and many binding lawes of her sister's making: yet like a palme, under all these bur- thens,[4] she raiseth her selfe prince-like : and upon notice of her agent's disgrace abroad, his servants being put into the Inquisition by the Spaniard ; her merchants surprized in America, contrary to the League between Charles the fifth and Henry the eighth ; which gave free traffique : *In omni- bus, et singulis Regnis Dominiis, Insulis,* not- withstanding that astronomicall, or rather biaced division of the world by the Pope's lines, which— contrary to the nature of all lines—only keep

---

[1] M, omits. G. [2] P, 'Maries'. G.

[3] P, omits 'at home' : M, spells 'faccon' G.

[4] P, 'burdens'. G.

latitude for the advantage of Spain : she—I say —upon these insolencies, receives the Hollander, and protects him from the[1] persecution of the Duke of Alva : settles these poore refugees in Norwich, Colchester, Sandwich, Maidstone, and South-hampton.

Yet againe, when this faith-distinguishing duke appealed to her selfe : she binding her heart for better or worse, to the words of her Contract ; summons her afflicted strangers to depart. Their number was great, their time short ; and yet their weather-beaten soules so sensible of long continued oppressions in their liberties and consciences, as— by the opportunity of this ostracisme—they in their passage surprised Brill, Flushing, and diverse other towns, expulsing the Spaniards ; and by this brave example, taught and proclaimed a way of freedome to all well-affected princes and provinces, that were opprest.

Wherein it may please the reader to observe, that Henry the Third of France, being one in the same league, and belike upon change of heart, which ever brings forth new questions, demanding whether mutuall defence against all, extended to the cause of Religion ? was presently answered by her ;

---

[1] P, omits 'the' : M, spells 'persecucon'.   G.

that she both treated and concluded in the same sense ; and if it were required at her hands, would performe every branch of it to her uttermost. The French king hereupon makes war with the Protestants : Monsieur his brother secretly protects them by Casimire.

Againe about that time, at the request of the Spanish king, she guards his Navy into Flanders ; where it being lost, and she requested by the same king to lend him her owne ships, for recovery of the maritime townes fallen from him : this blessed lady both denyes this crafty request of a conqueror, and withall providently refuseth any of his ships to be harboured in her ports. Yet in honour of her ancient league with the house of Burgundy, she publisheth the like inhibition to her beloved and safe neighbours of[1] Netherlands. And instantly, with a strong judgment in ballancing of forraigne princes, perswades the king of Spain to make peace with the Hollanders, and on the other side disswades those many wayes[2] distressed Hollanders from joyning with France. As I conceive, thinking that kingdome— manumised[3]

---

[1] P, 'the'. G.
[2] P, omits 'many wayes'. G,
[3] = manumitted, freed. G.

from us in[1] tyme—might through the conjunction of Holland's[2] shipping and mariners, with their disciplin'd land-armies of horse and foot, prove more dangerous enemies, either by way of invasion or incursion[3]—as I said once before—then that king's glorious standard, borne amongst his barbed horse and light foot, had hitherto done, either in our enticed undertakings or abandoned retraits.

Besides it is worthy of reverence in this queen, that she was never[4] afraid, or ashamed to avow[5] the quarrell of Religion for a ground of her friends or enemies.

And though in the charity of a Christian prince, even in the danger of a growing faction at home, especially buttressed with such strange partyes abroad,[6] she was content to let devout conscience live quietly in her realmes : yea[7] when they began[8] to practise disunion in the[9] Church, as their Jesuit-

---

[1] P, 'by'. G.

[2] P, 'of the Holland'. G.

[3] M, omits 'or incursion'. G.

[4] P, 'never was', G.

[5] P, 'averre'. G.

[6] P, omits 'especially ...... abroad'. G.

[7] P, 'yet'. G.

[8] M, 'begun'. G.

[9] P, omits 'the '. G.

ed spirits naturally affect to doe : then to shew that she was as well servant to God, as by him king over peoples, she tyed the head of the sacrifice perchance a little closer to the hornes of the altar. And made those spirits that[1] would not know the true God altogether, to have some kinde of sense or smart of His religious lawes ; howsoever they were dead and sacrificed to the growing supremacy of the Roman miter or conquering scepter of Spaine ; ordain'd—as she thought—by excesse of playing fast or loose with God and the world ; in time, one to devoure another ;[2] ambitious and superstitious subtleties being an abysse or sea, where the stronger infallibly devours the weaker.

Herevpon[3] she makes a publique League for defence of Religion, with the king of Scots, Denmark, and the princes of Germany ; perswades a marriage between Scotland and Denmark ; exileth all Jesuites, and seminary priests by act of Parliament ; makes it felony to harbor any of them in England, or for the English to send any of their's beyond the seas, to be trained up among them.

---

[1] P, 'which'. G,   [2] P, 'the other'. G.
[3] P, omits ' hereupon '. G.

After[1] the loss of Antuerpe, she resolutely under-
takes the protection of the Netherlanders, and to
distract the Spaniard—as I said before—sends
Drake to the West Indies, with 21 Ships, who
surprised Domingo and Cartagena.   And immediately after his returne, with spoile and triumph
—to prevent all possibility of invasion—she sets
him to sea againe, with commission to burne all
ships, gallyes, and boats, along his Spanish coasts.
Who, in the same voyage, breaks through diverse
of his gallyes in the Bay of Cales, appointed to
withstand him; takes, burnes, or[2] drownes
100 sayle laden with munition and victuals.
From thence in his way from[3] Cape St. Vincent,
he surpriseth three forts: burnes ships, fisher-
boats and nets; and then making for the Azores,
hee there takes a carricke comming from the East
Indies.

The next yeare—as treading in his steps—
Cavendish returnes from his voyage[3] about the
world, with the spoiles[4] of nineteen ships and of
many small towns in America.

---

[1] P, 'Upon'.   G.

[2] P, grossly misreads 'and'.   G.

[3] P, similarly misreads 'to' and spells 'Capo'.   G.

[3] P, 'journey'.   G.   [4] P, 'spoile'.   G.

This and such like providence did this miracle of princes use in all her Wars, whereby her Wars maintained her wealth, and that wealth supplyed her War. So as she came ever in state, when she demanded aid from her House of Commons. Neither did she fetch or force presidents from her predecessors in those demands: but made her self a president to all posterities, that the love of people to a loving princesse is not ever cautiously[1] ballanced, by the self-pittying abilities of man-kinde: but their spirits, hearts, and states being drawne up above their owne fraile[2] selfnesse, the audit is taken after; and perchance summ'd up with a little smart to themselves, wherein they glory.

Neither did she, by[3] any curious search after evidence to enlarge her prerogatives royall, teach her subjects in Parliament, by the like selfe-affections, to make as curious inquisition among their Records, to colour any encroaching upon the sacred circles of Monarchy: but left the rise or fall of these two ballances asleep, with those aspiring spirits, who—by advantage of State, or time taken—had been authors of many biaced motions.

---

[1] P, grossly misreads 'curiously'. G.
[2] M, omits. G.   [3] M, 'after'. G.

And in some confused Parliaments amongst the
Barons' Wars, even forced her ancestors, with
one breath, to proscribe and restore; to call out
of the House of Commons, by writ, to the Upper
House, during the cessation : where[1] one man's
sudden advancement proves envious to foure hun-
dreds[2] of his equals ; and from the same, not truly
active, but rather passive vaine, to imprison and
release injudicially[3], sometimes[4] striving to master
the multitude, by their nobility, then again
waving their nobility[5] with the multitude of people;
both marks of disease, and no healthfull state in
a Monarchy.   All which she providently foresaw
and avoided ; lest, by the like insensible degrees
of misleading passions, she might be constrained
to descend, and labour the compassing of disorder-
ly ends, by a mechanicall kinde of University-
canvasse.

So that this blessed and blessing lady, with a
calme minde, as well in quiet as in stiring[6] times,
studied how to keep her ancient under-earth
buildings, upon their first well-laid foundations.

---

[1] P, misreads 'Sessions : Wherein'.   G.
[2] P, 'hundred'.   G.   [3] P, 'unjudicially'.   G.
[4] P, 'sometime'.   G.   [5] P, 'the Nobility'.   G.
[6] P, 'stirring'   G.

And if she found any stray'd, rather to reduce them back to their originall circuits, then suffer a step to be made ouer[1] those Time-authorized assemblies. And by this reservednesse, ever comming upon the stage, a commander and no petitioner,[2] she preserv'd her state above the affronts of nobility or people; and according to birthright, still became a soveraigne judge over any dutifull or encroaching petitions of nobles or commons.

For this lady, though not prophetically, yet like a provident princesse, in the series of things and times, foresaw through the long lasting wisdome of government, a quintessence, howsoever abstracted out of Morall Philosophy and humane lawes, yet many degrees in use of mankinde above them. She, I say, foresaw, that every excesse of passion exprest from the monarch in acts, or councells of Estate, would infallibly stir up in the people the like cobwebs of a popular spinning, and therefore from these piercing grounds, she concluded that a steady hand in the government of soveraignty, would ever prove more prosperous, then any nimble or witty practise, crafty, imper-

---

[1] P, inserts 'or besides' after 'over'. G.

[2] P, oddly has 'Petitionet': M, spells 'peticoner'. G.

ious, shifting, or forceing[1] humors possibly could doe.

Againe, in the latitudes which some moderne princes allow to their favorites, as supporters of government, and middle wals between power and the people's envy ; it seems this Queen reservedly kept entrenched within her native strength[2] and scepter.

For even in the height of Essex, his credit with her, how far was she from permitting him— like a Remus— to leap over any wall of her new-built anti-Rome ; or with a young and unexperienced genius to shuffle pulpits, parliaments, lawes and other fundamentall establishments of her kingdomes, into any glorious apparances of will or power ?   It should seeme[3] foreseeing, that howsoever this unexpected racking of people might for a time, in some particulars, both please and adde a glossy stick to enlarge the eagle's nest ; yet that in the end all buildings above the truth, must necessarily have forced her two supremacies of state and nature, to descend, and through[4] irregularities acted in her name, either

---

[1] P, 'practise.... .. forcing'. G.
[1] P, 'strengths'. G.   [2] P, 'a foreseeing'. G.
[3] M, misreads 'though'. G.

become a sanctuary between the world and inferior persons' errors ; or—as playing an after-game
with her subjects, for a subject—constraine her
to change the tenure of commanding power into
a kind of unprincely mediation. And for what ?
Even vainely[1] to intreat her people, that they
would hope well of diverse confusions : howsoever
they might seem heady, nay ignorant passions :
and such as threatned not[2] lesse then the[3] losse of
native liberties, descended upon her people, by
the same prescription of time and right, by which
the crowne had descended upon her selfe and her
ancestors ;[4] with a probable consequence of many
more shaip-pointed tyrannies to raigne ouer[5] them
and their freedomes, then their happily deceased
parents ever tasted or dream't of.

Besides, admit' these flatterings and threatnings
of hope and[6] feare —which transcendent power is
sometimes forced to worke by—could have drawne
this excellent princesse and her time-present subjects to make brasse an equally currant standard

---

[1] P, ' vanity '. G.   [2] P, ' threatens no '. G.
[3] P, ' a '. G.
[4] M, omits, ' and her ancestors '. G.
[5] P, omits ' to raigne '. G.
[6] P, ' or '. G.

with gold or silver, within her sea-compas'd dominions; yet abroad, where the freedome of other
soveraignities is bounded with[1] Religion, Justice,
and well-waigh'd commerce amongst neighbour-
princes, she foresaw, the least thought of multiplying self-prerogatives there, would instantly be
discouered[2], discredited and reflected back, to stir
up discouragement in the softest hearts, of her
most humble and dutifull subjects.

Therefore contrary to all[3] these captived and cap-
tiving apparances, this experienced governesse of
ours published to the world, by a constant series
in all[4] her actions, that she never was, nor neuer[5]
would be overloaden with any such excesses in
her person, or defects in her government, as might
constraine her to support, or be supported by a
monopolous use of favourites; as if she would make
any greater than her selfe, to governe tyrannically
by them.

Nay more ; so far off was she from any luke-
warmnesse in Religion. as—if a single testimony
may have credit—that blessed Queen's many and
free discourses with my selfe, ingeniously bare re-

[1] P, ' by '. G.   [2] P, omits. G.
[3] M, omits. C.   [4] P, omits. G.
[5] P, ' ever '· G.

cord ; that the unexpected conversion of Henry the Fourth fell fatally upon him, by the weaknesses of his predecessor Henry the Third, and the dissolute carriage[1] of his favourites. Who like lapwings, with the shels of authority about their necks, were let loose to rome[2] over all the branches of his kingdome, misleading governors, nobility, and people, from the steady and mutuall restes[3] of lawes, customes, and other ancient wisdomes of government, into the wildernesses of ignorance, and violences[4] of will. Amongst which deserts[5], all fundamentall changes—especially of Religion—in princes, would be found—as she conceived—the true discipline of Atheisme amongst other[6] subjects ; all sacrifices, obedience, being[7] excepted, being but deare-bought knowledges of the serpent, to expulse kings and people once againe out of mediocrity, that reciprocall paradise of mutuall humane duties. Prophetically concluding, that whosoever will sell God to purchase the[8] Earth, by making that eternall Unity of many shapes, must in the end make Him of none : and so bee

---

1 P, 'miscarriage'. G.   2 = roam: P, 'runne'. G.
3 P, 'rest'. G.   4 P, 'violence'. G.
5 P, 'defects'. G.   6 P, 'theis'. G
7 P, omits. G.   8 P, omits. G.

forced with losse, contempt and danger of[2] trafficke
not for a coheire's[3] place, but a younger brother's;
in that Church, at whose wide gates he had—
with shame enough—already turned in.   And
under conditions of a servant, rather then of a
sonne, be constrained for his first step to set up
the Jesuits' faction, providently suppressed by
himselfe before, and therein to shake the Sorbonists,
faithfull supporters in all times of crowne-sove-
raignty, against these slave-making conjunctions
betweene the Spaniard and his Chaplaine.   Nay,
yet with a greater shew of ingratitude, his next
step must be to suppresse those humble soules,
who had long supported him, whilest he was King
of Navarre, against that murthering holy-water
of Spanish Rome.   Lastly, to shew that no power
can rest upon a steep, hee must precipitately be
forced to send embassadors to Rome—with his
sword in his scabbard—servily begging mercy
and grace of such reconciled enemies, whose endlesse ends of spirituall and temporall supremacy
—this princesse knew—would never forgive any
heavenly truth, or earthly power that should oppose
their combination.   Finally she concluded that

---

[1] P, 'to'.   G.   [2] P, 'an heire's'.   G.

holy[1] Church of Rome to be of such a Bucephalus
nature, as no monarch shall euer be[2] able to be-
stride it, except onely the stirring Alexanders of
times[3] present, wherein the world is passing,[4]
finely overshot in her own bow.

Wherefore to end — as I began — with the case of
Essex, was not this excellent princesse therein a
witnesse to herselfe, that she never chose or cherished favourite, how worthy soever, to monopolize[3]
over all the spirits and business of her kingdome; or to imprison the universall counsels of
nature and State, within the narrownesse of a
young fraile man's lustfull or inexperienced affections? not thinking any one, especially a subject,
better able to doe all then herselfe. Whence,[5]
like a worthy head of a great body, she left the
offices and officers of the crowne free to governe
in their owne predicaments, according to her trust :
reserving appeales to her selfe, as a sea-mark to
warn all creatures under her that shee had still a
creating or defacing power inherent in her crown
and person, above those subalterne places by which
shee did minister universall justice. And though

---

1 P, grossly misreads ' hollow '.   G.
2 P, ' be ever '.   G.   3 P, ' time'.   G,
4 M, omits.   G.   5 P, ' where '.   G.

her wisdom was too deep to nurse or suffer faction amongst those great commanders and distrib-
uters of publique rights : yet was shee as carefull
not to permit any aristocraticall cloud or pillar to
shew or shadow forth suspicious,[1] or false lights
between her and her people.

---

[1] P, misprints ' superstitious '.   G.

CHAP.[1] XVI.

GAINE in her houshold affaires she kept the like equall hand,[2] ballancing the sloth or sumptuousnesse of her great stewards and white staves, with the providence and reservednesse of a lord Treasurer, kept up their[3] tables for servants, sutors, and for honor's sake in her own house; not suffering publike places to be made particular farmes of private men, or the honor of her household to be carried into theirs : and withall, by the same reverend auditor, shee watched over the nimble spirits, selfe-seek-inges,[4] or large-handednesse of her active secretaries; examining their intelligence, money, packets, bils of transportation, propositions of State, which they offer'd up by their places, together with sutes of other nature,[5] in her wisdome still sever-ing the reall[6] businesses from the specious but narrow selfnesse of inferior officers.

---

[1] Printed 'Cap', as before. G.
[2] P, 'hands'. G.   [3] P, 'the '. G.
[4] P, 'selfe-seeking'. G.   [5] P, 'Natures'. G.
[6] P, 'deep businesse'. G.

Besides, all these were examined by reverend magistrates, who having bin formerly issuers of her Majestie's Treasure in the secretaries places, did now worthily become governours of her finances, as best able to judge betweene the selfenesse of place or person, and the reall necessities of her State and Kingdome. A fine art of government by well-chosen ministers successively to wall in her Exchequer from the vast expence of many things, especially upon forraigne ambassadors, which—she knew—could neither bring reverence nor thankfulnesse to the[1] soveraigne.

Under which head of forraigne and domestique ambassadors, the answer wherewith that majesticall lady entertained the Polacke,[2] expected a treating ambassador, but proving—as she told him—a defying herald, is never to be forgotten amongst[3] princes, as an instance how sensible they ought to be of indignity, and how ready to put off such sudden affronts, without any[4] prompting of councellors ; and[5] againe worthily memorable amongst[6] her subjects, as a demonstrative argument

---

[1] P, 'their'   G.

[2] P, misprints 'Polarke'.   G.

[3] P, 'among'   G.   [4] P, 'a'   G.

[5] P, omits. G.   [6] P, 'among'.   G.

that she would still reserve Moses' place entire to
her selfe,[1] amongst all the distributions of Iethro.

And to go on with her domestique affaires, how
provident was she, out of the like caution, and
to the same end, that even hee who oversaw the
rest, might have his owne greatnesse overseen and
limited too.   Whereupon she forgot not to allay
that vast power and[2] jurisdiction of a[3] Treasurer's
office, with inferior officers of her finances, and
perchance under an active favourit's eyes[4] kept
her owne ; besides she watched and checked him
in his marriage made with Paulet his predecessor,
reserved that man's accounts and arrears as a rod
over his grandchild's alliance, qualified and
brought the fines of his many and great copyhold-
ers[5] to easie rates, would never suffer any proposition to take hold,[6] of uniting the Dutchy of
Lancaster to her Exchequer, what narrow reasons
soever[7] were alleaged of sparing and cutting off
the multiplicity of officers, with their wages and[8]

---

[1] M, omits ' entire to her selfe '. G.

[2] M, omits 'power and'. G.

[3] P, 'her'. G.   [4] P, 'eyes '. G.

[5] P, 'copyholds'. G.

[6] M, omits ' to take hold .' G.

[7] M, omits ' whatsoever '. G.

[8] M, omits. G.

ignorances or corruptions, all chargable and cloudy
paths, which the dealing with princes' moneys
doth as naturally bring forth, as Africa doth
monsters. But like a provident soveraigne, knowing that place in a Monarchy must help as well to
traine up servants, as to reward and encourage
merit; she constantly—to that end—keeps that
chancellorship of the Dutchy entire, and would[1]
not make the rewarding part of her Kingdome
lesse, to overload her private[2] Exchequer with
any addition of instrumentall gaine amongst
under-officers, into whose barns those harvests are
inned[3] for the most part.

Again with the same caution in all her doings
she made merit precious, honour dainty, and her
grauntes[4] passing rare, keeping them—as the Venetians doe their curiously refined gold—to set an
edge upon the industry of man, and yet—like
branches of creation—sparingly reserved within
the circle[5] of her throne, as inherent and tender
prerogatives, not fit to be left at randome in the
power of ambitious favourites, or low-looking

---

[1] P, 'will'. G.   [2] P, omits. G.
[3] = stored. G.
[4] P, grossly misreads 'graces'. G.
[5] P, similarly misread 'circuit'. G.

councellors, whose ends are seldome so large and[1] safe for the publique, as the native prince's councells are, or ought to be.

For the[2] clergy, with their ecclesiasticall or civill jurisdictions, she fashioned the Arches and Westminster Hall, to take such care one to bound another, that they in limiting themselves enlarged her regallities,[3] as the chiefe and equall foundations of both their greatnesses; she gave the superior places freely, lest by example she should teach them to commit symony with their inferiors, and so adde scandall in stead of reputation to God's Word, whose allowed messengers they affect to seem.

Her Parliaments she used to supply her necessarily expended treasure, and withall, as maps of orders or disorders through her whole Kingdome. In which reuerend[4] body—as I said before—she studied not to make parties or faction, advancing any present royallist out of[5] the nether House to stir up envy against[6] her self among[7] all the rest, and so publish the crowne to use personall prac-

---

[1] P, 'or'. G.   [2] P, 'her'. G.
[3] P, 'their Royalties'. G.   [4] P, 'reverent'. G.
[5] P, 'in the'. G.   [6] P, 'upon'. G.
[7] M, 'amonge'. G.

tises of hope or feare, in these generall Councells of her Kingdome, but by forbearing art was never troubled with any artificiall brickwals from them ; so as their need and fears concurring with her occasions, made their desires and counsels concurre too, and out of those equall and common grounds forced every man to beleeve his private fish-ponds could not be safe, while[1] the publique state of the Kingdome stood in danger of any[2] present, or expectant extremity.[3]

Her Councell-board—as an abridgement of all other jurisdictions—she held up in due of[4] honour, propounded not her great businesses of State[5] to them with any prejudicate resolution, which once discouered, suppresseth the freedome both of spirit and judgment, but opens her selfe clearly, heares them with respect, observes number and reason, in their voices. and makes a quint-essence of all their concords or discords within her selfe, from whence the resolutions and directions came suddenly and secretly forth for execution.

To be short, she kept awe stirring over all her

---

[1] P, ' whiles '.   [2] P, omits.   G.
[3] P, ' extremities '.   G.   [4] P, omits.   G.
[5] M, ' estate '.   G.

Courts, and other cheife[1] imployments, as her antidote against any further[2] necessity of punishment ;[3] in which arts of men and government, her
nature, education, and long experience, had made
her become excellent aboue both sexes.

Againe, for the regiment[4] of her grandees, at
home, she did not suffer the nobility to be servants
one to the[5] other, neither did the[6] gentry weare
their libertyes[7] as in the ages before. Their number and wealth was moderate, and their spirits
and powers counterpoised with her maiestracy,[8]
from being authors of any new Barons' Wars,
and yet reserved as brave halfe paces between a
throne and a people.

Her Yeomendry, a state under her noblesse,[9] and
aboue her peasants — proper to England — she
maintained in their abilities, and never gave them
cause to suspect, she had any intent, with extraordinary taxes out of the course of Parliaments, insensibly to impoverish and make boors or slaves of
them, knowing that such a kind of champion

---

[1] P, omits. G.   [2] P, 'further'. G.
[3] P, 'punishments. G.   [4] Government, rule. G.
[5] P, 'another '. G.   [6] P, 'her'. G.
[7] P, 'liveries'. G.   [8] P, 'Majesty'. G.
[9] P, 'nobles '. G.

countrey, would quickly stir up the nobility it selfe, to become doubtfull of their owne fences; and by consequence in danger, not only of holding lives, lands, goods, and liberties at their soveraigne's indeffinite pleasure, but by suspence of them[1] nursing and protecting Parliaments, to have all other native birthrights, viz. pulpits, lawes, customes, voyces of appeale, audits of trade, humble and reverent mention of coronation oaths, legall publishers, and maintainers of War, true maps of diseases and cures through her kingdome, with many other mutuall ciments of honour and use, between soveraigne and subjects, like to be confounded, or at least metamorphosed into prerogative taxes, wherein the people neither have voyces, nor valuable returne   I say, this home-borne princesse of ours making her prospect over these wildernesses of will and power, providently for her selfe, and happily for us, refused the broad branch of Pythagoras, his[2] Υ, and chose that narrower, but safer medium of State-assemblies, concluding that these two honourable houses, were the only judicious, faithfull, and industrious favorites of unincroaching monarchs.

So that it appears she did not affect, nor yet

---

[1] P, 'those' G.   [2] P, omits. G.

would be drawne —like many of her ancient neighbours, the French kings—to have her subjects give
away their wealth after a new fashion, viz. without returne of pardons, ease of grievances, or comfort of lawes, lest her loving people might thereby
dream of some secret intent to endemnize[1] their
lives, wealth, and freedomes, into a ship of Athens,
of which the name being old, and all riders,
sleepers, and other timbers new, they were to be
shipped downe a streame of the like nature ever,
and yet never the same.[2]   Besides not to be shipped
into that ship as mariners, souldiers, saylors, or
factors, but rather as slaves and[3] conquered out-
laws, with great dishonour to the legall and royall
stiles[4] of monarchicall government, as she conceived.   From which example of chaste power,
we that live after this excellent lady, may with
great honour to her ashes resolve, that she would
have been as adverse[5] from bearing the envy of
printing any new lines of taxes,[6] imposition,[7] proclamations, or mandats—without Parliaments —
upon her ancient cælestiall and[8] terrestriall globes,

---

[1] P, 'indennize'. G.   [2] Cf. our Index under 'Athens.' G.
[3] P, 'or'.   G.   [4] P, 'estate'.   G.
[5] P, ' adverse'.   G.   [6] P, 'taxe'.   G.
[7] P. ' impositions' : M, spells 'imposicōn '. G.
[8] P, 'or'.   G.

as her humble subjects possibly could be, or wish her to be.[1]

Now if we shall examine the reason of her cutting between lawes, king's powers,[2] and the[3] people's freedome, by so even a thread, what can it be, but a long and happy descent within the pedegrees of active princes, together with the moderating education of kings' children in those times; or lastly[4] a quintessence of abilities, gathered out of those blessed and blessing mixtures of nature, education, and practice, which never faile to lift[5] man above man, and keep him there, more then place or power shall by any other encroaching advantages ever be able to doe.

In which map, as in a true perspective glasse, this provident princesse seeing both her owne part, and her people's, so equally, nay advantageously, already divided and disposed, shee thought it both wisedome and justice to leave them ballanced and distinguished as she found them; concluding that the least change of parallels or meridian lines newly drawne upon any[6] ancient globes of monarchall

---

[1] M omits "or . . . . be". G.

[2] P, 'powers'. G.   [3] M, omits. G.

[4] P, 'in a'. G.   [5] P, 'lift up'. G.

[6] P, 'any the'. G.

government, in absence of Parliaments,—would like the service of God in an unknown language—prove prophaned or misunderstood; and consequently such a map of writing and blotting, of irregular raising and depressing, disadvantagious matching of things reall, and humours together, as must multiplie atheisme in humane duties, cast trouble upon her Estate for lacke[1] of reverence at home, and provoke this heavy censure through all the world—Spaine only excepted—that she endeavoured to raise[2] an invisible tyrant above the monarchs;[3] and to that end had made this step over lawes and customes into such a dangerous kind of ignorant and wandring confusion, as would quickly enforce mankinde, either to live like exhausted creatures, deprived of all[4] sabboths, or like barren earth, without priviledge of any jubile, which metamorphosing prospect—as she[5] thought—would resemble Circe's guests, and[6] transforme her people into divers shapes of beasts; wherein they must lose freedome, goods, forme,[7] language and kinde, all at once. An inchanted

---

[1] P, 'want'. G.   [2] P, the 'raising of'. G.
[3] P, 'monarch' G.   [4] P, omits. G.
[5] P, 'they'. G.   [6] P, omits. G.
[7] P, grossly misreads 'fortune'. G.

N

confusion, imaged by the poets, to warne princes
that if they easily be induced to use these
racks of wit and power indefinitly, and thereby
force a free people into a despairing estate, they
must even in the pride of their governments,
looke in some sort to be forced againe, either to
sacrifice these Empsons and Dudleyes, as the most
popular act such princes can doe, or else with that
two-edged sword of Tyranny, irregulerly[1] to
claime[2] a degree yet higher then the truth, to
maintaine these caterpillars in eating, or offering
Religion, lawes, &c., to the covetous, cruell, or
wanton excesses of encroaching Tyranny, as
though God had made all the world for one.

Nay more, it pleased this provident Queen even
curiously to foresee, what face her estate was like
to carry, if these biaced humours should continue
in a[3] long raigne over us, viz. contempt to be cast
over the majesty of the crown, feare among the
people, hate and envy against the reverend magistrate, entisement of domestique spirits to mutine[4]
or forraigne to invade upon any occasion, the
Court it selfe becomming like[5] a farme, manured

---

[1] P, 'irregularitie' G.   [2] P, 'climbe'. G.
[3] P, 'any'. G.   [4] P, 'mutiny'. G.
[5] P, omits. G.

by drawing up, not a sweate,[1] but even the browes
of humble subjects; and lastly the Councell-boord,
that glorious type of Civill Government, compelled to descend, and become broakers[2] for money,
executioner[3] of extremity, better acquainted with
the merchant, or mechanicall scraping revenues of
sicke and exhausted kingdomes, then foraigne
treaties, equall ballances of trade, true grounds of
maufactures, mysteries of importation and export-
tion, differing strengths and weaknesses in[4] crownes,
alteration of factions or parties with advantage,
danger of alliances made to benefite[5] the stronger,
the steady—though sometimes intermittent—undertakings of the conqueror, with all things else
that concerne *Magnalia Regni*, and so apt instruments not reverently to shew princes the truth,
but rather self-loving creatures full of present
and[6] servile flatteries, even to the ruine of that
Estate under which they liue and doe enjoy[7] their
honours.

Which confusion of place and things being
cleerly imaged within her, perswaded this lady to

---

[1] P, grossly misprints 'sweet'.   [2] P, 'Broker'.   G.
[3] M, spells 'execucōner'.   G.   [4] P, 'of'.   G.
[5] P, 'the benefit of'.   G.   [6] M, omits '.   G.
[7] P, 'wherein .... enjoy'.   G.

restrain the lauish[1] liberties of transcendency, within lawes and Parliaments, as two unbatter'd rampires against all over-wrestings of power, or mutinies of people, and out of these grounds to conclude prince-like, with her fore-fathers, that *superstructiones antiquæ nec facile evertuntur, nec solæ ruunt.* In that[2] axiome making manifest to the world, that Time-present's children, with their young and unexperienced capacities, are much too narrow moulds, for any large branches of well-founded monarchies to be altered, or new-fashioned in, the new and old seldome matching well together, let the ciment of seeming wisdome on either side[3] appear never so equall.

Now from[4] the right use of these high pillars, if we shall descend to inferior functions, we there find her—like a working soule in a healthfull body—still all in all, and all in every part. For with[5] the same restraining providence, she kept the crowne from necessity to use imperiall, and chargable mandates upon her people, when she had the[6] most need of their service, contrary to the wisdome of all governments;[7] neither did

---

[1] P, grossly misreads 'slavish'. G.

[2] P, 'this'. G.   [3] M, omits. G

[4] P, 'for'. G.   [5] M, 'which', G.

[6] P, omits. G.   [7] P, 'government'. G.

she by mistaking, or misapplying instances—
gathered out of the fatall conquests of her ancestors—parallell her present need and levies with
theirs, but wisely considered that the king and the
people were then equall[1] possessors of both
realmes,[2] and so in all impositions contributers to
themselves at the first hand.

From which grounds, like a contented and a
contenting soveraigne, she acknowledged these
differences to be reall, and accordingly by an
equall audit taken from her itinerant judges, with
the justices inhabiting[3] every county, after she
was well informed of her subjects abilities and
her enemies threatnings, she then, by advice of
her Privy-Councell summon'd her Parliaments,
demanded ayd, and was never refused ; in returne
of which loving and free gifts, she disposed those
extraordinary helps to the repayring and provisionall supplying of her forts along the coasts[4]
with offensive and defensive munitions, she stored
her office of the Ordinance[5] as a royall magazine
to furnish the whole Kingdom in extremity, and
when there were no Wars, yet kept[6] she it full, as

---

[1] P, ' equally '.   G.   [2] P, misprints ' kealmes '.   G.
[3] P, ' in every '.   G.   [4] P, ' coast '.   G.
[5] P. ' ordnance ' and so onward.   G.
[6] P, ' she kept '.   G.

an equall pledge of strength and reputation, both abroad and at home.

Lastly, this princesse being confident in these native sea-walls of ours, fit to beare moving bulwarkes in martial times and in civill traffiques to carry out and in, all commodities with advantage; she double-stored her Navy-magazines with all materials, provided before-hand for such workes and things, as required time, and could not be bought with money; besides, she furnished her Sea-arsinals with all kind of staple provisions, as ordinance, pitch, rosin, tar, masts, deale-boards, cordage, &c. for the building and maintaining[1] her Navie, flourishing in multitude of ships for War and Trade.

And as the life of that vast body, she for encrease of mariners, gave princely countenance to all long voyages, knowing they would necessarily require ordnance, men[2], munition, and burthen; and further to encourage this long-breathed worke, she added out of her Exchequer, an allowance of so much in the tun for the builders of any ships upwardes[3] of so many hundred tuns; she cherished

---

[1] P, 'of her'. G.

[2] P, grossly misreads 'new'. G.

[3] P, 'upward'. G.

the fisher-boats with priviledges along her coasts, as nurseries of sea-men ; brought Groenland,[1] and Newfound-land fishinges[2] in reputation, to encrease her stock of mariners, both by taking and trans-porting what they took far off.

And for the governours of her Navy under the admirall, as well in times of warr as peace,[3] she chose her principall officers out of the gallantest Sea-commanders of that time, whose experience she knew taught them how to husband and guide her Muscovy-Company, in generall provisions, not as partners[4] with her merchants but to gouerne instrumentall servantes and services with skill—the Master shipwrights—not only[5] inbuilding, but restraining the Ship-keepers riot or expence, in harbour and at Sea, how[6] to furnish or marshall[7] ships and mariners in all kind of sea-fights to their best advantage.

Besides, through the same men's judgments, she made all directions pass for the divers moulds

---

[1] P, ‘Groniland ’: now ‘ Greenland ’.   G.

[2] P, ‘ fishing ’.   G.   [3] P, ‘ peace as war ’.   G.

[4] P, ‘ partner ’.   G.

[5] From ‘ but ’ on to ‘ only ’ from MS. for first time.   G.

[6] M, omits.   G.

[7] P, grossly misprints ‘ martiall ’.   G.

required in shipping betweene our seas and the Ocean; as the drawth of water, high or low, disposing of ports, cleanly roomes for victuals, conveniency[1] of deckes for fight, or trade, safe conveyance for powder, and all other munitions,[2] fit stowage for[3] sea-stores, according to the difference of heats or colds in the climes they were to reside in, or passe through.

Againe, as well to instruct the captaines in their particular duties, as to keep a hand of government over the large trust and charge committed unto[4] them, in all expeditions, the ship with her furniture, tackle[5] and men, the gunners'[6] roome and all munition of that kind, the boat-swain's provision of anchors, cables, canvas, and sea-stores, the purser's, steward's, cook's roomes, touching victuals, were delivered to the captaines by bill indented; the one part kept with the officers of the Navy at home, the other in the hands of every private captaine to examine his accounts by when he return'd: of which I[8] my selfe am witnesse,

---

[1] P, 'convenience'. G.

[2] P, 'munition': M, spells 'municōns'. G.

[3] P, 'of'. G.   [4] P, 'to'. G.

[5] P, 'tackling' G.   [6] M, misreads 'gunner'. G.

[7] P, 'with'. G.   [8] P, omits. G.

as being well acquainted with the use of it in the imploymentes of[1] my youth, but utterly unacquainted with the change since, or any reasons of it. Besides like a provident lady who knew Place, for the ease of crownes, must serve both to reward meritt and to encourage it with other like motiues mentioned before, in the gouernment of the Exchequer, she kept her Cinque Portes seucred from the greatnes of the Admiralty, though she knew the principal vse and end in keeping of them devided were taken away by tyme and other changes through her sister's neglect and our former vnfortunate losses in Fraunce.[2]

Lastly, this great[3] governesse could tell how to worke her high[4] admirals—without noise—to resign their letters[5]-patents, when the course of times made them in power, and gaine, seeme or grow too exorbitant; yet kept she up their command at sea, and when they were there, made them a limited or absolute commission under the great seale of England, sometimes associating and qualifying

---

[1] P, omits ' the imploymentes of '. G.

[2] This considerable paragraph ' Besides ...... Fraunce ' is here given for the first time from the MS.   G.

[3] M, omits. G.   [4] M, ' greate '.   G.

[5] M, ' lres. Fattes.' : P, omits ' letters '.   G.

their[1] place, with a Councell of war of her own choice, and ever guiding the generalities of the voyage with instructions proper to the business, and to be published at sea in a time prefixed.

Out of which caution in her principall expeditions, she striving—as I said—to allay that vast power of place with some sencible[2] counterpoise, many times joyned an active favorite with that sea-Neptune of her's, making credit, place, and merit, finely competitors in her service ; besides, she well understanding the humours of both, temper'd them so equally one with another in her latter expeditions, as the admirall being remisse and apt to forgive all things, Essex severely true to martiall discipline, and loath to wound it by forgiving petty errours under that implacable tyrant Mars, in all likelihood her Fleet could hardly be over sailed or under ballasted, and consequently the crowne—in her absence—was sure to be guarded by[3] more eyes than two, to prevent confusion in martiall affaires, where every ship proves beyond the amendment of second thoughts, and so fatall to that state which paies and negligently ventures.

---

[1] M, omits. G.
[2] P, 'insensible'. G.   [3] P, 'with'. G.

The merchant-state[1] of her kingdome was oppressed with few impositions, the Companies free
to choose their owne officers, to fashion their trade,
and[2] assisted with the name and countenance of
embassadors, the custome and returne of their
industry and adventures, contenting them in a
free market without any nearer cutting of people's
industry to the quick.

The Flushingers, and Dunkerkers in succession[3]
of time, it is true, did much afflict their traffique,
though with smal strength; whereupon she first[4]
travelled to suppresse them by force, but found the
charge grow infinite, and the cure so casuall, as
she joyned Treaty with the sword, and set her
Seas by that providence and industry, once againe
at liberty from all molestation or danger of pyrates.

Her Universities were troubled with few mandates, the Colledges free in all their elections,
and governed by their own statutes, the grosse,
neglect of using the Latine tongue she laboured[5] to
reforme, as well for honour of the Vniversities, as
for her own service in all Treaties with forraign
princes; she studied to multiply her civilians with

---

[1] P, 'part'. G.   [2] P, omits. G.
[3] M, 'successe'. G.   [4] M, omits. G.
[5] P, 'studied'. G.

little charge, and yet better allowance to their profession. In a word, she preserved her Religion without waving, kept both her martiall and civill government intire[1] above neglect or practice, by which, with a multitude of like instances, she manifested to the World, that the well governing of a[2] prince's own inheritances, is—in the cleare house of Fame—superiour to all the far-noised conquests of her over-griping ancestors, since what man lives, conversant in the calenders of estates, but must know, that had not these wind-blown conquests of ours happily been scattered, they must in time have turned the moderate wealth and degrees of England into the nasty poverty of the French peasants ; brought home mandates in stead of lawes, waved our freedomes in Parliaments with new christned impositions, and in the end have subjected native and active Albion to become a province, and so inferior to her owne dearly-bought forraign conquests, being forced to yeeld up the superlative works of power, to the equall lawes of Nature, which almost every where—America excepted—proclaimes the greater to be naturally a law-giver over the lesse.

---

[1] M, omits. G.   [2] P, omits. G.

CHAP.[1] XVII.

ET as this wise and moderate governesse was far from incroaching upon any other prince's dominions, so wanted she not[2] foresight, courage nor might, both to suppresse all insolencies attempted against her selfe, and to support her neighbours unjustly oppressed, whereof by the reader's patience I will here adde some few instances.

She had no sooner perfected her virgin triumph over that sanctified and invincible Navy, and by that losse published the Spanish ambition, weaknesse, and malice to all Christendome, secured her owne estate, revived the Netherlands, confuted the Pope, turned the cautions[2] of the Italian princes the right way, and amazed the world; but even then to pursue that victory, and prevent her enemie's ambition, which still threatned the world with new Fleets; then—I say—did this active lady conclude, with advise from her Councell, and applause of her Kingdome, to de-

---

[1] 'Cap as before. G.   [2] P, 'neither'. G.
[3] P, 'caution'. G.

fend her selfe thenceforth by invading, and no more attend the Conqueror's pleasure at her owne doores.

Out of which resolution she first sent forth the Earle of Cumberland, who attempted the surprize of Porto Ricco, accomplished it with honour, and so might have kept it, had not disease and disorder proved more dangerous enemies to him, then the great name and small force of the Spanish did.

Againe to prevent danger, not in the bud but root, she tooke upon her the protection of Don Antonio king of Portugall, sent Sir John Norris, and Sir Francis Drake, with a royall Fleet, and eleven thousand men to land, seconded with the fortune and countenance of the Earle of Essex ; they tooke the base town of the Groyne, and when they had overthrowne all that came to succour it, and burnt the countrey, then marched they on to Lisbone, and in that journey sacked Peniche[1], wasted villages, and provinces, entred the suburbs of Lisbone, even to the gates, took East Cales[2] and burnt threescore Spanish hulkes full of provisions.

---

[1] P, ' Penicke '.   G.
[2] P, ' gates of the High Towne '.   G.

And to the same end, she did, and still meant succesively to maintaine a Fleet of her owne ships and her fast friends the Netherlanders[1] upon his coasts, not only to disturbe the returne of victuals, munition, and materials for War, with which the Empire, Poland, and the Hanse townes did usually, and fatally—even to themselves—furnish this growing monarch, but withall to keep his Navy which was riding and building in many havens, from possibility of getting head in any one place to annoy her; and thirdly to set such a taxe upon the wafting home of his Indian Fleets, as might—in some measure—qualifie that fearfull abundance which else was like enough to spread infection through the soundest councels and councellors of all his neighbour-princes.

In the[2] meane time, the French king Henry the Third—heartned by her example and successe—did encounter the Guisards, a strong faction depending upon Spaine. And when he was made away by treason, and the leaguers[3] in armes under the Spaniard's protection, then did the Queen providently take opportunity to change the seat of her Warres, and assisted Henry the Fourth,

---

[1] P, 'Netherlands'. G.   [2] M, 'this'. G.

[3] P, 'League'. G.

the succeeding king, by the Earle of Essex, untill he was able to subsist by himselfe, and till, by her support, he was strengthned, both to over-throw the League, and become a second ballance against the great and vast desires of Spain.

Neither did she rest here, nor give him breath, but with a fleet of one hundred and fifty sayle, and a strong land-army, sent the Earle of Essex and the admirall of England to invade Spaine it selfe; they tooke Cales, spoiled his Fleet of[2] twenty gallyes, and fifty nine ships, the riches whereof were valued at twelve millions of duckets. Im-mediately after, imployed she not the Earle of Essex with a Fleet to the Islands? In which voyage he sacked Villa Franca, and[3] tooke prizes to the value of foure hundred thousand duckets at the least.

Now when this Spanish invader found himselfe thus well paid with his owne coyne, and so forced to divert the provoked hand of that famous queen held over him, by stirring up Tirone in Ireland; —to which end he sent money and forces under Don Iohn d' Aquila, even[3] then that lady, first by Essex, and after by Montjoy, overthrew

---

[1] M, omits.   G,   [2] P, omits.   G.
[3] M, 'and even'   G.

the Irish, and sent home the Spaniard well recom-
penced with losse and dishonour for assisting her
rebels.

By which and the like active courses of hers, in
successive and successefull undertakings, that
provident lady both bare[1] out the charge of all
those expeditions, requited his invasion, clipped
the growing wings of his fearfull monarchie[2] and
made his credit swell through all the money-banks
of Europe, causing withall as low an ebbe of his
treasure.

Againe, by this imprisoning of the lyon within
his owne den, she did not only lessen his reputation—a chiefe strength of growing monarchs—but
discovered such a light as perchance might have
forced him in time, to dispute the titles[3] of his
usurpations at home, and have given Portugall,
Arragon, and Granada[4] opportunity to plead their
rights with Castile in the Courts of Mars, if God
had either lengthened the dayes of that worthy
lady who understood him, or Time not neglected
her wisdomes too[5] suddenly, by exchanging that

[1] P, ' bore '. G.
[2] P, misreads ' the fearful wings of this growing monarch '. G.
[3] P, ' title '. G.   [4] Misprinted ' Granoda '. G.
[5] P, ' wisdome so '. G.

active, victorious, enriching, and ballancing course of her defensive wars, for an idle—I feare—deceiving shadow of peace. In which whether we already languish, or live impoverished, whilst he growes potent and rich, by the fatall security of all Christendome, they that shall succeed us, are like to judge freely.

Thus you see how our famous Iudith dispersed the terrour of this Spanish[1] Holofernes, like a cloud full of wind, and by a princely wakefulnesse, preserved all those soveraigne States that were in league with her, from the dangerous temptations of power, wealth, and[2] practice, by which the growing monarchs doe often intangle[3] inferior, but yet soveraigne princes. And amongst the rest, from that vsuall[4] traffique[5] of his leiger embassadors, who trained up in the nimble exchange of intelligence, grow to be of such a Bucephalus nature,[5] like Rome, as I said before, a body of those[6] members, as the Alexanders of their time can only mannage, and make use of; instance Mendosa, in whom she had long before discovered and discredited all practises of those specious imployments of conquerers' agents.

---

[1] P, omits.   G.   [2] M, omits.   G.
[3] P, 'the inferior'. G.   [4] P, 'usefull'.   G.
[5] P, 'so like'.   G.   [6] P, 'such'.   G.

Besides in honour of her be it spoken, did not this mirrour of justice, by restraining that un-naturall[1] ambition of getting other princes rights, within the naturall bounds of well-governing their[2] owne, become a beame of such credit, as most of the kings or States then raigning, freely yeelded; both to weigh their owne interests within the scales of her judgment, and besides to assist her in bounding out the imperiall meeres[3] of all princes by that[4] ancient procession[5] of right and power.

Lastly, did she not purchase the like reputation even amonge[6] the heathen, and by it destroy[7] a nest, which this aspiring monarch began[8] to build in the seraglio[9] of Constantinople; for she thinking it no wisdome to looke on, and see his Spanish pistols pierce into so huge[10] a mountaine of forces, and dispose of them at his pleasure,

---

[1] P, grossly misreads 'naturall'. G.

[2] P, 'her' G.

[3] = boundaries. So Bacon in 'Essayes' (56) where 'meere-stone is = landmark. See Mr. W. A. Wright s edition as before. G.

[4] P, 'by the'. G.

[5] P, 'precession . G.

[6] P, 'amongst'. G.

[7] P, 'destroy d'. G.

[8] M, omits. G.

[9] M, 'Seraglia . G,

[10] P, 'high'. G.

providently opened the stronger monarch's eyes to discover how craftily the weaker wrought his ends at the cost of all defective, or sleepy princes about her.

Yet did not this soveraigne lady intercept his designes from under any goddesse-shield—whom Homer makes the Grecian worthies shoot, and hit —but displanted him by a gallant factor of her merchants in a league of traffique, and prevailed to make his embassador landed at Ragusa, housed in Constantinople, and all under protection of Ferrat, chiefe-Visier, yea upon[1] a contract of thirty thousand zecchins[2] already paid him, glad to returne, and shippe himselfe away, with more expedition then he landed.

Besides which reputation given to her name by the Grand Signior in this particular, she generally got power to keep this fearfull standard of the halfe-moon waving in such manner over all the king of Spaine's designes, as he durst move no where against his neighbour-Christian-princes, for feare of being incompassed within the horns of that[3] heathen crescent.

---

[1] P, 'yet, and upon'.   G.
[2] M, oddly has 'chickeens'.   G.
[3] B, 'the'.   G.

But these things swell, and require a more authenticall History, to continue the memory of that wonder of Queens and women; in honour of whose sacred name, I have presumed thus to digresse, and admonish all Estates by her example, how they may draw use and honour, both[1] from the dead and liueing,[2] the change of times having no power over reall wisdomes, but infinite over the shadowes of craft, and humours of petty States, which commonly follow the greater bodies, as they are unequally extended or contracted about them.

Wherefore now to conclude these heroicall enterprises abroad, together with the reformation[3] of her State at home, the refining of the English standard[4] embased by her sister, the preservation of her crown-revenue intire, her wisdome in the change of lawes, without change of dangers, the timely and princely help she gave to Henry the Fourth when he had nothing but the towne of Diepe left him, his credit and meanes being utterly exhausted, and so that brave king, being[5] ready, either to take sea and escape, or flye for

---

[1] M, omits. G.   [2] P, 'the living'. G.
[3] P, 'reformations' : M, spells 'reformacon'. G.
[4] The coinage. G.   [5] P, omits. G.

succour into England, her constant establishment
of Religion in Ireland, driving the Spanish forces
divers times from thence, who were maliciously
sent as well to stirre up her subjects to rebell as
to maintaine and support them in it, together
with the former recited particulars, howsoever
improperly dispersed, or bundled up together, yet
are in their natures of so rare a wisdome, as I
beleeve they will be still[1] more and more admired
—and justly—in that excellent princesse, even
many ages after her death.

Thus have I by the reader's patience, given
that Ægyptian and Roman tragedy a much more
honourable sepulture, then it could ever have
deserved, especially in making their memory[2] to
attend upon my soveraigne's herse, without any
other hope of being, then to wait upon her life
and death, as their maker did, who hath ever since
been dying to all those glories of life which he
formerly enjoyed, under the blessed and blessing
presence of this unmatchable Queen and woman.

Now if any man shall demand why I did not
rather[3] leave unto the world a complete history
of her life, then this short memoriall in such

---

[1] P, 'still be'. G.   [2] P, 'memories'. G.
[3] M, omits. G.

scatter'd and undisgested minutes, let him receive
this answer from a dead man, because I am confident that[1] noe flesh breathing—by seeing what
is done—shall have occasion to aske[2] that question, whilest I am living. Presently after the
death of my most gracious Queen and mistress,
the false spirits and apparitions of idle griefe
haunted me exceedingly, and made all things
seeme either greater or lesse then they were; so
that the further[3] I went, the more discomfortable I
found those new revolutions[4] of time, to my decayed
and disproportioned abilities; yet fearing to be
cursed with the fig-tree, if I bare[5] no fruit, I rouz-
ed up my thoughts upon an ancient axiome of
wise men; *si quicquid offendit, relinquimus cito;
inerti otio torpebit vita;* and upon a second
review of the world, called to mind the many
duties I ought[6] to that matchlesse soveraigne of
mine, with a resolution to write her life[7] in this
manner.

First, curiously[8] to have begun with the uniting
of the Red and White Roses, in the marriage of

---

[1] P, omits. G.   [2] P, ' of asking '.   G.
[3] P, ' farther '.   G.
[4] P, grossly misreads 'resolutions'.   G.
[5] P, 'bore'.   G.   [6] = owed.   G.
[7] M, ' on '.   G.   [8] P, 'seriously '.   G.

Henry[1] the Seventh.   In the like manner to have
run over Henry the Eighth's time, untill his severall
rents in the Church, with a purpose to have demurr'd more seriously upon the sudden change to[2]
his sonne Edward the Sixth, from superstition of
the establishment of God's ancient, catholique, and
primitive Church.   Those cobwebs of re-conver-
sion in Queen Marye's dayes, I had no[3] intent to
meddle with, but only by pre-occupation to shew,
that princes, captived in nature, can seldome keep
anything free in their governments, but as soyles
manured to bring forth ill weeds apace, must live
to see Schisme arise in the Church, wearing out
the reall branches of immortall truth, to weave iu
the thin leaves of mortall superstition, and to
behold in the State all their fairest industries
spring and fade together, like ferne seed.   Lastly,
I intended with such spirits, as age had left me,
to revive my self in her memory, under whom I
was bred.

Now in this course, because I knew, that as
the liberality in[4] kings did help to cover many
errours, so truth in a story would make good
many other defects in the writer, I adventured

---

[1] P, ' Hen '· G.   [3] M, ' not '. G.

[2] P, ' in '. G.   [4] P, ' of '. G.

to move the Secretary, that I might have his favour to peruse all obsolete Records of the Councell-chest,[1] from those times downe as near to these as he in his wisdome should think fit ; hee first friendly required my end in it, which I as freely delivered him, as I have now done to you.

Against her memory he, of all men, had no reason to keep a strict hand, and where to bestow a Queen Elizabeth's servant with lesse disadvantage to him-selfe it seems readily appeared not; so that my abrupt motion tooke hold of his present counsell. For he liberaly granted my requestes[2] and appointed me that day three weeks to come for his warrant, which I did, and then found in shew a more familiar and gracefull aspect then before, he descending to question me, why I would dreame out any[3] time in writing a story, being as likely[4] to rise in this time as any man he knew; then in a more serious and friendly manner examining me, how I could cleerly deliver many things done in that time, which may perchance be construed to the prejudice of this.

---

[1] In the MS. this word is divided by the end of the page, and ' Chamb^r.' is the catchword, although 'chest' follows on the next page. G.

[2] P, ' request '. G. [3] P, 'my'. G.

[4] P, 'like'. G.

I shortly made answer, that I conceived a[1] histor-
ian was bound to tell nothing but the truth, but
to tell all truths were both justly to wrong and
offend not only princes and States, but to blemish
and stir up against himselfe, the frailty and
tendernesse, not only of particular men, but of
many families, with the spirit of an Athenian Timon;
and therefore shewed my selfe to be[2] soe far from
being dicouraged with that objection, as I took
upon me freely to adventure all my own goods in
this ship, which was to be of mine[3] owne building.
Immediately this noble secretary, as it seems,
moved, but not removed with theis[4] selfenesses of
my opinion, seriously assured me, that upon
second thoughts he durst not presume to let the
Councell-chest lie open to any man living, without
his Majesty's knowledge and approbation,

With this supersedeas, I humbly took my
leave, at the first sight assuring my selfe this
last project of his would necessarly require sheet
after sheet to be viewed, which I had no confidence in mine[5] own powers to abide the hazard of;
and herein it may please the reader to beleeve me

---

[1] P, ' an '.   G.   [2] P, omits ' to be '.   G.
[3] P, ' my '.   G.   [4] P, ' those '.   G.
[5] P, ' my '.   G.

rather by these pamphlets, which having slept out my own time, if they happen to be seene here-after, shall at their own perill rise upon the stage, when I am not ; besides, in the same proposition I further saw, that the many judgements, which those embryoes of mine must probably have past through, would have brought forth such a world of alterations, as in the end the worke it selfe would have proved a story of other men's writing, with my name only[1] put to it, and so a worship of time, not a voluntary homage of duty.

Further,[2] I cannot justifie these little sparkes, unworthy of her, and unfit for me ; so that I must conclude with this ingenuous confession, that it grieves me to know I shall—as far as this apology extends—live and dye upon equall tearmes with a Queene and creature so many waies une-quall, nay, infinitively superiour to me, both in nature, and fortune.

---

[1] P, ' to put '. G.   [2] P, ' Farther '. G.

CHAP. XVIII.

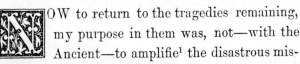OW to return to the tragedies remaining,
my purpose in them was, not—with the
Ancient—to amplifie[1] the disastrous mis-
eries of man's life, where orders,[2] lawes, doctrine
and authority are unable to protect innocency
from the exorbitant wickednesse of power, and
so out of that melancholy[3] vision, stir vp[4] horrour,
or murmur against Divine Providence : nor yet
—with the moderne—to point out God's revenging
aspect upon every particular sin, to the despaire
or confusion of mortality ; but rather to trace out
the high waies of ambitious governours, and to
shew in the practise of life[5] that the more audacity,
advantage and good successe such soveraignties
have, the more they hasten to their owne desolation and ruine.

So that to this abstract end, finding all little
instruments in discovery of great bodies to be seldome without errour,[6] I presumed, or it rather

---

[1] P, ' exemplifie '.   G.

[2] P, 'order'.   G.

[3] P, ' melancholike'.   G.

[4] P omits.   G.

[5] P, omits ' of life '.   G.

[6] P, ' errours'.   G.

escaped me, to make my images beyond the ordinary stature of excesse, wherein again that women are predominant, is not for malice, or ill talent to their sexe; but as the[1] poets figured the vertues to be women, and[2] all nations call them by feminine names, so have I described malice, craft, and such like vices in the person[3] of shrews, to shew that many of them are of that nature, even as we are, I meane strong in weaknesse ; and consequently in these orbes of passion, the weaker sexe, commonly the most predominant; yet as I have not made all women good with Euripides, so have I not made them all evill with Sophocles, but mixt of such sorts as we find both them and our selves.

Againe, for the arguments of these Tragedies, they be not naked and casuall, like the Greeke and Latine, nor — I confesse — contrived with[4] variety and unexpected encounters of the Italians, but nearer leveled to those humours, councels, and practices, wherein I thought fitter to hold the attention of the reader, than in the strangeness or perplexedness of witty fictions; in which

---

[1] P, omits.   G.

[2] *Ibid*.   G.

[3] P, 'person's.   G.

[4] P, 'the variety '.   G.

[5] P, ' these '.   G.

the affections or imagination, may perchance find exercise and entertainment, but the memory and judgement no enriching at all; besides, I conceived those delicate images to be over-abundantly in all languages already.

And though[1] my noble friend had that dexterity, even with the dashes of his pen to make the Arcadian antiques beautifie the margents of his works ; yet the honour which—I beare him record— he never affected, I freely[2] leave unto him, with this addition, that his end in them was not vanishing pleasure alone, but morall images and examples—as directing threds—to guide every man through the confused labyrinth of his own desires and life.   So that howsoever I liked them[3] too well—even in that unperfected shape they were —to condescend that such delicate—though inferior—pictures of himselfe, should be suppressed ; yet doe I[3] wish that work may be the last in this kind, presuming no man that followes can ever reach, much lesse goe beyond that excellent intended patterne of his.

For my own part, I found my creeping genius more fixed upon the images of life, than the

---

[1] P, omits.   G.   [2] P, omits.   G.   [3] P, ' not too '.   G..
[4] P, ' I do '.   G.

images of wit, and therefore chose not to write to them on whose foot the black oxe had not already trod, as the proverbe is, but to those only, that are weather-beaten in the sea of this World, such as having lost the sight of their gardens and groves, study to saile on a right course among rocks and quick-sands; and if in thus[1] ordaining and ordering matter and forme together for the use of life, I have made theis[2] Tragedies no plaies for the stage; be it known, it was no part of my purpose to write for them, against whom so many good and great spirits have already written.

But he that will behold these acts upon their true stage, let him look on that stage wherein himself is an actor, even the state he lives in, and for every part he may perchance find a player, and for every line—it may be—an instance of life, beyond the author's intention or application, the vices of former ages being so like to these of this age, as it will be easie to find out some affinity, or resemblance between them, which whosoever readeth with this apprehension, will not perchance thinke the scenes too longe,[3] at least the matter not to be exceeded in account of words.

---

[1] P, 'this'.   G.   [2] P, 'these' G.   [3] P, 'large'.   G.

Lastly, for the stile; as it is rich or poore, according to the estate and ability of the Writer, so the value of it shall be enhansed, or cried downe, according to the grace, and[1] capacity of the reader, from which common fortune of bookes, I look for no exemption.

But to conclude, as I began this worke, to entertaine and instruct my selfe, so if any other find entertainement, or profit by it, let him use it freely, judge honcurably[2] of my friend, and moderately of me, which is all the returne that out of this barren stock can be desired or expected.

---

[1] P, 'and the'.   G.
[2] MS honorble = honourable.   G.

finis.

III.

Additions to Life of Sidney.

Appendix.

A. ONE OF THE "TWO PASTORALLS MADE BY SIR PHILIP SIDNEY, NEUER YET PUBLISHED.

Vpon his meeting with his two worthy Friends and fellow-Poets, Sir Edward Dier, and Maister Fulke Greuill".[1]

(SEE INTRODUCTORY NOTE, *ante.*)

OYNE Mates in mirth with me,
Graunt pleasure to our meeting :
Let Pan our good God see,
How gratefull is our greeting.
Ioyne hearts and hands, so let it be,
Make but one Minde in Bodies three.

Ye Hymnes, and singing skill
Of God Apolloe's giuing,

---

[1] From "Davidson's Poetical Rhapsody. 1602. (Mr. Collier's reprint.)   G.

Be prest our reedes to fill,
With sound of musicke liuing.
  Ioyne hearts and hands, &c.

Sweete Orpheus Harpe, whose sound,
The stedfast mountaynes moued,
Let heere the skill abound,
To ioyne sweete friends beloued.
  Ioyne hearts and hands, &c.

My two and I be met,
A happy blessed Trinitie ;
As three most ioyntly set,
In firmest band of Vnitie.
  Ioyne hands, &c.

Welcome my two to me,   E.D. F.G. P.S.
The number best beloued,
Within my heart you be,
In friendship un-remoued.
  Ioyne hands, &c.

Give leaue your flockes to range,
Let vs the while be playing,
Within the elmy grange,
Your flockes will not be straying.
  Ioyne hands, &c.

Cause all the mirth you can,
Since I am now come hether,

Who never ioy, but when
I am with you together.
　Ioyne hands, &c.

Like Louers do their Loue,
So ioy I, in your seeing ;
Let nothing mee remoue
From alwayes with you being.
　Ioyne hands, &c.

And as the Turtle-Doue
To mate with whom he liueth,
Such comfort, feruent loue
Of you, to my hart giueth.
　Ioyne hands &c.

Now ioynèd be our hands,
Let them be ne'r a sunder,
But linkt in binding bonds
By metamorphoz'd wonder.
　　As should our seuer'd bodies three
　　As one foreuer ioynèd bee."

The second Pastoral is entitled " Disprayse of
a Courtly life" which furnishes only these two
stanzas bearing on the triple friendship :

　　" Therefore Pan, if thou mayst be
　　Made to listen vnto me,

Grant, I say (if seely man
May make treaty to god Pan)
That I, without thy denying,
May be still to thee relying.

Only for my two loues' sake,   SIR ED. D. AND

In whose loue I pleasure take,   M.F.G.

Only two do me delight
With their euer-pleasing sight,
Of all men to thee retaining,
Grant me with those two remaining."

B. PEPYS:

BY LORD BRAYBROOKE, 4th (1854) Ed.   III 336-7 : pp. 340-1 :
(SEE INTRODUCTORY NOTE, *ante*)

1667-8. Jany. 1st. " Dined with my Lord
Crewe, with whom was Mr. Browne, Clerk of
the House of Lords, and Mr. John Crewe. Here
was mighty good discourse, as there is always :
and among other things, my Lord Crewe did
turn to a place in the Life of Sir Philip Sidney,
wrote by Sir Fulke Greville, which do foretell the
present condition of this nation, in relation to
the Dutch, to the very degree of a prophecy ;
and is so remarkable that I am resolved to buy
one of them, it being, quite throughout, a good
discourse."

Jany. 2nd. " To Westminster Hall, and there staid a little : and then home, and by the way did find with difficulty, the Life of Sir Philip Sidney. And the book-seller told me that he had sold four, within this week or two, which is more then ever he sold in his life of them : and he could not imagine what should be the reason of it : but I suppose it is from the same reason of people's observing of this part therein, touching his prophesying our present condition here in England in relation to the Dutch, which is very remarkable."   (Cf. or Indices under *Holland*.)

C. ZUTPEN.

FROM WILLIAM GAMAGE'S "LINSI-WOOLSIE OR TWO
CENTURIES OF EPIGRAMMES, 1613." (SEE INTROD-
UCTORY NOTE, *ante*)

Epig. 49.

" To Zutphen, a towne in Gilderland, at the be-leagring of which the renown Sir Philip Sidney was killed.

I wist not which thy fame or infamie ?
Doth more exceede, in causing Sidney's fall :
But yet, I rather thinke thy fame, for why
Before that time thou hadst no fame at all."   G.

IV.

A Letter to an Honourable Lady.

A Letter to an Honorable Lady.[1]

CAP. 1.

Right Honourable Lady,

YOV are desirous, in regard of the trust you repose in me, to vnderstand mine opinion, how you should carry yourself through that labyrinth, wherein it seemes time and mischance haue imprison'd you. It was a wisdome among our Ancestors not to deale betweene the barke and the tree, otherwise than with confessors, shrifts, and such like superstitious rites, as—discharging ourselues—did vainely charge others with our desires. But the twine is so strong, wherewith your worth and fauour

---

[1] See Introductory-Note to this Volume for account of a MS. from which corrections of the folio have been taken. These corrections are nearly all silently adopted in the text, but noted at end of the Letter. They are rather numerous, and put right some glaring oversights. G.

haue bound me, as I will imagine our predecessors aphorismes in that point, to be rather a
modesty out of sloth or ignorance than any precept to guide our loues or liues by. For first, the
liberality of knowledge makes no man poorer; and
then the charity is much more meritorious, that
releeues distressed mindes, than distressed bodies.
Therefore to break through these mists—with how
little wisdome soeuer, yet with reuerent goodwill—I must first compare the state you were in,
with that wherein you stand now: then your
nature with your lord's: and lastly, the priuiledges of a wife, with the authorities of a
husband.

When you married him, I know for your part,
hee was your first loue; and I iudge the like of
him. What the freedome and simplicity of those
humours were, euery man is a witnesse, that hath
not forgotten his own youth. And though it be
rather a counsell of remorse than helpe, to lay
before you your errors past; yet because they
teach you to know, that time is it which maketh
the same thing easie and impossible, leauing
withall an experience for things to come; I must
in a word lay occasion past before you.

Madame, In those neere coniunctions of society,
wherein death is the onely honourable diuorce,

there is but one end, which is mutuall ioy in
procreation ; and to that end two assured waies :
the one, by cherishing affection with affection :
the other, by working affection, while she
is yet in her pride, to a reuerence, which hath
more power than it selfe. To which are required
aduantage, or at least equality : art, as well as
nature. For contempt is else as neere as respect:
the louingest minde being not euer the most louely.
Now though it be true that affections are relatiues,
and loue the surest adamant of loue ; yet must it
not be measured by the vntemperate elne[1] of it
selfe, since prodigality yeelds fulnesse, satiety a
desire of change and change repentance : but so
tempered euen in trust, enioying, and all other
familiarities, that the appetites of them we would
please may still be couetous, and their strengths
rich. Because the decay of either is a point of
ill huswifery, and they that are first bankrupt
shut vp their doores.

In this estate of mindes, onely gouerned by the
vnwritten lawes of Nature, you did at the beginning liue happily together. Wherein there is a
liuely image of that Golden Age, which the alleg-
ories of the poets figure vnto vs. For there

---

[1] Ell, measure. G.

Equality guided without absolutenesse, Earth yeelded fruit without labour, Desert perished in reward, the names of Wealth and Pouerty were strange, no owing in particular, no private improuing of humors, the traffick being loue for loue; and the exchange all for all : exorbitant abundance being neuer curious in those selfe-seeking arts, which teare vp the bowels of the Earth for the priuate vse of more than milke and hony. Notwithstanding, since in the vicissitude of things and times, there must of necessity follow a Brazen Age, there ought to be a discreet care in loue : in respect the aduantage will proue theirs that first vsurpe, and breaking through the lawes of Nature, striue to set downe their owne reaches of will.

Here Madame, had it beene in your power, you should haue framed that second way of peace, studying to keepe him from euill, whose corruption could not be without misfortune to you. For there is no man, but doth first fall from his duties to himself, before he can fall away from his duty to others. This second way is, that where affection is made but the gold, to hold a iewell farre more pretious than it selfe : I meane respect and reuerence; which two powers, well mixed, haue exceeding strong and strange variety of working.

For instance, take Coriolanus, who—Plutarch saith—loued worthinesse for his mother's sake. And though true loue containe them both, yet because our corruption hath, by want of differences, both confounded words and beings, I must vulgarly distinguish names, as they are current.

The wayes to this respect and reuerence—as shaddowes to the bodies of worth—are placed not in the sense, but vnderstanding; where they stand vpon diverse degrees, and strengths of reason, not to be approched with the flattering familiarity of inferior humours; as hauing no affinity with desire and remorse, high or low estate : whence we see kings sometimes receiue them not from their vassals, but rather pay them as tributes to them. In this mystery lies hidden that which some call—applying it to matters of estate—the Art of Gouernment ; others the art of men; whereby equality is made vnequall, and freedome brought into subjection. Example, all soueraigne Estates commanding ouer other men, borne as free as their rulers ; and those soueraignes ruled againe, by the aduantage of worth in their inferiors.

Into this superiority—noble Lady—it seemes your husband hath stept before you, not by any councell of worth, which with a naturall motion drawes respect and reuerence vpward; but by a

crafty obseruing the weakenesse of men, wherewith men are best acquainted. For as our desires
are more vntemperately earnest than women's;
so are our repentances more stronge and easily
inclined to change, if not to loathing. Of which
' forbidden tree ' when the affections haue once
tasted, presently as in the Brazen-Age, naked Eue
must hide her shame, sowe that she will reape,
and no more enioy the full measure of reciprocall loue, but be stinted with the vnconstant proportions of Power and Will. Because the knowledge of euill doth euer teach the first offender to
seeke aduantage; and so when they haue sinned
against the true equalities of loue, to take priui-
iledge in the false sanctuaries of place, person,
sexe or time; deceiuing the truth with that which
should defend it. Here Diuision drawes out her
vnreconciled paralels, to make the vnity of man
and wife, to become lesse one; and then it followes, that they which yeeld most doe not command most, as before in the lawes of naturall
affection : but contrarywise, they that giue, enrich them that take, they that loue must suffer,
and the best is sure to be worst vs'd. Because
the ends of society are no more now to loue or
equally participate, but absolutely to rule; and
where that is the contention, what need statutes

or recognizances to tye those humble natures,
that passe away the fee-simple of themselues,
either with selfe-louingnesse or superstitious
opinion of duty ? For it is with them, as with
the riuers that runne out their waters into the
sea Caspium ; the more goodnesse, the lesse returne.

Vpon this step, it seemes, your husband stood,
when he began to thinke of something more than
mutuall enioying ; as drawing the familiaritie of
natiue affections vnder the affected absolutenesse
of a husband's power. Here false pleasure—which
springs and withers with our flesh—began, as
gluttony doth, to kindle new appetite with variety
of meates. Here comes in change of delights and
delight in change ; the riches of desire in that
it hath not ; the triumphs of opinion, which though
the flesh of any one bee a true map of all flesh,
yet doth it racke vs still with idolatrous longing
after strange and vgly images of it. For the
restlesse confusion of Error hath this plague,
that her peace must be still in the power of
others, where Nature hath placed both the way
and guide of true peace within our selues. But
who are they that can walke this milky way?
Not those vnconstant spirits, which are wandred
into the wildernesse of Desire ; nor those, whose

vgly prospect is vnrepentant horrour; whose senses
are but spies of Conscience vpon their faults;
their reasons purchased into bondage, by offers of
their seruant-affections; and whose informing
consciences stand, like tormentors, with stained
tables[1] to giue in open euidence of secret deformity.
No Madame, this milken way is for those single
and simple spirits, who foolish and ignorant in
euill, thinke the passage to it hard, if not impossible; or when they idly slip, doe yet recouer,
with a regenerate industry; not ioying, as those
other vagabond soules, after they haue deceiued
themselues, to stray abroad and deceive others.

This is a generall description of the fall of
mindes; wherein there is notwithstanding an infancie and a man's estate : because as easie as the
euill is, yet no man growes by and by to her
extremities. Besides, there are degrees and differences, according to the state, frame, and mixture
of humours in the body : some inclin'd to one
frailty, some to another; some languishing, some
violent; some proper to ages, fortunes, times,
with such exceptions as are in particulars vnder
all vniuersall rules.

---

[1] = tablets or books of Memory.   G.

CAP. 2.

SINCE therefore in this glasse you may see where you were and where you are; there rests now a consideration of the limited authorities of a husband and the priuiledges of a wife; upon which I will not stand long: because you poore wiues doe in that, runne a common fortune with those estates, which by vsurpation of time or violence, haue nothing left of their former conquests or greatnesse, but fame and ruine. So as I will not vainely trauaile to winne that againe, which corruption and confusion haue won of you and the truth; but onely make mention of their names or natures in passing, as they serue to your end ; and open those other three wayes, which in the falne estate, wherein you stand, offer themselues to your aduantage. The first is to mend him : the second, to master both his euill and his estate : the third, to please him.

Vnto amends—miracles being aboue our power —there is required either the authority of credit or fauor. For credit, how you should haue any by the truth, where it hath none, his faults to himselfe and you, are pregnant witnesses. What

Q

little fauor you haue, if you repeate the story of
his life to your selfe, it will be manifest. For
first—you know—his deuotion and affection,
are long since carryed from you to his mistresse ;
by which reuerend name men commonly call
those whom they meane, by corrupting, to make
their seruants. And though shee, either out of
craft or coldnesse, deny him the enioying of her
body ; yet is that no aduantage to you : to him it
is the art of his ruine. For vnsatisfied desire is
too earnest for counsell, too confident for mistrust,
too omnipotent for remorse. So as, right like
the poeticall image of Phaeton, it inflameth
the whole horizon of man's nature with irregular
and disproportion'd notions. What wonderfull
effects those entising denials haue wrought, there
are records in euery age. The same poets make
in the chastity of Diana, Endymion our example.
Hippolytus, with his constant refusall of Phædra
and his deuotion to Phœbe, a martyr. The fable
of Ixion, where instead of Iuno he embrac'd a
cloud, begetting monsters in strong imagination ;
with many moe.[1] All which doe but expresse
how farre greater wonder we stand in of this
well-disguised ashes, your flesh, while the wheeles

---

[1] More : a poetical rather than a prose form. G.

of desire are woond vp, than when they are run
out with enioying. For in this crafty forge are
framed wanton modesty, entising shamefac'dnesse,
faint reproofes, with what other charmes soeuer
are fit to stirre vp the blindnesse of our selfe-loue
or pitty.

But methinkes—noble Lady—I euen now see
your face blush, while your thoughts tell me, that
your lord's affections haue so many vents, as there
is no danger of breaking the vessell with fulnesse ;
nor yet of multiplying deuotion, by restraint. It
is true that liberty disperseth, and so makes the
streames of fantasie lesse violent. Notwithstanding
Dotage is an unscrutable depth; it puts seales to
blancks, makes contradictories true, and sees all
things in the superlatiue degree. To be short, it
is a prospect into the land of Ignorance ; which—
they say—no man can describe, but he that is past
it. Nay, it is such a kinde of enchantment, as
makes the easinesse of others endeere her bewitching refusalls. Satiety, which iudgeth with scorne,
yet honours her ; impossible being no more
able to qualifie desire, than intreaty to reuiue it.
So as you being already bankrupt in his fauour,
in this course of amends, I will onely aduise you
to pray, if your faith serue : or if you will goe
farther, I must bring against you the fatall doomes

of Sisyphus, rowling the stone ; Belides filling the sieue ; with the poet's phrases of catching the wind ploughing the seas, and such like metaphoricall hyperboles, as describing infinite and impossible, lay them to your charge. Therefore— worthy Lady—remember Æsop ; seeke not your husband against the streame, vntill he be dead.

To master his mind, which is the second way, hath yet in the fore-front some more possibilitie. For the evill is malitious and yet subject ; changing, because imperfection cannot stand alone ; amorous, for that euerything seemes louely, compared with the deformity of euill it selfe. But it may please you to remember, that Inconstancy hath so strong a wall of craft about it, as it is hard by sophistication of wit, to master the experience of euill : it being old borne with vs, and acquainted with euery corner, accesse, and recesse of our mindes. Besides, it comes not into the nature of man with cleare and open euidence, as true their's doe ; but as vsurpers, whose vnderminings are hardly to bee seene, while they may bee preuented ; and when they are seen, beyond cure or contention. For the being of euill being nothing but onely a depriuing of the good, and the captiuing of our free-will-lights to the workes of darknesse ; it must needs come to passe, that when

her conquering venimes[1] are once distilled through
all our powers, and wee won with our selues, that
there can bee no thought within vs to heare or
entreat ; and without vs, though Authority may
cut off the infection of ill example from others,
yet can it no more take away the diuel's part in
vs, than call vp the dead.   Out of which I conclude: whatsoeuer cannot be mended—·without
authority—cannot be ruled.

Now if you will examine the preeminences of a
husband's estate, you shall soone discouer what
huge armies of vsurpation, custome, municipall
lawes, are in this strife of mastering him against
you; truth in some degree, fortune, and opinion
vniuersally.   Archimides held that it was possible
by art to remoue the vnremouable Earth, if he
could find vpon what basis he might fix the foot
of his engine: the same doubt I may make to
you, which is, where you will lay the ground of
that strength, which should master him?   If
upon his humours; then—as I said—the centre
is craft, the circumference inconstancie ; neither
strong vertues nor vices; but changing and
irregular fantasie ; as vnfit to rule, as hard to be
ruled ; especially since ill-nature and good fortune

---

[1] Venoms.   G.

learn easily to know their strengths, and like proud cowards, tyrannize where they find Right in the guard of loue or weakenesse. If vpon his estate, then doe you assaile him in his strength. For hee is by lawes aboue you: the words of your contract, obedience; of his, loue; the reuenew his, Liberty his friend, Honour scarce indifferent, Fame against you; protesting euer on the side of strength, not of right.

So as contention with superiors is but that which the poets figure in the fable of Anteus wrestling with Hercules, wherein they feigne him euer too weake, while he was lifted from his earth, and his onely recouery of strength by fall-ing to it. This earth of your estate is patience and humility; aboue which what light desire, or offence soeuer doth lift you, lifts you aboue the priuiledges of a wife, and with more harme and losse, will at the last make you fall, to vnderstand your own estate.

If you trust not these prophane images, I will lay a diuine before you; that you may see iniust and impossible haue like condemnation both in Nature and Grace. When the fleshly Bablyonians went about to preuent a second deluge, and so, with man's power to limit God's; they purposed to raise a tower equall to the heauens, thinking thereby, that God should either fauour their dwellings or destroy His owne. What came vpon them? Marry, a 'confusion of tongues' to the end, that they which understood not their Maker, might much lesse vnderstand themselues : An excellent course of the Wisedome, to punish vaine ends by fruitlesse labors. And sure the like destiny lies wrapt vp still, to fall vpon those, that for want of measuring their desires with the circumstances of time, estate, and worth, doe vndertake the giants Warre, and so burie themselues in their owne earth. Therefore by my consent—honourable Lady—you shall in stead of mastering him, master your selfe ; and auoid that other violent course, which requires wilfull vrging, seruile patience, broken shame, with all kinds of indecorum ; such as the worst speed best with; and yet so, as they that winne their ends, are sure to lose their honours. Yea, the truth is in euery part such a proofe of it selfe, as whoso will narrowly obserue the complexions of those wiues, that vsurpe vpon the authority of their husbands, shall see, that the very change of the office, workes almost a metamorphosis in nature ; the woman growing mannish, and the man womanish. For it is most true that ages and sexes haue their distinct lawes ; so as the fame is not the same in both, but diuerse ;

as the wise man saith vertues be in men and women.   Our fame lying in hazard, armies, bloud ;
theirs in silence, modestie, restraint : our reputations not easily shaken, and many wayes repaired;
theirs, like glasse, by and by broken, and impossible to bee healed.   Since therefore your owne
genius, honor, and impossibilitie, do all oppose
against this aduentrous practise, let vs leaue it ;
and conclude with the poet, that

> Who so will the deuil's master bee,
> Must haue a minde more mischieuous than he.

The last point, which is to please, hath in it a
face both of divine and humane duty ; possibilitie
in the censure[1] of rumour, that speakes most and
knows least.   Besides, the meanes that are vsed
in it, as vowes, prayers, sacrifice, obedience, &c.,
are all milde counsells ; and such as rather enrich
than impouerish those that vse them.   Let vs
therefore striue to wade through, or swimme ouer
the depth of pleasing : in which there are two
branches, either to please him with your selfe, or
with his owne humours.   To please him with
your selfe — considering the map wee haue already
described his nature in — I thinke you must be
sometimes short, sometimes long ; now faire, now
browne ; wanton, modest, and al at once.   For

---

[1] Judgment.   G

they must take on many shapes, that will please
a man of many mindes ; sense being there a judge,
motion'quiet ; and their felicity in such wandring
desires, as onely ioy till they doe enioy. So as
these two excellent mediators, Worth and Merit,
can be no more to them than light is to blindnesse,
or musicke to the deafe. Nay Beauty it selfe,
which is the obiect of vncorrupted sense, is nothing vnto these sensuall natures; who are so
bewitched with this disease of nouelty, as
vnwealdy fatnesse, discoloured skinne, and such
like vncouth prouokers of appetite, are often
dearest vnto them.   What hope then to stay
or fixe this vagabond lust ?   Since as those shadows that goe before the bodies which make
them, can neuer by the same bodies be ouer-
taken: so these shadowy natures haue neither
strength enough to leaue worshipping of others,
nor to esteeme those that worship themselues ;
but like smokes, kindlinge with euery flame, are
dissolued againe into euery new ayre about them.

The second of these branches is, to please him
with himselfe.   For the better understanding of
which course, if we doe examine the wayes that
common subjects doe hold vnder the vnquiet nature
of Power; we shall finde that waye doth corrupt
vs, in not working a largenesse, but narrownesse of

heart : and so making vs, like the little flies, apt
to couet after the flattering light, wherein we
burne. For vpon this stage, if superiors delight
in lust, panders are the ministers of credit : if in
wealth, the sparing negative voyces be the counsels of aduancement ; if they be iealous, then the
deprauing corporations, which keepe downe all
spirits of hope, or encouragements of honor, with
false narrow axioms of tyranny, are the charmers
we must giue eare vnto : helping to drowne our
superiours in the inundation of their owne follies,
and make their thrones a grange, wherein there
shall be nothing but selling of honour, to purchase
scorne abroad, and seruile feare at home. For it
is most true that the iealousie of vnworthinesse
in power is so infinite, as where sloth, ignorance
or basenesse haue once giuen it leaue to giue law,
it endures none vnder it, but such as are either
outwardly deformed, and so borne with their owne
crosses ; or inwardly defective in wit and courage;
the right estate of those mindes, which though
they be borne free in the lawes of Nations, are
yet slaues in the narrow moulds of their owne
affections ; or lastly, such, as in the extremitie of
want, or obscurenesse of birth, must be long prent-
ises to their superiors. How vgly a prospect
such rootes and branches must be to all free

mindes, you shall easily see, if it please you to looke vpon the poeticall mappe ; wherein the painter liuely describing a pageant of worldly vanities, with the plagues and deformities of euery sinne, represents mishapen humane shapes vnto vs ; either long tayles, clouen feet, hornes, or such like antikes, as with too many, or too few members liuely represent vs the monstrous births of Error. And when you haue exactly view'd it, I dare vndertake you shall not see in that mappe so horrible and fearefull images to the soules of men ; as you shall in those tyrannical courts to the bodies, and fortunes of the worthiest, and not without danger to the Libertines. Since as true worth is euer iealous to the fearefull nature of tyrants : so are extreme vnworthinesses a scorn, both to their pride, and power.

Now Madame, by the ill example and dangerous consequence in these misgouern'd courts of princes, you may comparatiuely see what such by-wayes will worke in a priuate family ; faults hauing there no purple to couer them, nor yet great hopes to excuse errors. So that, the ends and instruments, being both of necessity base, and neither with vertue nor fortune redeem'd from the scorne of seruile vices ; it must needs be with them as with the sinkes and vessels of dishonour, which

they that vse are asham'd to haue appeare.   Besides, the reproach will be greater in meane
estates ; because there they want the helps of
feare, which mak[e]s Murmur wary how shee
speakes aloud of Power ; and redeemes imperfections with rewards of magnificence and liberality.
Againe, if you will needs corrupt your selfe, to
make the line you leuell by more crooked ; then
must your first step be ouer the shoes in shame.
For you must combine with his mistris, who will
perchance measure you forth some part of that,
whereof the whole is yours : I meane your husband's loue.   And whether she will, in this false
glasse of his dotage, discouer your fall of spirit,
and so teach him to be more absolute, it is doubtfull ; because the more sandy the foundations
of craft be, the more charge and care is euer to
be vsed in building vpon it.   Moreouer, this is
one essentiall difference, betweene the counsell of
Honour and Craft ; that if the successe of subtility
be euill, it doth blast and blacke the stocke it is
grafted in, where the counsell of Honour doth in
mischance it selfe, improve the reputations of
them that bee gouerned by it.

Therefore—as I said—if you will aduenture
vpon these vnsound counsels, which haue base
conditions, hazarding successe and infallible

infamy; you must first deface honour, shame, religion, and all other honest limits in your selfe: because it is an vnprosperous and half-witted course, to thinke of remorse, after counsell taken to haue good by the deuill. And who but those natures that can be as euil as they list, are fit to guide themselues by that iron industry, wakefull faithlesnesse, aduantageous contracts, which they must passe through that intend to master, or please corrupted Power? The conclusion, and end of my counsell therefore is, onely to perswade you, that you neuer study to be wiser than the truth; and so neither striue to master, mend or please him.

CAP. 3.

OW if I leaue you here, I haue onely laid before you a glasse of disquiet, and rais'd vp such mists of opinion, as make your woes seeme greater, and thereby—like an ignorant Criticke—rather dissolu'd those rests you had, than erected you any new. But though there be lesse labour and art required in ouerthrowing than establishing—the common errors of men giuing authority to censurers, and a reputation of piercingnesse to the reprouers—yet my selfe-end being nothing but your fauor, and my true end your good ; how vnequall soeuer my spirits be, to build you any certaine felicity vp on this broken foundation, yet shall they bee sufficient, I hope, to pull downe those ruines of yours, that threaten·— while you labour vnder them—to fall upon you, or while you peice[1] with them, suddenly to fall away; and so leaue you weaker, with the trauell and charge of many thoughts. For it is most true, that as the old and new agree together in nothing,

---

[1] = Make peace . G.

so the mixtures of good and euill are incompet-
ible. Therefore Madam, Let me digresse a little,
and remember that the metall[1] you are made of is
earth, your habitation a world ; both mortall, and
so no perfection at all to be expected in them :
those petty shadowes of rest which are there,
being full of temptation, lets, or dangers ; which
I must take notice of, both to diminish your expectation that else will proue an enemy to you ;
and besides to warne your steady mind, that a
slip is not strange in an icie way.

To beginne therefore with our flesh. Euer
since the curse of bondage, which God breathed
out vpon the first sinne, each degree of life in it
is onely a change and variety of seruitude. The
child's innocency being in weakenesse, his food in
the nurse, his frailties vnder the rod ; man vnder
man, his faults vnder lawes, rewards vnder will;
nothing constant but the inconstancy of the euil,
and her appearance of liberty the extremest of all
bondage. Nay, to goe further, the vniuersall
corruption of inferior elements is such, as euen
worldly wisedome it selfe workes but as our vulgar
physicke doth, which passing through the imperfections and contrarieties of our natures and dis-

[1] So elsewhere " oare " : see Glossarial Index. *s.v.*   G.

cases, doth helpe and hurt together; still multiplying the curse of our fall, in the false changes of diseases and cures, appetites and opinions. Neither can the confluence of worldly things yeeld any other rest or stability, than such as is in the kingdome of sleepe, where the best is but a dreame. Because where imperfection is, there disquiet must be; and where disquiet gouernes, there Nature is as apt to wander, as to be weary. Nouelties—like instants—come and passe; that which we desire proues like to that we haue enioy'd; the faire deceiues, and the vntasted is onely pleasing. Wee may therefore as well seeke fish vpon the mountaines, trees in the sea, as peace in flesh: which is only a promise to them that care not to finde it there. To proue this : if we obserue the progresse betweene God and vs, in his first Testament, the Sabbath is there annexed to the condition of sixe dayes labour, not of rest : here a figure only, hereafter a being; in this life a thing we taste of by faith, performed in eternity to them that haue passed through this flesh as an inne, not as an habitation. So as this body, this composition of elements, is but onely a purgatory of the soule, either to cleanse or corrupt, as the affections of it looke vp or downe.

And Madame, now that wee haue done with

this fleshly prospect, if we consider the world, we shall finde that to be vnto a man—like a sea to an island—full of stormes, vncertaineties, violence; whose confusions haue neither iustice nor mercy in them. If we examine the motiues that caused the man to make art his nature, and borrow wooden feet to walk ouer her mouing waters; we shall finde them to haue beene necessity, couetousnesse, curiosity, ambition, and some such other enemies to rest, as with false greatnesses—while men could not endure little things—inforced them through paine and danger, to suffer all the torments of vncertainty. To apply which comparison Madame, you shall see the same impatient humours are they, who hauing first wearied vs within, doe after perswade vs to seeke peace in the world without; where we being forced to wrestle with others, because we could not ouercome our selues, in stead of one euill are constrain'd to encounter many. And iustly; since where in all inward wayes to peace, man needes no lawes but God's and his owne obedience; if he once goe into trafficke with the world, his desires are there bound with the snares of Custome, the heauy hand of Power, the enammels of Authority, which conceale—as the poets say—vnder the golden garments of Pandora, all the venome

of her brazen tonne. And in that bottomelesse pit
of humours shall we not finde deceit as infinite as
desire, Honour but the throne of Care, Prosperity
both the child and mother of Labour, ? To be
short, we shall there finde—though too late—
that all fortunes and misfortunes are but moulds
of momentary affections, spunne out with proportion or disproportion of time, place, and natures.
So as since no estate can priuiledge this life from
death, sicknesse, paine—Power it selfe being alike
feared and fearefull—must we not thinke to
gather our roses among thornes, and consequently
the world to be a flattering glasse, wherein man
rather sees how to change, or adorne his euils,
than any way to reduce or amend them ?

Through this false Paradise—noble Lady—we
must therefore passe, as Vlysses did by the enchanted desarts of Circe ; stopping our eares and
closing our eyes, lest our rebellious senses, as apt
to flatter as to be flattered, chance to take part
with the diuersity of beguiling obiects, and so
lead our misty vnderstandings captiue to perdi-
tion. The company of Vlysses—like multitudes
stronge in sense and weake in reason—by making
loue to their owne harme, were with open eares
and eyes, transformed into sundry shapes of beasts:
the poets figuring to vs, in them, the diuerse

deformities of bewitching frailties, wherewith
for lacke of diuine grace or humane caution, they
get power to ensnare vs. And in this captiuity,
let no ignorance seem to excuse mankinde; since
the light of truth is still neere vs, the tempter
and accuser at such continuall warre within vs,
the lawes that guide, so good for them that obey,
and the first shape of euery sinne so vgly, as whosoeuer does but what he knowes, or forbeares
what he doubts, shall easily follow nature vnto
grace: and if he in that way obtaine not the
righteousnesse of eternity, yet shall he purchase
the world's time and eternity, by morall fame.
For obedience, not curiosity; as in heauenly, so in
earthly things, is the most acceptable sacrifice of
mankind. Because this inherent tribute of nature
vnto power—like a reuealed light of vniuersall
grace—refines man's reason, rectifies his will,
turnes his industries and learnings inward againe
whence they came, ioynes words with things,
and reduceth both of them to their first beings.
To conclude, this is that inward fabricke, by
which we doe what we thinke and speake what
wee doe.

Now Madame, In this narrow path, your helps,
both against inward assaults and outward temptations, must be those moderate sweet humours

which I haue knowne to bee in you and some of
yours. This moderation of desires being a farre
freer and surer way, than the satisfying of them
can bee : Repentance following the one and Peace
the other; the one course making Nature go as
well too fast backe, as forwards; and so must
consequently offend others with that which first
offended themselues : where these moderate affections doe with a naturall harmony please themselues; and then must not the ayre of that
vntroubled world naturally yeeld peace to euery
creature that breathes in or about it? Besides,
this moderation brings forth few desires, strong
humblenes to pay the tributes of power, patience
as an armour against oppression, truth as a sacrifice : whereby the world which giues but what
it hath and the euill of others, that desires to
oppresse or infect; can the hardlier finde meanes
to trouble them, or colour why they should study
to doe it. My counsell is therefore Madame, that
you enrich your selfe vpon your owne stocke;
not looking out-wardly but inwardly for the
fruit of true peace, whose rootes are there; and
all outward things but ornaments or branches,
which impart their sweet fruits with the humble
spirit of others.

Yet noble Lady, because you are a woman and a

wife; and by the lawes of both these estates, in some measure ordain'd to liue vnder meane and supreame authority: my intent is not, while I perswade you from the captious labyrinth of practise; to leaue you without such reasonable latitudes, as passengers haue in their trauailes, who when they cannot clime ouer steepe mountaines, find means to go about them, and so by length cut away the danger or possibilitie of precipitation. In which course Madam, because presidents are osteemed the best guides for humane ignorance to follow, I will first lay before you the opinions of worthy men, borne vnder tyrants, and bound to obey, though they could not please; the comparison holding in some affinity betweene a wife's subiection to her husband and a subject's obedience to his soueraigne. Brutus would leaue nothing in his mind fearefull to Power, nor in his fortune exorbitantly to be coueted; as resolute either to be safe by innocencie or contempt; or if both failed yet to haue extremity a warrant against extremities. Some haue thought the way of security to be in not vnderstanding the abstruse courses of Power. Others aduise vs—with the moone—to acknowledge all our light to the sunne. Some would haue vs imitate the spheres, who carried about with the violent course of the First Mouer, doe yet steale

on in their naturall with slow and vnsensible
motion; with many of like nature, which I for-
beare to number, in respect that no man gouern
his life wholly by precepts.   Humane wisedome
it selfe varying with circumstance of occasion,
place, time, and nature; and so neither the same
in all things, nor still the same in any.

CAP. 4.

THEREFORE Madam, lest you should thinke I would foolishly conclude the state of all minds in the aphorismes of a few; I will leaue this bondage of precepts, to walke in this larger field, and through an vnproper comparison of diuine and humane power together, shew you by humility a way into the one and by discreet constancy a passage out of the other. For as the two authors differ in the disproportion of infinite good and finite euill ; so doe their workings within vs. The one makes faith a wisedome, the other infidelitie a freedome : the one giuing abilitie to walke ouer the deepe sea of God's commandements, which while they seeme impossible proue easie ; the other drowning weake faith in the shallow dewes of mistrust, vanity, selfenesse, and such other irregular hum- ours, as while they seeme easie, proue impossible : my intent being, by this mappe, noble Lady, to make you affraid of trusting your peace in a leak- ing ship of humane power and affections. Because all things there are so gouern'd by the two false

rudders of hope and feare, as though—like the
boat of Charon—they refuse no passinger, yet
carry they none ouer either into rest or honour.
In example of diuine power; when God led the
children of Israel out of bondage into the Land of
Promise, to witnesse His omnipotencie, He vsed
the miracle of cloud and pillar; one to lighten
darkenesse, the other to shadow the beames of
glory : which two signes the people of God had
reason to adore ; since it is credible that Hee who
created the world should be in loue with His
worke; and consequently Hee not curious to deceiue, in Whose power it was to create, maintaine,
and destroy. Besides to giue all, and take nothing, proceeds of an vncaused goodnesse, and so
necessarily of an vnabusing.

The princes of the Earth haue two like ensignes ;
viz. feare and hope : the pretence of the one,
to awake our dull spirits out of the idle sleepes
of ignorance to serue the ends of actiue spirits ;
the other, to keepe the exorbitant desires of multitudes vnder the seruice and cautions[1] of supreme
Will. Of these humane clouds and pillars we
haue more reason to be iealous. First, in respect
that whatsoever is created, is affraid of disolution,

---

[1] Misprints 'cautious'. G.

and so in loue with it selfe. Then because wee know, that as many riuers must lose their names, to make vp one sea : so absolutenesse must winne and keepe aboue, with the losse of all, or at least many branches of vniuersall freedome. And therefore the fox did not conclude amisse, when he saw his fellowes' steps march towards the lion's denne, and none returne, *Nos hæc vestigia terrent.* But more clearly to discerne these gilt or painted fetters, from a true golden freedome, let vs examine the specious wisedomes of man's absolute gouernments : and for the most part wee shall find them to maintaine that which is stollen by craft ; vsurpations by might ; and for a further enlargement of their narrow foundations, to stroake vs with our owne hands, threaten vs with our owne strengths, and reward vs with the spoyles of our owne fortunes.

Yea, so much they abhorre equality from whence they came, as they clime ouer Law, Religion, and Truth, to keepe more and more aboue that sweet orbe of humane and equall peasing[1] lawes. If then euen the coward and foolish spirits doe feele enough to acknowledge this, of what haue we more cause to be iealous, than of these two

---

[1] Poising, as before. See Glossary-Index. **G.**

cloudy pillars Hope and Feare ? Since by no other
racke can the nature of man be more highly im-
proued to the aduantage of Power and disaduantage
of his natiue freedome : the one bewitching, the
other amazing vs, the one mastering the strength
of number with a multitude of scattered desires,
the other entising or forcing vs to giue away our
rights for feare to lose them : both—as they say
of Esop's dogge—making vs forsake the true flesh,
to catch at the reflexion of shaddowes. So that
the best course for vs inferiors is, neither—like
little children—to play away our times with the
babies[1] which we our selues haue made, nor yet
to feare the antickes of our owne painting—since
we lend the hornes and nayles which make them
vgly ; but rather to suppresse desire and affections
within our selues, by which we shall wither Hope
and Feare—two crafty spies of Power—giuing
intelligence what may be forced within vs, hereby
to enhaunse the tributes of tyranny, till it haue
drawne vp our browes after our sweat, and giuen
lawes to thirst, as well as drinking. Therefore
Madame, vntill the smarts of sense haue so vnited
will and vnderstanding, as all men in like fortunes
may haue like ends, till the beasts beginne to

---

[1] Dolls. G.

know their strengths, the vnwritten lawes blot out the written, and the temporall cease vnder the eternall ; there is neither in your's nor in any other subiection, any true peace to be gotten by trust of superiors ; nor honour by strife against them. Whence may I not demonstratiuely conclude, that wakefull Power must needs winne of all inferiors, who striue or venture to win of it ?

Now Madame, when Nature in her vniuersall knowledge foresaw this distresse or taxe, like to fall vpon her freedome ; she, which is no stepmother to any of hers, straightwaies gaue Honour more wings than one, to the end, those which cannot haue it in commanding, might haue it in obeying ; and those that want power to doe nobly, may yet finde latitudes to suffer nobly in. Out of this came the wise-man's words, deliuered vnto vs from the trauailes of his minde : that there are times to rest, and times to labour ; times to be well, and times to be sicke ; times to hope, and times to vnhope, &c.[1] In which vnhoping time you must resolue to finde your selfe, and by counsell of the Wisedome, limit all vnquietnesse of desires ; lest they being vnseasonable, adde shame to your other misfortunes. Let nothing therefore

---

[1] Ecclesiastes iii., 1—8. G.

makeyou hope, where an ecclipse of many humours
hath darkened your sunne. Trust not; for vn-
loulinesse and vnworthinesse are euer vnsafe.
Venture not; for besides that this fortune is in it
selfe misfortune, power being too hard for right,
the very multitude, who judge of actions by
the whorish conduct of effects, will by and by
censure them that vndertake and prosper not,
either vainely to haue fixed impossible ends to
themselues, or foolishly neglected the meanes;
and from these grounds euer conclnde Aduersity
in the wrong, and Prosperity in the right. If
your ladyship desire a reason of this error, it is
because men's common iudgements vpon common fame neither will, nor indeed can, well examine the different constellation betweene your
husband's nature and your's; your merits, his
demerits : but will infallibly sticke fast in the
skinne and outside of estates, preeminces and
authorities; iudging well of that in their folly,
which in their basenesse they resolued to worship

To be short; the wit of people is so many times
vnder the truth and their care so much lesse than
their wit; as it is with them euer a lesse fault to
doe iniury than to haue ill lucke.

Therefore noble Lady, I cannot aduise you either

to complaine or mutinie against the stronger; for the one discouers inconsiderate weaknesse, the other languishing errors : but rather as the vegetable things in the wisedome of Nature doe, so aduise your ladyship to doe : which is draw all your sap in this Winter of thoughts, downe to the root; and be content to want leaues, till the sweet Spring of time or occasion come to inuite them vp againe. For besides that these iuries of common opinion will euer when they doe best, looke vpon law, and not equity, vpon custome, not on nature, strength, and not right : euen the clearest humane iudgements will hardly conceive so monstrously of mankind, as shall be sufficient to acquit you and condemne your husband. The reason is : because these extremities of good or euill will not easily be beleeued to raigne in these middle natures of flesh and blood : in respect that God hath decreed the angels to heauen, the diuels to hell ; and left the Earth to man, as a meane creation between these two extremes. So that he must be a kinde of diuell himselfe, that can easily beleeue there should be diuels raigning within or amongst vs. Besides Madame, how vncomely it were for you—like the crow— to goe out of your arke of duty, and discouer extraordinary seas of vanity in your husband, the

lawes of honour will tell you. Let God " the
searcher of hearts " and Time the " discouerer of
faults," moue those links of shame and punishment, whereto our errors are tyed ; and let it be
enough for you henceforwards not to worship
idols, " who haue eyes that see not, and eares
that heare not." For, as they say, when euery
particular dies, he hath his owne doome ; though
the generall doomes-day bee to come : so may I say,
to whatsoeuer your husband hath to all the world
else, he hath neither life, loue, nor sense to you.
Therefore since power lies in him, desire and
dutie in you ; pay your tribute, doe your homage,
and make your reward to bee the secret peace of
well-doing ; cutting off all other thoughts of rest
by him, who not hauing it in himselfe, cannot
possibly bestow it vpon others. For by that
meanes your honour will bee safely guarded from
these muddy visions of Hope, which—as I said—
is one chiefe pillar in incroaching power ; and in
which the fooles of the world, sleeping away their
liberties, doe vainely make Authorities their
heires.

Now that we haue shaken your hopes, the next
chiefe engine of power is terror : a breath which
seemeth to pierce neerer, and not to leaue vs safe
or free within our selues. Because it hath slander

at commandement, spies, accusers, violence, and oppression ; which fooles vnderstand not and base men giue ouer-much reuerence vnto. Against these I can onely say this; that they be the fires in whose heat Worthinesse is re-purified ; and by whose light the glories of it are farthest seene. So as for these violencies of temptations, I perswade you to make Iob your example; a type whom God gaue the diuel leaue to persecute in his goods, his children, and in his person with such infirmities of body, as had both paine and lothsomenesse in them. And marke againe in the same afflicted Iob, in whom the excellent wisedome of constancy is figured; hee neither did sacrifice to his euill angell, nor studied amends or reliefe at the hands of his tempter, but walled his flesh with patience, and his conscience with innocencie: leauing to the diuell that which was his ; I meane his body, and fortune, subiect by Adam's discreation to the prince of sensuality. And what small power the princes of this world haue ouer the resolutions of faith, honour, or nature, examine — if it please you—by those paines, which your selues suffer for children, hereticks for opinion, pride for fame, feare for feare; wherein the rod makes the child endure the corrosiue. So as the vnmeasurable measures

of these things haue some resemblance with the
infinite yet mercifull Word of God ; wherein the
lambes may safely wade, while the vaste bodies
of the elephants shall be drowned [1] Beleeue therefore with the wise ; that betweene misty obiects
and more misty senses, many things doe rather
terrifie than oppresse ; and so force fraile mankinde often to labour more in opinion than in
things.   To goe farther in this example of Iob ;
you may remember that it was his wife that bade
him " Curse God and dye :" in her sexe, the Scrip-
ture expressing weaknesse, and in weakenesse,
the boast of rage, and childish violences of passion :
yet did Iob refuse the counsell, but not the wife :
the way of righteousnesse being to hate the
vices and not the persons ; lest contrary to the
duties of charity and affinity, we should make
our selues a warre with all flesh.

Now, to deale more particularly with this
threatning power ; there are but three wayes in
which it can be heauy vnto you.   Ill dealing

---

[1] JOHN DAVIES of Hereford in his "Muses Sacrifice"
(1612) thus quaintly puts it :

  " Though camels there may swim and gnats may ford,
  Yet both may drown if—there—too bold they be".

                                      (p 62).   G.

with your selfe : a hand vpon your children : or separation   For your children, remember the image of Cecropia , in whose narrow and vnlouing nature, there is yet expressed an vnmeasurable and bewitched loue of her owne.   Besides, the rule is vniuersall ; that where there is no worth within, merits—like cyphers—stand for nothing ; because it must be a spark that can be made a fire with blowing.   Rest therefore your religious and motherly care in this, neither vpon merit nor demerit. but onely vpon his selfe-loue, which is such an vnseparable knot betweene frailty and her owne, as it is vnpossible either to adde or substract anything from it.   And be confident, that while your husband remaines subiect to his selfe-affections, there will euer be partiality within him, to keep his children safe from dis-inheriting.

For your selfe : if in your estate he restraine you; first, consider you haue lost his loue, a thing farre more pretious to your mind—I know —than his fortune can be.   And you haue lost withall the experience of that losse, if you haue not learnt by it to beare the rest more easily. Besides, it is desire that makes poore or rich ; so as where you can feele necessity, the measure of enough or too little, is in your owne moderation :

s

and in this according to the old prouerbe, 'no body hurt but by their owne excesse.' Againe, of all the apostles, remember who it was that carried the purse;[1] and whether the errour bee a destiny to the office or officer; it is childish to complaine and madnesse to striue with disaduantage.

But perchance this credulous selfe-pittie—which euer makes opinion more or lesse than the truth—may perswade you, that these imprisonments of fortune doe really both imprison Honour and Nature. Wherin—for answere—be pleased to consider; that there is none so poore, but hee may haue liberall thoughts; of wisedome, as much vse as of the elements: for shee is patience in misfortune and moderation in good. Chastitie needes no purple to become it selfe: and as for deuotion, princes can neither command, nor forbid it. Besides, affliction is rather a spurre than a bridle to that vertue; our flesh being like a toppe which only goes vpright with whipping. Lastly, pleasure it selfe is not banished out of bondage; since there may be peace within, and fame without, to the sincere conscience: so that the error is onely man's, in his not seeking rest

---

[1] Judas: Matthew xxvi. 47. G.

in that fortune vnder which hee liues ; but in change, which is euer in the power of others. To proue this, let vs goe a little further, and examine of how many complexions this pleasure is ; some finde it in labour, others in ease; some in women, others in bookes, &c. So as there being no truth, but opinion in it ; fortune can haue aduantage of those excellent-tempered natures, that when they may not chuse delights, can yet make them to themselues. And whoso are not indifferent to this indifferent humour, are but like little children, that crie when their parents or fellowes take their toyes from them. Yea, so subiect is our life to the oppressions of power, chance, and negligence, as the practise of times will shew ; that hee who cannot endure to lose, can much more hardly endure to liue.

Of separation, which is the last, I will bestow few words : because I am wel acquainted with your goodnesse and seuere lawes ouer your selfe. Besides, I know your husband's nature, which is rather weakely than strongly euill ; full of respects, desires, feares ; iealous and carelesse : factious, and vnresolute ; rather inclining to craft, than violence. What bee the counsels of such natures ? Whispering, murmur, conspiracy in speech, slander ; sweare and breake ; loath, and

keepe, ; dispraise, and loue ; a tyrant—in words—
valiant ouer a wife. And from thence all the
harme, onely a threatning of those excellent humours in you, which vnacquainted with the degrees
of euill—while you thinke him worse than hee is
—are amazed ; and when you hope for better,
wounded with being deceiued in him. But learne
to know for your owne ease, that euery man,
though hee would, yet cannot become excellently[1]
evill at once ; since both weeds and herbs are more
or lesse perfect in their kindes ; according to the
temper of earth and ayre, wherein they grow. So
that your ladiship may bee assured it is vnpossible for his hollow and wauing[2] minde to goe ouer
the shame and opposition of the world ; the swarme
and faction of wiues ; the courage and credit of
your priuate friends ; and the customes of England
to a diuoree ; though you were as ill as he would
haue you : much lesse hauing a well-gouerned
innocency, with all these other humane guards,
to breake thorough.

---

[1] = completely, in an ill sense. So late as *Hume* it
was so read, *e. g.* he speaks of Elizabeth as 'an *excellent*
hypocrite'. G.

[2] Wavering, changeable. : see Glossary-Index (waue'd).
G.

CAP. 5.

F you therefore stand firme against the temptations of feare and hope, there remaines an excellent end in your passage, to which all those necessities and misfortunes are no other kindes of lets, than raine or stormes vpon the land be, which cannot stay resolued passengers, though it moyle[1] their clothes, and make their way slippery. This end is, to haue the honour of being an excellent wife: in which womanlike ambition, the principall actor is obedience; an attribute from inferior to superior duties. I speak not of loue, since that wonderfull affection must be stirr'd either by extraordinary worth, or by a naturall sympathy of loue againe; both which obiects I thinke your estate in your husband to be very barren of, and therefore aduise you to nothing vnnecessary, or vnpossible. To satisfie ourselues that obedience is necessary, let vs againe examine the nature of authority: and we shall finde it to bee, a commanding power, that hath relation to

---

[1] = foul. G.

the obedience of inferiors. And then if we consider from what root it springeth, we shall find it to be out of nature in some things, in others from a lauish giuing away of our owne liberties. Thirdly, that prescription, which binds equals, still giues superiors an increase of freedome. Fourthly, that custome priuiledgeth humours aboue Nature, so as Time must pull downe that which aduantage and Time hath established. Out of which particulars I thinke we may conclude obedience to be necessary; and that they who striue to remoue the vnremoueable rockes with chaines, draw themselues to the rockes, but not the rockes to them.[1] Neither in this question is the difference betweene supreme or meane authority materiall, nor what diuerse foundations they haue; since it falls out in Power as it doth in Knowledge; that who is any thing at all, is all the world aboue vs. Therefore Madame, be pleas'd to weigh what folly it is for a subiect vnder a prince, or a wife vnder the yoke of a husband, to striue alone with the strong corporation of Power: since in obedience we need ouercome but one—our selfe I meane—where in these other contentions, we must serue many masters, worship

---

[1] See Indices under ' rocks '. G.

equals, flatter inferiours, and trust in strangers : that course being—as I haue shewed—subiect besides to treachery, ignorance, and inconstancy of instruments ; together with mischance, which hath greatest rule in all these vnruled hazards. The fearefull examples of those men that haue walked this icie path and been vnfortunate, by disproportion between their natures, places, and times they liu'd in, are innumerable. Seianus vnder Tiberius, the Duke of Guise vnder Henry of France, many of our dukes and Barons vnder our owne kings, in that false stage of our Barons' Warres. All which I shortly lay before you, because your estate is — I said—such a modell of subjects' estates vnder princes, as man's little world is of the great, differing onely in more or lesse.

That obedience is iust, the customes of Nations and lawes of Nature will assure you; who giue the mightier preeminence, and the stronger, rule. Againe, those excesses which arise out of Authority, are they not either rods of trials which we inferiors must kisse, and that God onely may burne, which made them ; or else mists of mutinous selfe loue, which deceiue, and make man as well misunderstand his diseases, as their remedies ? And so by misplacing equality and inequality, at once ruine both publike and priuate security. These

be indeed meteors, that encourage man to vnder-
mine gouernement, examine soueraignity, and
measure the arcana of all estates by the crooked
line of our owne opinions. Now Madame, if you
please to apply this to your selfe, it hath this
instruction in it; that if because you are vnequall
and haue aduantage of your husband in loue,
chastity, piety, sincerenesse, you will thinke your
selfe equall with him in liberty, wealth, and
power;—whereof some are proper by nature to
his sexe, as a man, some by ordinance vnto his
person, as a husband;—you shall erre in confusion
of merit, while you doe not distinguish vertue
from vertue, right from right; but out of selfe-
loue's counsels, striue to haue equality in one
become an equality in all. In which false path,
the iron pot doth often meet with the earthen; and
then you know which is broken. Besides Madame,
in these contentions betweene crafty strength and
well-beleeuing weakenesse, spies must be maintain'd and rumour paid, to the watching of errors
and vncouering of shame in your owne nest; which
quire of foule spirits, if the inferiours be so foolish
to coniure vp, the superiours will euer take aduantage by; authority giuing authority to vntruths:
so that all strifes with superiours must needs proue
idle, where we cannot; and vnnoble, where we

may not either stand or leaue with the prosperity of Honor. Therefore, let vs conclude, that necessity is the law of Time ; and consequently whatsoeuer is iust, to be onely and really wise.

If you desire an example of this obedience, which I vrge you to, it may please you in that arch-story of loue, to read the licentious affection of Antonie toward Cleopatra :[1] where you shall see, that if his vertuous wife Octauia had striuen to mark his dissolutenesse :—Augustus was her brother and his competitor in the Empire ; whereby right and strength, might with some possibility haue lifted vp her ambition and reuenge, from the barren grounds of duty. If she had striuen to please him with change, whom she could not keepe from it; the pride of Rome did then manifest variety of delights, and the seruile instruments of Time and Greatnesse, would soone have had an eye to their gaine and her fortune. If she would have rowled the stone of Sysiphus, and studied with merit to call backe his loue; she was as yong, equall in beauty, stronger in honour ; but euer the same, which—she knew—was not so pleasing

---

[1] Probably the reference (in thought) was to his own yet un-destroyed Tragedy : but I like to think he alluded to Shakespeare. G.

to him, as the same in others.   Besides, she had
the colour of estate to enammell all reuenges vpon
his vngratefullnesse. Notwithstanding, this worthy
lady would neuer yeeld to aduenture her honour
vpon the dice of Chance, nor vainly seeke to haue
power ouer him, that had none ouer himselfe ;
but diuiding her innocency from his errors with
the middle-wall of a seuere life, she remained still
his good angell with Octauius ; temper'd publike
iealousies and all aduantages of priuate wrongs ;
and to be short, was content, when she could not
doe the workes of a well-beloued wife, yet to doe
well, as becomes all excellent women.   In which
course of moderation, shee neither made the world
her iudge, nor the market her theater, but contented her sweet minde with the triumphs of
patience, and made solitarinesse the tombe of her
fame : which fame, as true to her worth, and
enuious to his lasciuiousnesse ; hath multiplied her
honour and his shame, to liue—as you see—many
ages after them both.

Where, if on the other side she had, with her
first thoughts, descended into the counsells of
impatiency, pleaded distresse in teares, and wrongs
in complaint ; who sees not that she had therein
not onely lost greatnesse of reputation—the true
shadow of great hearts ; but stirred vp Murmur,

which handles all things; but either neuer concludes any, or at least concludes in the worst
part? And so perchance, by ouer-acting, might
haue brought her right and his errors into an
equall ballance. For it is most true, that exorbi-
tancies of passions doe many times—like players
vpon stages—represent the office of a king, in the
person of a begger; Aristides' constancie, with
the weakenesse of Philautus; and the resolute
courage of Turnus, with the cowardise of Nicias;
acting that which they are not; and consequently, either out of felt or adopted impressions, vainely striuing to deny Chance her tributes,
Error her changes, and Tyranny her iniustice;
fall suddenly into that kind of weakenesse, which
vnder Power must be forced to endure many
stormes and burdens; because it could not endure
the petty and incident passages of life. Therefore
good Madame, Since I haue shewed you by reasone,
that obedience is iust and necessary; by example,
that it is possible; be not restiue in their weak
stubburnesse that will either keepe or lose all:
but thinke what folly it were for a man, in the
naturall decaies of age, not to goe because he cannot runne: and beleeue that it will proue the
like kind of headinesse in a wife, to forsake herselfe, for his ill that hath already forsaken her.

Therefore noble Lady, proceed constantly to your
end; beare and deale with these weakenesses of
your husband's; not with hate of your selfe or of
him : but as mothers doe with the wantonnesse of
children; who cry not to still them, nor threaten
imperfection and malice with one rod, but first
take away the offence, then suffer them to enioy
those toyes they delight in. For looke what a
mother's loue is towards her children, the like is
a husband's power ouer a wife : they will not
punish, you cannot.

To confirme this more clearely; let vs examine
the commodities that arise out of this iust and
necessary obedience. The poets, who sometimes
vnder clouds of beasts, describe the beastly courses
of degenerate men, tell you that Iupiter after he
had many wandering pilgrimages from heauen
downe to the Earth, brought still some of that
earthly metall vp with him; so as his affection
became diuided and euery day lesse kind to Iuno.
She—as a goddesse—acquainted with his power,
and with all the tempestuous powers of lust,
found that she, which hitherto had brought to
passe many things by his loue, could now worke
nothing by it. Neuerthelesse wisely considering
that all affections mixt betweene heauen and
Earth, haue wauing hopes, reuenge, desire, feare

and repentances in them, which contrariety of
passions had likewise their times, and places of
raigne—Sensualities in man not being made of
one, but many humors—out of these peircing
grounds, shee neither forsakes her ends, nor takes
vpon her that languishing despaire, which made
the first monke, nor that earnestnesse of rage,
which is euer reuenged of it selfe; but where
strength of credit failed, shee there vseth the
traffique of wit; obseruing his humours and their
changes; learning out of them so to temper and
allay one thought with another, now bearing, now
vrging, that—as those graue authors affirme—
Carthage was long kept vp by Iuno's industry, in
despite of Venus, her constant ambition to build
Rome vpon the ruines of it : which proues, that no
man being made all of loue, they haue not lost all,
that haue—how vnhappily soeuer—lost it. The
art wherewith she thus wrought Iupiter, lay
vndisclos'd ; as the faults of Power doe; selfeloue
couering them within and flattery without : vnder
which two veyles the will of supreme Authority
is many times stolen away ; and the lion's skinne
become the foxe's priuiledge : the agents going
still vnpunished, because it is not stealing, but
stealing ill, which husbands as well as princes
take offence at.

Therefore noble Lady, as the straight line shewes both it selfe and the crooked: so doth an vpright course of life, yeeld all true wayes of aduantage, aud by mastering our owne affections, anatomizeth all inferior passions, making knowne the distinct branches out of which the higher powers of kindnesse, respect, and admiration doe arise. A mappe, wherein we may by the same wisedome of moderation, choose for our selues that which is least in the power of others. Besides, it plainly discouers that iealousie acknowledgeth aduantage of worth, and so becomes the triumph of libertines; that griefe is the punishment of wrong, or right ill vsed. Curiosity euer returnes ill newes; Anger how great soeuer it seemes, is but a little humour, springing from opinion of contempt; her causes lesse than vices, and so not worthy to be loued or hated; but viewed, as liuely images to shew the strength and yet fraility of all passions—which passions being but diseases of the minde, doe so disease-like thirst after false remedies and deceiuing visions; as the weake become terrified with those glow-worm lights, out of which wise subiects often fashion arts to gouern absolute monarchs by. For Madame, as nourishment which feeds and maintaines our life, is yet the perfect pledge of our mortality : so are these light-moued passions true and assured notes of little natures, placed in what great estates soeuer. Besides, by this practise of obedience, there grow many more commodities. Since first, there is no losse in duty; so as you must at the least winne of your selfe by it, and either make it easie for you to become vnfortunate, or at least finde an easie and honourable passage out of her intricate lines and circles. Againe, if it be true, which the philosophers hold, that vertues and vices, disagreeing in all things else, yet agree in this; that where there is one *in esse*, *in posse* there are all : then cannot any excellent faculty of the minde be alone, but it must needs haue wisdome, patience, piety, and all other enemies of Chance to accompany it; as against and amongst all stormes, a calmed and calming *Mens adepta*.

CAP. 6.

NOW worthy Lady, If you please from this humble mountaine, vnto which no panting desire can ascend, but thoughts of long breath; I say, if it please you to pause and make your prospect backewarde, ouer the courses we haue past; which are the impossibility to amend, danger to master, casualty to please; then our metall, and that of the world's we liue in; lastly, the iustice, necessity, and commodities of obedience: you shall see the proportions betweene one excellency and all other are such, and the lets vnto them of such affinity: as he that hath ouercome, or profited in any, is in an easie way to more perfection in them all. Out of which grounds Madame, from a good wife to an excellent creature, the trauaile must needs proue pleasant and familiar. Yet because they that rest in fame or vertue, keepe not the estate they were in, but decline; let vs from this humble pinacle cast our eyes before our feet, and looke to the euen or vneuennesse of this well-shadowed path, we are to pass thorough. Wherein our first prospect

must be ouer our owne natures, examining our
strengths and weakenesses, with our desires and
ends ; then the particular differences and contrarieties of other men's humours, which—as instruments in the workman's hands—must proue helpes
or hindrances, according to the art or ignorance of
those that vse them. In the consideration of
which we shall finde some spirits narrow, and
woond all vpon one wheele; others vpon many:
diuers pleas'd—like children—with little things;
while the greater bodies must haue greater mindes
to moue them : some—like Heraclitus—bewailing
the world with the teares of selfe-pittie ; others
—like Democritus—iouially laughing at griefes
and affliction ; rather with an easinesse of nature
than any strength of worth or counsell : chance
the end of many, and change of more: together with
the libertine or seruile effects of too many or too
few distinctions, or respects in our morall liues. To
be short ; in the whole view of mankinde, you
shall obserue onely such nice diuision and differences, as there are in the kingdome of beasts ;
where some are rauinous and spoyling; others
weake and apt to bee prey'd vpon : their strengths
and weakenesses diuerse wayes laid ; some in one
member, some in another : all subiect alike to
deliuer their skins to those deceiuers which are

T

aboue them; but dangerously enuious to equals
or inferiours. To conclude; when they are wilde,
ill neighbours, worse friends; but excellent seruants when they are tamed. Out of which diuer-
sitie of natures and affections, wee may gather
againe, that euen those misfortunes or afflictions,
which be diseases to some are vnto others health
or cure: error and offence in the mindes of men
comming from as diuerse causes, as imperfections
doe in the sight; either by too much vniting or
dispersing the beames. So that many may say as
truely with comfort; Iniurie often makes way for
better fortune, as others may with griefe, what
tyrant hath taken away our godhead from vs?

Now Madam, If you apply this to your selfe,
it hath this morality in it; to let you know, that
without your husband's vnkind dealing, you
would perchance haue doted too much in the
worship of one man; neglecting for that one
humour, all other wayes of honour, as bewitched
affections vse to doe. So that lest the other excellent powers of your minde should bee in vaine
to you and to the world; it seemes, euen by the
prouidence of mischance, you are driuen from
these narrow sanctuaries of selfe-affections, which
imprisoned you; to take into your heart new
idea's, larger ends, and nobler wayes. And in this

new deliberation, it will be no impertinent counsell; first, to examine the difference of worths
required in seeking to winne one or the world; or in
a third progresse, by losing both, to winne credit
with God. In which mysticall worke the fine
mixture of grace and nature together, makes it
more easie to mend our errours, than before it was
to couer them; and consequently our flesh as
capable to receiue the immortality of good, as it
was to run headlong vnder the eternall curse of the
sinne. Againe, since it is flesh onely that receiues
immortality of good or euill; and vpon the same
flesh no heauier tax laid in these worthier courses
than you were charged with before; I meane
a resolution to turne all things within and without you to the best: noble Lady, gather your
powers together, and know that where, in the
former imprisonment of thoughts, reason, wrong,
and occasion were all kept subiect to an ouer-
tender affection in our selues, they shall in
this bee set at libertie, and spread as farre as
the limits of nature or grace, can possibly be
extended. Besides, in all the course of choice or
chance, whosoeuer will but compare what aduantage the strength of one mouer hath ouer another,
he shall see all hardnesse and inequalitie in the
wayes to bee reconciled in the force and preemin-

ence of the mouers : so as pleasure hauing a weake
entrance and an easie adamant ; Honor, a crabbed
first step, but an omnipotent object ; the light goes
as easie upward, as the heauy downe.

To beginne therefore with the first, which is
the winning of one; there is in that course
required neither exact vertue nor vice; but a happy
temper in both, to a nimble vse of either. Here
yeelding, soothing, seruing, must be our sacrifices ;
humours our study; and wee bound—like shadowes—neither to be shorter, nor longer, than
befitteth those bodies we resolue to worship : so
as the most factious spirits, are often the most
fortunate in these courses. For as in coynes it is
the stampe, not the metall that goes currant;
that which is gold here, going perchance euery
where else but as copper, so doe the vnworthy
choices of fauour often make Nature's meanest
creations for superlatiue. Nay more, if by the influence of a good destinie, wee chance to honour
a worthy man ; yet shall wee but take on and not
take in worth by that traffique: and then how can
they truly merit, that doe well for any respect,
but goodnesse it selfe ? This was it, that made the
piercing iudgements of times past, note a difference betweene the affability of Scipio and Cæsar; it
being artificiall in this to his end, and in the other

a naturall sweetnesse of bowels ; in the one an art of ambition, in the other noblenesse and ingenuity. Whereby wee may conclude ; that it is no great inriching of man's nature to bring forth pleasing fruits to one land-lord, how fantasticall or imperious soeuer. Besides, these humour-hunters onely muster those affections of minde, which are not honourable in the large extents of Truth, but in the narrow limits of Opinion ; and thereby sometimes make vs creatures to our equals ; seruants to vnworthinesse ; lesse than our selues, by seeking to winne a man perchance worse than our selues ; rather improuing craft than wisedome, seruitude, than honour. In all which, true worth must necessarily suffer allay, as being changed from generall approuings to particular ; and thereby forced to imprison Nature within municipall and seruile humours or constitutions.

The second part, which is the winning of the world, hath many and large respects in it : since therein our mediator must be Fame, a spirit neuer entreated but commanded vp ; our study Honour, as a pledge which the world doth trust and beleeue in ; Magnanimitie, must bee our scepter, wherein the equall finde strength and the inferiour protection; Liberalitie, that all desires may hope ; Iustice, which distinguisheth right from estate, or persons ;

Mercy, that frailty may not despaire with such
like great strengths of minde, as are vniversally
currant, and doe giue euidence to the world that
wee despise those pettie things which the rest doe
wonder at; and by affecting the generall loue of
all men, bring forth that which all men loue in
vs. Besides, the end is more noble to winne reuerence than to yeeld it; to create than pay tribute;
the powers of the mind that are vsed more strong,
as doing and not suffering affections; the proportion of the meanes larger and of more difficulty,
requiring better formes, perfecter health, and
greater strengths : because in our ends, we embrace the ends of all men; and thereby are
aduanced without preiudice or discontent to any.
Hence, from equalities of Nature, grew vp all
estates of superiority; this is that seruing of the
multitude, which commands them; this is to
be least and greatest; one, and rule many :
yea, euen in that great art, which hath ever
flourished in the brauest spirits and most flourishing ages; and which being forgotten by the corruption, or vicissitude of times—as the most excellent
sciences haue beene—is growne strange among
men; and which being but renewed in shew, the
vaine world—made to bee deceiued—will without
suspition embrace; as a liuely picture of her ancient pompe and greatnesse.

Againe, since the nature of the multitude is not vnlike the Earth; which—not made for it selfe—while it lies common, brings forth nothing to enrich, but conceales many treasures under her skinne and bowels; and on the other side, owned or manured, yeelds reward for his paines that husbands her: since—I say—these two being paralell'd; euen as the first authors in all innouations, while they mend not, but change the complexion of passions, shall find audacity in vndertaking the hardest of their worke; as being forced to bee presidents to themselues: so againe, the consequence must of necessitie proue faire and easie, in respect that noueltie is euer as welcome, as fearefull; and the whole flocke apt to follow the first sheepe. In which vndertaking to become an example, hath something in it worthy of aduenture. Therefore, if you compare the winning of one and the world together, you shall finde the world exceeds one both in number, weight and measure; and then as our English prouerbe saith, "The more cost, the more worship".

From this second step if you will climbe up to the third, and though with absurdity, yet for vnderstanding's sake, compare finite and infinite together; I meane the winning of the world with the worship of God, the centre with the circumference, Him that made all things with that which was made of nothing; the ends differ no more in excellency, than the wayes and meanes to attaine it doe. For in the one we worke with our owne strengths, which are but weaknesses: in this with His, that is omnipotent; in the first with flattering promises, that will deceiue; in this with Him that is greater than all things, and onely equall with His word; as whose each part is of His owne assence, indivisible, infinite, and eternall. . . . . . .

Not finished.

VARIOUS READINGS, &c., FROM THE ORIGINAL (CORRECTED) TRANSCRIPT.

1. Page 234, line 22, 'makes', not 'maketh'.
2. page 235, line 19, 'ill for the misprint 'all' of the folio.
3. page 238, line 4, 'stronge' for the misprint 'strange' : and so onward.
4. page 239, line 13, 'begunne', not 'began'—an early form.
5. page 240, line 6, 'open' not in folio.
6. page 240, line 7, 'is' not in folio.
7. page 240, line 23, 'exceptions', for the misprint of folio 'expectations'.
8. page 243, line 16, 'mood' for 'degree', but erased.
9. page 244, line 6, originally 'doe not (with Æsop) seeke your husband', &c, but corrected in text.
10. page 244, line 23, 'cure' for the misprint 'care' of folio.
11. page 245, line 10, spelled 'preheminence' : see Index of Words.
12. page 249, line 20, 'kindlinge' for 'kindled 'of the folio.
13. page 251, line 19, originally 'ill' and changed to 'mis-gouerned' as in text.
14. page 251, line 20, originally 'theise', but corrected 'suche'.
15. page 252, line, 3, 'hope and' written but erased by the Author.
16. page 252, line 14, 'his', carelessly dropped in folio.

17. page 257, line 12, originally 'with' but corrected to 'through', as in text.

18. page 257, line 14, 'impatient' for the odd misprint of 'impotent', in the folio.

19. page 257, line 18, originally 'that', but corrected to 'because we'.

20. page 259, line 23, originally 'feele', but changed to 'thinke'.

21. page 261, line 16, 'a' for 'her'.

22. page 262, line 1, 'with' for the ungrammatical 'which' of the folio.

23. page 264, line 23, 'those' for 'these'.

24. page 268, line 27, 'advise you, *as I have sayd*'. The italics inserted, but again erased by the Author.

25. page 269, line 16, 'the' for 'these'.

26. page 270, line 24, 'your' for the careless 'our' of the folio.

27. page 270, line 26, 'seemes' for 'seemeth'.

28. page 273, line 13, 'vnpossible' not 'impossible', as in folio.

29. page 274, line 25, 'his' for 'this' of folio.

30. page 274, line 14-17, here the folio reads confusingly, as follows : " of *Wisdome* as much vse as of the *Elements*. For shee is *patience in Misfortune*, and moderation in good Chastitie, needes, &c."

31. page 283, line 17, 'or would not' inserted and erased again.

32. page 284, line 10, 'an' for 'a'.

33. page 287, line 6, 'selfe' for 'flesh', as misprinted in folio.

34. page 288, line 6, 'mend' for 'amend'

35. page 289, line 15, 'and' dropped in folio.

36. page 289, line 23, 'are' dropped in folio.

37. page 291, line 10, 'the' dropped in folio.

38. page 291, line 24, 'chance' for 'change'.

39. page 293, line 7, 'muster' for 'master' of folio.

40. page 295, line 5, 'owned' for 'moued' of folio.

41. page 296, line 12, 'Not finished' added by the Author
in the manuscript in old age. See description of the
MSS. onward. G.

V.

Letter to Greuill Varney on his Travels.

A Letter written by Sir Fulke Greuill to his Cousin
Greuill Varney residing in France; wherein
are set downe certaine rules and obseruations,
directing him how he may make the best vse of
his Trauels.[1]

Y good Cousin, according to the request
of your letter, dated the 19. of October,
at Orleance, and receiued here the 18. of
Nouember, I haue sent you by your Merchant
[£30 sterling] for your present supply, and had

---

[1] A Manuscript copy of this Letter is contained in a
MS volume in University Library, Oxford, [I. 13. 152 :
pp 13-17.] entitled "A Collection of Letters, Speeches
&c., of great Statesmen and Scholars". According to the
Catalogue it formerly belonged to a William Goswell.
At close I have noted various readings compared with the
text of 1633. Some of these, as the filling in of the sum
in line 5th, the signature &c., would seem to indicate
access to the original. Another MS copy is preserved in
the British Museum. G.

sent you a greater summe, but that my extraordinary charges this yeere haue vtterly vnfurnished
me.

And now Cousin, though I will be no seuere
exacter of account, either in your money or time,
yet for the loue I beare you, I am very desirous
both to satisfie my selfe and your friends, how
you prosper in your Trauels, and how you find your
selfe bettered thereby, either in knowledge of God
or the world; the rather because the daies you
haue already spent abroad are now sufficient both
to giue you light how to fixe your selfe an end
with counsell, and accordingly shape your course
constantly vnto it. Besides, it is a vulgar scandall
of trauellers that few returne more religious than
they went out. Wherein both my hope and
request is to you, that your principall care be to
hold your foundation, and to make no other vse
of informing your selfe in the corruptions and
superstitions of other Nations, than onely thereby
to engage your owne heart more firmely vnto the
truth. You liue indeed in a country [which is]
bigarre, of two seuerall professions, and you shall
returne a nouice from thence, if you be not able
to giue an account of the ordinances, progresse,
and strength of each in reputation and party, and
how both are supported, ballanced, and managed

by the State, as being the contrary humours, in the temper or predominancy whereof the health or disease of that body doth consist.

These things you will obserue, not onely as an Englishman, whom it may concerne to know what interest his country may expect in the consciences of her neighbours, but also as a Christian, to consider both the beauties and blemishes, the hopes and dangers of the Church in all places.

Now for the world, I know it too well to perswade you to diue into the practices thereof : rather stand vpon your guard against all that tempt you thereunto, or may practise vpon you in your conscience, your reputation, or your purse. Resolue that no man is wise or safe, but he that is honest. And let this perswasion turne your studies and obseruations from the complement and impostures of this debauched age to more reall grounds of wisedome, gathered out of the stories of Time past, and out of the gouernement of the present State.

Your guide to these is the knowledge of the Country and the People among whom you liue.

For the Country : though you cannot see all places, yet if as you passe along you enquire carefully, and further helpe your selfe with bookes that are written of the Cosmography of those parts; you shall thereby sufficiently gather the strength, riches, trafficke, hauens, shipping, commodities, vent; and the wants and disaduantages of all places.   Wherein also for your own vse hereafter and for your friends, it will be fit to note their building, furniture, their entertainements, all their husbandry, and ingenious inuentions in whatsoeuer concerne either pleasure or profit.

For the people: your trafficke among them while you learne their language will sufficiently instruct you in their habilities, dispositions and humours; if you [a little] enlarge the priuacy of their owne nature to seeke acquaintance with the best sort of strangers, and restraine your affection and participation from your own country men of whatsoeuer condition.

In the story of France you have a large and pleasant field in the three lines of their kings, to obserue their alliances and successions, their conquests, their wars, especially with vs, their counsels, their treaties, and all rules and examples of experience and wisdome, which may be lights and remembrances to you hereafter, to iudge of all occurrents at home and abroad.

Lastly, for the gouernment : your end must not be like an Intelligencer, to spend all your time in fishing after the present newes, humours, graces,

or digraces of Court, which haply may change before you come home ; your better and more constant ground will bee to know the consanguini-
ties, alliances and estates of their princes : the
proportion betweene the nobility and magistracy,
the constitutions of the Courts of Iustice, the
state of their Lawes ; as well for the making as
for the executing thereof ; how the souerainty of
the king infuseth it selfe into all acts and ordinances : how many wayes they lay impositions and
taxations, and gather reuenues to the crowne ;
what be the liberties and seruitudes of all degrees;
what discipline and preparations for wares ; what
inuentions for increase of trafficke at home, for
multiplying their commodities, incouraging arts
or manufactures, or of worth in any kinde : also
what good establishments to preuent the necessities
and discontentments of the People, to cut off
suits-at-law and duels, to suppresse theeues and
all disorders.

To be short, because my purpose is not to bring
all your obseruations to heads, but onely by these
few to let you krow what manner of returne your
friends expect from you, let me for these and all
the rest, giue you this one note, which I desire
you to obserue as the counsell of a friend : Not to
spend your spirits and the pretious time of your

U

trauaile, in a captious preiudice and censuring of all things, nor in an infectious collection of base vices and fashions of men and women, and generall corruptions of these times; which will be of vse onely among Humorists for iests and table-talke : but rather straine your wits and industry soundly to instruct your selfe in all things betweene heauen and earth, which may tend to vertue, wisedome, and honour, and which may make your life more profitable to your Countrey, and your selfe more comfortable to your friends and acceptable to God.

And to conclude, let all these riches bee treasured vp not onely in your memory—where Time may lessen your stocke—but rather in good writings and bookes of accompt ; which will keepe them safe for your vse hereafter. And if in this time of your liberall traffique, you will giue me any aduertisement of your commodities in these kindes, I will make you as liberall a returne from my selfe and your friends here, as I shall bee able. And so commending all your good endeauours to Him that must either wither or prosper them, I very kindly bid you farewell.

Your very louing Cousin,
FVLKE GREVILL.

From Hackney this 20. of Nouember, 1609.

VARIOUS READINGS, &c. FROM OXFORD MANUSCRIPT, as *ante*.

I. page 301, line 1, 'cousen'.

2. page 301, line 2, '18th' for '19th' of October.

3. page 301, line 5, 'merchant £30 sterling': this I have filled in in our text.

4. page 302, line 2, 'yeare hath'.

5. page 302, line, 3, 'mee'.

6. page 302, line 4, 'Cousen....noe....Exactor'.

7. page 302, line 5, 'accompt....the mony'.

8. page 302, line 8, 'Trauells'.

9. page 302, line 9, 'better therby'..

10. page 302, line 10, 'dayes....spent already'...

11. page 302, line 12, 'propound' for 'fixe'.

12. page 302, line 20, 'then only'.

13. page 302, line 21, 'harte....friendly'.

14. page 302, line 22, I have here filled in 'which is': 'bigare' = bigger is spelled with a capital B.

15. page 302, line 25, 'accompt'.

16. page 302, line 25, 'progresses'.

17. page 302, line 26, 'credit'—which seems preferable to 'parity'.

18. page 303, line 2, Misreads 'of' for 'or'.

19. page 303, line 3, 'diseases'.

20. page 303, line 4, 'only'.

21. page 303, line 5, 'to know' not in MS.

22. page 303, line 7, 'their,' for 'her'.

23. page 303, line 7, 'to' not in MS.: 'bewties'.. 'daungers'.

24. page 303, line 13, 'you' not in MS.

25. page 303, line 15, 'nor' .. 'hee'.

26. page 303, line 19, 'wisdome'.

27. page 303, line 19, 'times'.

28. page 303, line 20, 'gouernment'.

29. page 303, line 23, 'the' not in MS. : 'amongst' ..
     'wee'.

30. page 303, line 26, 'farther' .. 'help'.

31. page 303, line 27, 'Commogrophie'.

32. page 304, line 2, 'trafique' .. 'havings'.

33, page 304, line 6, 'buildings, Furnitures..there'. (*bis*)

34. page 304, line 8, 'profit or pleasure'.

35. page 304, line 9, 'trafique'.

36. page 304, line 12, 'humers'.

37. pags 304, line 12, I have filled in 'a little' from the MS.

38. page 304, line 13, 'of'.

39. page 304, line 18, 'three lyves of three kings'.

40. page 304, line 27, the fishing'.

41. page 305, line 1, 'happily'.

42. page 305, line 3, 'ground'.

43. page 305, line 7, 'for' not in MS.

44. page 305, line 8, ; as I have given in our text.

45. page 305, line 12, 'bee their',

46. page 305, line 14, 'trafique'.

47. page 305, line 18, 'the' not in MS.

48. page 305, line 20, 'discords'.

49. page 305, line 24, 'this'.

50. page 305, line 27, 'the' not in MS.

51. page 306, line 1, 'trauells'.

52. page 306, line 1, 'censure'.

53. page 306, line 5, 'of'.

54. page 306, line 10, ' acceptable '.
55. page 306, line 15, ' accoumpts '.
56. page 306, line 16, ' self ,
57. page 306, line 19, ' this kind '
58. page 306, line 24, ' very ' not in MS.
59. page 306, line 25, ' Fulk Grevyle '.   G.

VI.

Short Speech for Bacon:
with Introduction

CONTAINING

Additional Materials

FOR

Life of Lord Brooke.

NOTE.

The short Speech for BACON is given in the State Trials and COBBET's Parliamentary History, and the like. It needs to be read in relation to the very remarkable Speech of Yelverton, and the others, as well as to Wraynham's own. The reference to 'duells' springs out of Wraynham's use of the illustration—very imprudently—and "Foorth's Case" is adduced by Yelverton as precedent for the kind and extent of punishment awarded to Wraynham.

As stated in the Introductory-Note to the present Volume I bring together here references from various sources that must be utilized in the ultimate Life of Lord Brooke :

I. 𝔉𝔯𝔬𝔪 𝔇'𝔈𝔴𝔢𝔰 " 𝔍𝔬𝔲𝔯𝔫𝔞𝔩 𝔬𝔣 𝔱𝔥𝔢 𝔙𝔬𝔱𝔢𝔰, 𝔖𝔭𝔢𝔢𝔠𝔥𝔢𝔰, 𝔞𝔫𝔡 𝔇𝔢𝔟𝔞𝔱𝔢𝔰, 𝔗𝔢𝔪𝔭. 𝔔. 𝔈𝔩𝔦𝔷𝔞𝔟𝔢𝔱𝔥, 1693," (𝔣𝔬𝔩𝔦𝔬.)

1. 27th Eliz. 1584—5 : Thursday 18th February. Mr. Fulk Grevill, member of a Committee appointed to confer with the Lords touching the Bill of Jesuits, (p. 352.)

2. 26th February 159⅔.   Do., do., to consider of the dangers of the realm, and of speedy supply and aid to be be given to her Majesty : (p. 474.)

3. 28th February.   On a Committee against Recusants (p. 477) and another Committee to confer with the Lords (p. 481.)

4. 19th March.   Member of a Committee concerning George Ognell : (p. 503.)

5. 14th November. 39 and 40 Eliz., 1597. Member of a Committee to draw a Bill for reformation of abuses, occasioned by Licenses granted for marriages without Banes [= banns] asking : (p. 556.)

6. 18th November.   Do. do.   The Bill concerning the hospital of Warwick was read the second time, and committed to the knights for Warwickshire : (p. 559.)

7. 23rd November.   On a Committee for repealing part of the Charter of the town of Yarmouth : (p. 562.)

8. 12th January.   On a Committee to restrain the making of malt : (p. 578.)

9. 14th January. One of a Committee on Bill for the revising, continuation, and explanation and perfecting of certain Statutes (p. 580.)

10. Same day.   Innovation of Lords ' misliked of' in ' not using any of their lordships former and wonted courteous manner' of receiving a deputation from the Lower House.   Greville among those appointed ' for further resolution thereupon'.   (p. 580.)

11. 20th January. Greville with others sent up to the Lords to confer on the Bill for the maintenance of husbandry and tillage. (p. 584.)

12. 23rd January.   Bill for the better measuring of

seven miles from the town of Great Yarmouth, delivered to Mr. Greville with the Committee's name. (p. 586.)

13. Same day. Greville and others appointed to attend a conference of the Lords on the service and defence of the Realm. (p 586.)

14. 31st January. Greville, one of a Committee on the Bill for the more speedy payment of her Majesty's debts. (p. 591.)

15. 43rd Eliz. 1601. 3rd November. Greville on a Committee on Bill for the better preserving of the breed of horses, and to avoid the common stealing of them. (p. 623.)

16. 11th November. Question whether the knights and citizens of London should be on a certain Committee. ' Mr. Fulk Grevil said, That a Committee was an artificial body, framed out of us, who are the general body; and therefore that which is spoken at the Committee, *evanescit*, it is gone, when the body which is the Commitment is dissolved ; and then every particular Committee is no more a part of the artificial body but of us the general body, when he hath his free voice as though he had spoken before." (p. 635.) The Committee was appointed and Greville was a member.

17. 12th November. On a Committee to go to the Lord Keeper. (p. 637.)

18. 20th November. On a Committee on Bill against taintering of woollen cloths. (p. 647.)

19. 8th December. A dispute touching the information against Mr. Belgrave: " Mr. Grevill said, I wish that in our Conferences we do not neglect our privileges, and that

we may be means of mediation, &c." (p. 673.) Greville and others appointed on a committee to confer with the Lords.

II. From the Calendars of State-Papers in the Record Office and Lambeth, &c., as enumerated in the Volumes covering 1547—1631, thus far published.

I. 1547-80 : LEMON (1856) :

1. October 22nd, 1557: Collection of loan in Warwick, by G. and others : (page 95.)

2. 1569 : Musters and military force of Warwick : Letters of deputation to G. and Sir Thomas Lucy, &c. : (page 358.)

3. April 8th, 1569. Declaration by G. and others of submission to the Act for Uniformity of Common Prayer and Service in the Church : (page 371.)

4. May 2nd, 1570. Letter of G. and others to Council on exactions by Price : (page 373.)

5. August 24th, 1573. G. and Lucy forwarding Musters : (page 466.)

6 May 25th, 1580. Musters delayed from 'sickness' of G. : (page 657.)

7. September 9th. 1590. Sir John Huband to Atey : 'desires to know if G. is to have the Mastership of the Game' : (page 675.)

II.   1574-85 : HAMILTON (1867) :

1. July 14th, 1580.   Letter of G. from ‘ Limerick, Ireland ’: exceedingly interesting letter on Ireland : (page 233.)

2. July 22nd, 1580.   N. White, master of the Rolls: curious notice of G.: ‘his cabin stored with books, sea-cards ’: (page 236.)

3. August 13th. 1580.   Waterhous to Walsingham: ‘ Mr. Greville is well ’: (page 243.)

4. September 20th, 1580.   Byngham to same : ‘ Mr. Foulke Greville to receive instructions ’ : (page 254.)

5. July 2nd, 1580.   G. to same: very important Letter from and concerning Ireland : (page 230.)

6. August 2nd, 1580.   *Ibid.*   *Ibid.* : (page 239)

III.   1575-88 : BREWER AND BULLEN (1868) :

Notices of G. *passim* in Letters of Pelham to Sir William Winter in Ireland : (pages 254-260-272-277-279 : P. calls him ‘my cousen ’: N. White to Leicester ‘ the bearer Mr. Spenser’ entertained on ‘ board ship ’ by G. and others. (page 280.) [May 11th, 1580 to July 21st, 1580.]

IV.   1581-90 : LEMON (1865) :

1. October 21st, 1585. G. to Council as ‘ Sheriff of Warwickshire’ on ‘ two recusants ’: (page 276)

2. April 12th, 1586.   G. and Lucy, certificate that a Mr. Smythe is not a recusant : (page 319.)

3.   November 1586.   G. important Letter to Walsingham on Sidneys ‘old Arcadia ’ and his translation of Du Plessy against Atheisim : (page 369.)   *⁎* I shall give

this Letter in my Introduction to the (intended) collected Poems of SIR PHILIP SIDNEY.   G.

5. March 1587. 'Grant of the office of clerk of the Signet in reversion to Mr. Greville, 19th February, 1577 : (page 399.)

6. January 14th, 1587.   Amyas to Walsingham : Lord President of Wales had taken away 'the fees from Mr. Greville' : (page 381.)

V.   1595-97 : GREEN (1869) :

1. 1596 : Toby Matthew to Carleton : G. ' censured, with much displeasure for spreading ' a letter : (page 331.)

2. June 24th, 1597.   Grant of the rangership of Wedgnock Park : (page 444.)

3. July 7th, 1597. Letter of Essex, Raleigh, Vere, &c., &c., to Cecil : 'pray further the motion which Fulk Greville is to make from us to the ' Queen ' : (page 451.)

4. July 10th, 1597.   Letter of Essex to same—concerning Fleet : 'If the Queen will dispense with his absence, get my cousen Fulk Greville the conducting of it, but if she will not let him, then.... ' (page 457.)

5. July 23rd, 1597. *Ibid.*   *Ibid.* : Letter sent to G. : (page 470.)

6. September 3rd, 1597.   Letter of G. and Sir Thomas Howard on sea-fight : (page 497.)

7. October 21st, 1596.   *Passim* : G. ' sick ' : (page 296.)

VI.   1589-1600 : BREWER AND BULLEN (1869) :

1. May 22nd, 1598. Cooke to Cecil : ' my uncle Greville has moved the Queen for Mr. Bowes' office : (page 54.)

2. June 15th, 1598.   Killigrew to Burghley ' Mr.

Fulke Greville has just brought me word of her Majesty's
pleasure that I should write you that there is a waiter's
room of the Custom-house fallen in, which she has long
determined might be bestowed upon John Speed, who has
presented her with divers maps' : (page 62.)

3. Notices as Treasurer of the Navy, *passim* : (pages
92-95-147-282—associated with Raleigh : Under January
1601 is a ' Satirical ballad of seven stanzas upon some principal personages about the Court at the latter end of
Elizabeth's reign ' including G : (page 542.)

4. Documents as ' Warrant to pay G. Navy treasurer
£12,850 4s. 2d. for charges of transporting 2,000 men to
Ireland, &c. : (page 136) estimates by G. of charges pp.
148, 371-2. payments and warrants : pages 134-136-149-
150(2) 156-7-203-275-292-293-376-382-437 (2) 506.

VIII. 1623—25 : GREEN (1859) :

1. Notices *passim* of Lord B. " added as a referee by
the king " Oct. 3rd, 1623 : page 87.—" Lords B. and
Belfast spoken of to succeed Lord Treasurer ", April 14th,
1624, page 213—precedence denied to an Irish peer over :
May 13th, 1624, page 244—Secretaryship : page 263—
letter to Lord B. page 332—a reference as to payment of
monies, page 360—Carleton January 13th, 1625—Incloses
Lord Brooke's invitation to Vossius, of Leyden, to come
ouer and supply a lectureship on Humanity at Cambridge :
page 446—July 31st, 1619, the Chancellor will sign no
warrants till money comes in " : page 555—copy [printed]
of " Five Years of King James " : (page 583).

2. Letter of, to the King, July 29th, 1624, on one Rey-
nolds : (page 316).

3. Official Letters to Conway : pp 10—85—282—293 (on "Falconry")—and important, November 26th, 1624 : "Hopes Sir Hatton Farmer will not succeed in getting confirmation of his surreptitious grant. Will think it hard in his old age, after 80 years' quiet possession, to be turned out by misinformation, and not even heard for himself" : (page 393).

4. Official Letters to Lord B : pp 4—56—214 (the King to, and others : April 14th, 1624, on the Palatinate : *Ibid Ibid* : (on "council of War") : page 220-295-6 (on French) —320-388-9-395 (on Harmer's grant " the king willed the matter to be ended by compromise ")—Other papers on this at pp 487-500-502.

IX. 1625-26 : BRUCE (1858) :

1. Official Letters relating to—pp 7-12-123 ('king's jewels for Buckingham going to Hague" Oct. 12th, 1625) 126-128-135-137-328-435-479-580.

2. Valuable Letters of : June 4th, 1625, page 37 Oct. 16th, 1625, " a prisoner to age and indisposition of body, these many days": page 125-October 26th, 1625 : " Age and sickness (the gentlemen ushers of death) had imprisoned him for a while " : page 133.

3. Official Letters to, 1-9 (April 13th, 1625 : the King "dispensing with his personal attendance in execution of his office of Secretary and Clerk of the Conucil and Signet in the Principality of Wales,")-19-127.

X. 1627—28 : BRUCE (1858) :

1. December 16th, 627—Bp. Wren to Laud " informing against Dorislaus" sent hither by Lord Brooke, whose domestic he now is " : p 470-and also 546.

2. Letter to, from Secretary Conway : " appointment as Deputy Vice-Admiral for the Isle of Wight" January 24th, 1627. Other Letters relating to this office 227-395-403-405-479-542 (2).

3. Letters of—June 2nd., 1627 from "Cowes" p 204-5 and another p 234.

4. Official Letters to—pp 29 173-242-394-448-545-566-572 (as ' deputy Vice-Admiral ').

XI: 1628—29 : BRUCE (1859) :

1. Letter of Viscount Dorchester to Earl of Carlisle : September 30th, 1628 : "Lord Brooke is dead of his wounds, given him by his man, who slew himself " :)p 340)

2. Letter of Secy. Coke to Secy. Conway : October 6th, 1628. on death of Lord Brooke and funeral : (p. 344-5).

3. Successor of Lord B. in the office in Wales : (p 477.)

4. „   „   as "Groom or Bedchamber " (p 581.)

5. Order of the proceeding to the funeral of Lord B : Oct. 27th, 1628 (p 362,)

6. Codicil of Will "whereby he charged his lands in Toft Grange, Forsdike and Algarkirk in co. Lincoln, with an annuity of £100 for the maintenance of a history lecture in the University of Cambridge and appointed Dr. Isaac Dorislaus, the first lecturer " : p 438.

7. Notices of *passim* a "deputy Vice-admiral" pp 40-117-136-152-172-208-392-415 (2)-565-

8. Official Letters to, pp 59-257-258-330-384-415-417-547 (2).

т

XII.　1629-31: BRUCE (1860):

1. Letter Feb. 26th 1631 Lieut. Beaulie to " Sir Fulke
Greville," (p 519) : (as if still alive !) and another March
18th, 1631, Nicholas to G: p 542.

2. Letter of Thome, successor of Lord B. in Wales

*** The above in the Indices are somewhat confusingly
and uncritically distributed as if among various Grevilles,
while the whole really refer to our Worthy.　Only my
late lamented friend MR. JOHN BRUCE is strictly accurate.

III.　"𝔉rom 𝔉irst 𝔅eport of t𝔥e 𝔅o𝔶al 𝔠ommis-sion on 𝔥istorical 𝔐anuscripts", 1870.

1. MONTACUTE HOUSE, Somersetshire (W. Phelips,
Esq.): a Letter by Sir Fulke Greville, 18th July, 1613,
containing instructions to Commissioners regarding certain moneys late of Prince Henry. (p 57.)

2. ICKWELL BURY, Bedfordshire (not Hertfordshire as
in the ' Report ') - a " 12mo Volume (end of 16th century)
contains [among other things] " The manner of Sir Philip
Sidney's Death, written by the Right Honourable Fulke,
Lord Brooke, 1586 ($9\frac{1}{2}$ pages). (p. 62.)

*** See our Introductory-Note to the present
Volume : by which it will be seen that the Commissioner (Alfred T. Horwood, Esq.) is mistaken in assigning it to the " end of 16th century ", inasmuch as Lord
Brooke received not his title until 1620.　It ought also
to have been recorded that it was not an original but
a copy.　The want of this distinction greatly lessens the
value of this otherwise acceptable " First Report."

3. The Corporation of Coventry. (p. 100.) I am indebted to Thomas Browett, Esq., Town Clerk, Coventry for accurate transcripts of the following MSS in his custody (*a*) Letter from the Mayor and his brethren to Sir Fulke Greville : 31st June, 1592 : (*b*) Letter of Sir Fulke to the Mayor, &c., 21st January, 1592 : (*c*) *Ibid* to *Ibid* : 15th Jnne, 1592. [These are to and from the elder Sir Fulke Grevill.] (*d*) Lord Brooke 13th March, 1622. These Letters are of much interest as shewing the pleasant relations of the lord of the manor towards Coventry.

** Our details supersede the very imperfect description in the " Report " of the Commissioner (H. T. Riley, Esq.)

IV. 𝔙𝔦𝔱𝔞 𝔡𝔦 𝔊𝔦𝔬𝔯𝔡𝔞𝔫𝔬 𝔅𝔯𝔲𝔫𝔬 𝔡𝔞 𝔑𝔬𝔩𝔞 𝔰𝔠𝔯𝔦𝔱𝔱𝔞 𝔡𝔞 𝔇𝔬𝔪𝔢𝔫𝔦𝔠𝔬 𝔅𝔢𝔯𝔱𝔦. 1868. 8𝔳𝔬.

In this intensely interesting " Life " of the extraordinarily brilliant and original Thinker, hitherto entirely unknown documents are furnished by its well-informed, and most conscientiously-laborious Writer. Chapter IX. (pp. 156—192) and relative Appendix, gives a graphic and specially suggestive glimpse of the England of the period, amusingly so of the dignitaries of Oxford. It is to be regretted that Bruno's friendship with Sidney and Greville is only meagrely and vaguely told. But the fact is given with glowing recognition. Here is one small morsel : " On Ash Wednesday of 1584 at a sumptuous banquet held at Fulke Greville's, according to the printed works of Bruno, or at the French ambassador's, according to

what is said in the Trial, Bruno took to argue before his guests—who were all doctors [learned] and English gentlemen—except Florio—about the Copernican theory. Florio sat opposite a cavalier, and had at his side Fulke Greville, and at his left Bruno." (pp. 173—4). Here is another, conveying a bit of literary news on Buckhurst: "In Windsor Castle and at Court in London, all the statesmen like Walsingham, Dudley, Sidney, Greville, and the flowers of the cavaliers who formed Elizabeth's retinue, spoke the Italian tongue, which was often used in the colloquies between the English ministers and the ambassadors of Spain and France. Lord Buckhurst was very well read in Italian literature. He wrote "Daniel" in Italian verse, not without elegance." (pp. 188—9.) Finally there is this: "Fulke Greville, a very dear friend of Sidney, and hence also of Bruno, and, like SIDNEY, fond of studies, of arms, of travel, held when still young the office of Secretary for Wales, and acquired great authority at Court and with the Queen. He offered hospitality to the Nolan [Bruno], who would perhaps have accepted it, had their friendship not been for a time broken, through the work of malignants. Bruno did not honour him with any of his dedications, and Greville takes no notice of him in his life of Sidney, nor in his other writings." (pp. 191-2.) Light is much to be wished on this (alleged) 'broken friendship': and again one sighs for family-papers that must surely be preserved. It is to be hoped that Berti's 'Life' will sooner or later find an English translator, and one who will take pains to enlarge and vivify the period of Bruno's residence in our country. So potential a soul, if also wayward, acute if ultra-speculative, honest if impul-

sively out-spoken to rashness, even bravado, demands
revelation to Englishmen of the new Facts in the stormy
Life and the tragic and dolorous martyr-end.

V. Letters of Vossius.

LORD Brooke intended this eminent scholar to be the first
occupant of his 'professorship' or Lectureship at Cambridge: and very pathetic Letters of his to Brooke are
preserved in the well-known Volume, which by-the-way
is quite a treasure-trove of contemporary allusions and
names. There are none of Brooke's to Vossius given. The
length of this 'Note' prevents our submitting certain
excerpts that we had prepared. The whole subject of the
History or " Humanity" chair in its institution and abey-
ance equally, needs thorough investigation.

VI. British Museum and Lambeth.

In my Memorial-Introduction I have given *in extenso*
the whole of the Letters of our Worthy known to be preserved in these two great national Repositories. In additional MSS. 18. 638, f. 3, is a long and important Letter
from THOMAS WILSON to Sir Fulke Greville sending a
translation from the Spanish. G.

Short Speech for Bacon.[1]

Sir Folke Grevill, Chancellor of the Exchequer:

"THIS court hath no intent to discourage the meanest subject of his lawfull appeal unto his Prince; for that were to disiherit the People of law, and the King of

---

[1] From "A Vindication of the Lord Chancellor Bacon from the aspersion of injustice cast upon him by Mr. Wraynham, containing the said Mr. Wraynham's representation of his own case, and the sentence pronounced upon him, together with the learned speeches of the Judges Hubbert [= Hobart], Coke, and other sages in the Law, Archbishop Abbot, and other reverend Prelates, the Lord Chamberlain, Earl of Arundel, Sir Fulk Grevill, and other noble Peers. Now first published from the original Manuscript. London, Printed for J. Peele at Locke's Head in Paternoster Row, 1725: p. 37 *et seqq.* See also Popham's Reports, 2nd edition, 1682, p. 137, and the "State Trials", 4th edition 1778, folio: Vol. VII., pp. 102—114. G.

the intelligence of the oppressor that might fall upon his people. But this case, I suppose not to be within the first. The matter in such case is but a review of an inferiour sentence in a superiour Magistrate, my Lord Chancellor of England, and that before he be heard, making the King his speedy executioner. But examine the nature of these accusations, and you shall find them mere scandals and impossibilities, as breaking of decrees, rewarding frauds and perjuries, palliating oppressors with greatness, wit, and eloquence. Why, my Lords, if this liberty should spread, then I desire the indifferent [=impartial] hearers to see in what a miserable case the subject stands, when the right of every man shall stand in the malignity and unquiet nature of every turbulent spirit? And, my Lords, the Judges, in what a case stand they, if by such clamours every delinquent shall be made a judge over them? And what privilege shall the King my master have? for if this humour should take a little head, will it not carry both him and justice into the field? And therefore I conclude, that this is severely to be punished; and is not a petition but a presumptuous challenge, and of so far a worse nature beyond duells, as honour and universal justice, is beyond particular right? And therefore I agree with him (Sir Edward Cooke [= Coke] that went before me, leaving all his good parts to mercy, and his ill parts to the censure of Foorth's case of 2 Jac."

Description

OF THE

Manuscripts of Lord Brooke

AT

Warwick Castle.

VII.

Description of the Manuscripts of Lord Brooke at Warwick Castle,

FORWARDED TO THE EDITOR BY THE EARL OF WARWICK AND BROOKE, WITH READINGS FROM THEM AND NOTES.

N our Prefatory Note, Volume I. (page x.) reference is made to certain MSS. of our LORD BROOKE, sold at the BRIGHT Sale in 1844, and ever since lost sight of. On the present EARL OF WARWICK AND BROOKE reading our remarks, he spontaneously, and with appreciative words informed me, that these manuscripts were in his possession, and that it would be a pleasure to entrust me with them. Gratefully accepting the offer, I have received and collated every volume, page, line, and word of these MSS. with the results shewn in the sequel. They consist of six volumes folio, bound in white vellum, and are, save a few worm-holes, in excellent preservation. They are not marked Volume Ist. onward: but the details of the contents &c., of the several volumes follow:

(*a.*) This is a very legible and careful Scribe's copy, with corrections by the Author himself, of the Poems of Monarchy, as given in the published " Remains " of 1670, viz :

§ 1. Of the Beginning of Monarchy, pp. 1 – 16, stanzas 1—45.

§ 2. Declinacōn of Monarchy to Violence, pp. 17—28, stanzas 46 – ·79.

§ 3. Of Weake-minded Tyrants, pp. 29 –37, stanzas 80—105.

§ 4. Cavtions against these weake extremeties, pp. 38— 51, stanzas 106 – 145.

§ 5. Stronge Tyrants, pp. 52—67, stanzas 146—191.

§ 6. Of Chvrch, pp. 68—83, stanzas 192—238.

§ 7. Of Lawes, pp. 84—111, st. 239 –321.

§ 8. Of Nobilitie, pp. 112-125, stanzas 322 –360.

§ 9. Of Com̄erce, pp. 126—147, stanzas 361—425

§ 10. Of Crowne⸵Revenve, pp. 148—161, stanzas 426 – 466.

§ 11. Of'Peace, pp. 162 – 179, stanzas 467—521.

§ 12. Of Warr.⸵pp. 180—199, stanzas 522 –579.

§ 13. The Excellencie of Monarchie compared with Aristocratie, pp. 200—210, stanzas 580—609.

§ 14. The Excellencie of Monarchie compared with Democratie, pp. 211—221, stanzas 610 -- 640.

§ 15. The Excellencie ⸵of Monarchie compared with Aristocratie and Democratie, ioyntlie, pp. 222— 230, stanzas 641—664.

Prefixed to the present Volume of the Works is a

double-page of Facsimiles, the first of which presents a specimen of the ' copy ', together with the
interlinear and erasing corrections of the Author.

Onward I exhibit the whole of such corrections
and various readings : but it may be mentioned
here, that the corrections found in Volume *a* and
throughout, must have been made when our
Worthy was young, corresponding as they do
with his handwriting while still Mr Fulke (or
Foulke) Greville.   Besides these earlier, there are
in all the volumes corrections made in old age.
A specimen of these is also given in our Facsimiles : see under No. IV.   At close of stanza
664 *(supra)* ''Sect. 15th " apparently changed
to " 16th " is the catch-word : but it is not re-
sumed elsewhere.   Fastened into this Volume is
a Navy-paper, from which is taken the facsimile
autograph in our Facsimiles, No. II.

(*b*) This is wholly in the autograph of the
Author himself, at different periods: and contains
the following, as in the folio of 1633 :

    1. Of Humane Learninge, 151 stanzas.   The
handwriting of this corresponds with the corrections in '' Excellencie of Monarchie ", as in
our Facsimiles.   Separately paged 1—51.

    2. Of Religion, 114 stanzas : separately
paged, 1—38.

3. An Inquisition upon Fame and Honor, 86 stanzas : separately paged 1—29.

4. A Treatie of Warrs, 68 stanzas : separately paged 1—23.

Nos. 2, 3, and 4 are in the autograph exhibited in our Facsimiles, No. III.   Compare the peculiar 'C' in the corrections in 'Excellencie of Monarchie", line 5th,' 'Carelesse' with the 'C' in 'Creation' in "Of Religion", line 6th.   But this is a later MS. than that previously described. On the fly-leaf of this Volume *b* is a corrective arrangement by the Author thus :

" Those treatises should be thus placed,

1. Religion.

2. Humane Learninge.

3. Fame and Honor.

4. Warre."

There are a number of blank leaves, and one blank leaf between each of the Poems.

(*c*) This is entirely in the autograph of the Author, as in Nos. 2 to 4 of *b*: and contains the Tragedy of Alaham, with a few slight corrections made in old age : pp. 166 and blank leaves.

(*d*) This is precisely correspondent with *c*, and contains the Tragedy of Mustapha : pp. 166 and blank leaves.

(*e*) This is a different Scribe's copy, with cor-

rections and markings made in old age by the
Author. It contains " Cælica ", as in the folio
of 1633 : pages 154. See Facsimiles, No. IV. for
example of these later corrections, &c. "Cælica"
from its biographic worth and passionateness is
perhaps the most important as certainly it is the
most substantively poetic of Lord Brooke's writings. Hence this Volume of the MSS. is of surpass-
ing interest. In their several places I note such
'various readings' as occur: but I would here
give further details not so readily exhibited in the
Notes. One of the sonnets from its curious
interlineations and alterations and re-alterations
calls for specific examination. In the MS. it is
numbered 79 (our 81): the latter half alone,
presenting these variations. Originally the first
line of this portion read,

" Dull spirittes again wth prayse sadd reall groundes."

' Sadd' seems first to have been erased, then
' reall', then over ' prayse' in old-age handwriting ' love' is written, and over ' sadd' is first
' fixt' (?) and then ' all', and over 'reall' is
' all' and an illegible word, and beyond it ' constant'. Lines 2nd and 3rd are as in the folio,
save slight othographical changes. Line 4th
begins ' As pow'r supreame spreades' with ' ac-
tyve' inserted. Line 5th originally stands,

"For as in Nature's wealth they are brought forth.'

Over ' as ' is written ' though ', over ' wealth ' is
' weyn ', over ' they ' is ' power ' over ' are ' is
' brings ' and over it again ' this another ' and
' the ' erased—all in old-age handwriting. Line
6th originally reads,

" Soe be they currant but on supreame worth ".

Over this, very illegible and erased, ' Yet . . .
still must make them' and ' currant' over ' supreame ' with other illegible words. Below this
line is the following,

" Can place or stamp make currant ought but worth."

as in the folio, and as had previously been under-
written in an earlier handwriting. It is scarcely
possible even with these details, to convey the
labour and mixture of these interlineations.

Turning now to the MS. volume, as a whole, I
have to make these notes on the arrangement and
markings throughout. Comparing the MS. with
the folio, No. 2 has a line drawn across it as if
intended to be cancelled, and so Nos. 4 (double
lines) and 6 (cross lines), the latter with ' stet ' in
pencil at bottom. But No. 6 of the MS. is No.
vii. of the folio, as of our reprint, No. vi., "Eyes,
why did you bring ", &c., not being in the M.S.

No. viii. is consequently No. 7 in the MS., and so
the numbers run on. No. 13 of the MS. (xiv. of
the folio and in ours) has two lines drawn across,
and in the margin but erased ' this 2 sonnetts '—
No. 14 (xv, as before) a mark above and below,
and in the margin, but erased ' In question to be
left out ', and below, ' this stands.' No. 15 (xvi.,
as before) two cross lines, and in margin ' yes, I
question', but erased : No. 16 (xvii., as before)
the same, and in margin ' question ', but erased,
and above, ' this stands '. No. 19 (xx., as before)
in margin ' question', but erased. No. 30 (also
xxx. in folio, from the misnumbering of xxviii. as
xxvii. : but xxxi. in our edition from correction
of the error, and so onward) ' question ' in margin,
erased. No. xxxi. of folio (our xxxii.) is not in
the MS. It begins ' Heauens see ', &c. No. xxxii.
of the folio (our xxxiii.) is No. 31 in the MS. ;
has two lines drawn across, and ' question ' in the
margin, erased. No. xxxiii. of the folio is No. 32
of the MS., and so the numbers run on. No. 38
(xxxix., as before) has two lines drawn across,
and so No. 44 (xlv., as before). No. 47 (xlviii.,
as before), a mark and ' stands ' in margin ; No.
52 (liii., as before) four lines across, and in
margin at top 'This out', and below ' This
stands'; No. 54 (lv.) the MS. furnishes a very

important addition, as given in the sequel in its place; No. 65 (lxvi., as before) a mark at top and bottom; No 67 (lxviii., as before) lines drawn across, and in margin 'question', erased. No. lxxv. of the folio (our lxxvi.) is divided in the MS. thus: From line 1st, "In the window of a graunge" to line 24th, "While thoughts", &c., is numbered 72: from line 25th, "Philocell entraunceèd stood", to end of. lxxiv. of the folio (our lxxv) is numbered 73. Then No. lxxv., of the folio (our lxxvi.) is No. 74. No. 75 (lxxvi., as before) has two marks, and in margin 'this I question' erased, and below but also erased, "Here wants sonnet 75, page 93: it follows page 113". Guided by the latter note, on page 93 is found the page-portion of No 74, as above, and at page 113, No 82 (lxxxiii, as before), "Who grace for zenith had", with blank page preceding it. No. 76 (lxxvii, as before) is marked and interlineated in hopeless confusion. It would serve no rewarding end to exhibit these. One specimen as above must suffice. On margin 'question' erased, and below, 'this stands'. No. 77 to 79 lines across: at end of 77 'this song stands' (as in our Facsimiles (No. IV.), and on margin of No. 78 'this stands', and No. 79 the same. After No. 81 (lxxxii, as before) is this foot-note in old age handwriting " this to come [?] after wth the rest " No. 82 (lxxxiii., as before) has two lines of the folio in one throughout. No. 101 is on page 142 misnumbered 102, but correctly 101 in next pages. By the omission of No . vi., ' Eyes, why ", &c., in the MS., the last is No. 108, not cix., as in folio, or cx., as in our text.

(*f*) This is by the same scribe as in *a*, with a few slight corrections by the author as in *c*, *d*, and *e*. It contains the Letter to an Honourable Lady [= Lady Rich] as in the folio of 1633 : pages 78, and a large number of blank leaves.

It will be observed that these six volumes of MSS. embrace the whole of the contents of the folio of 1633 and of the " Remains " of 1670, *id est*, the entire Works, with the exception of the Life of Sir Philip Sidney : for which ' Life of Sidney ' we have had the advantage of a MS. in Trinity College, Cambridge, as explained in its place.

Speaking generally, the orthography throughout differs from the printed text in the use of " ie " for " y " and " es " for " s " and the like. The stanza from the Poems of " Monarchy " (Of Religion " st. 1st.) in our Fac-similes, exemplifies the most of these variations, *e.g.* compared with the text of the " Remains "—faithfully reproduced by us (Vol. Ist. page 239)—there is in line 1st. ' manie ' for ' many ', ' lawes ' for ' laws ' ' raines ' for ' rains ' and so on. It would be endless and practically supererogatory, to record such merely orthographic differences, except in a few notable instances : and indeed it had been a question whether it should have been wise to have substituted another orthography for that of the original authoritative text, even if the MSS. had been in my possession at the time of printing our Volumes. The MS. orthography is extremely arbitrary. Thus in the " Beginning of Monar-chie " stanza 2d , line 1st. for our ' golden ' we read ' goulden ' but again in stanza 6th., lines 5th and 6th, it is twice ' golden ' (Vol. Ist. pp 5 and 7) and so with other words, as ' maister ' and ' master ', ' freinde ' and ' friend ' &c. &c. This very arbitrariness is of course an element in considering the transition-forms and formative-processes of our Language.

Looking now over the successive Volumes, I have to present the result of a personal collation of the whole. Many of the ' various readings ' will be found on examination to be interesting and valuable in themselves, and further, to correct and clear up the printed text of 1633 and 1670 : and in a few cases the necessary re-perusal has discovered to me oversights of my own text, which I beg may be put right in their places.   I am grateful that I do not require to draw very much on the indulgence of my Readers in respect of such ' escapes ' : on which as in all human work-manship, let an ancient Worthy speak : ' There be spots in the all-seeing sun, and it is therefore no admiration that our dim owl eyes pass over specks and stains of printing.   Please thee then Reader to forgive and correct these, in thy charity as thou dost the eye of day for his clarity : ' it being no strange thing for good scholars to be no good scribes ',—the latter bit being from dear old Henry Brome for Henry Beesley of Swanford in his " Soules Conflict "—not unworthy to be placed beside that of heavenly Dr. Richard Sibbes. That these required corrections may be made more readily I have tabulated in a fly-leaf to this volume, such as I should wish to be done *at once* : others of no great moment, are marked below and onward with an asterisk [*] in the 1st column after the number, and [†] in the 2nd column, those new readings from the MS. that specially commend themselves for acceptance.   G.

OUR VOLUME 1st, FROM THE TEXT OF
'REMAINS' OF 1670.

*** Though the Notes are necessarily not exactly opposite each other, the number on the one page will guide to its equivalent on the other.

	PAGE.	ST.	LINE.
1.	6	5	1 'those'
2.	*ibid*	5	3 'give'.
3.	8	11	6 'still made'.
4.	9	12	5 'Diomedes of Thrace'.
5.	9	13	6 'trophies'.
6.	11	18	1 'were'.
7.	12	19	5th and 6th.

" Power still affects more inequality,
Which made mankind more curious to be free ".

8.	12	21	4 'now blasted'.
9.	12	22	1 'do'.
10.	14	27	2 'his',
11.	*ibid*	27	3 'her self'.
12.	15	29	(*see opposite.*)
13.	16	31	2 'men'.
14.	16	33	4 'king'
15.	17	34	3

" Where that well happy mixt and confluence '.

16.	17	34	5 'wear'.
17.	18	37	2 'rights'.
18.	18	39	1 'move'.
19.	19	42	1 'So then'.
20.	20	43	5 'kings'.
21.	21	46	1 'the excentricks'.
22.	,,	46	4 'through'.
23.	22	49	3 'desires'.
24.*	25	57	2 'that great gift' : 'great' misinserted.
25.	26	60	3 'Are not'.
26.	26	61	3 'Cybele'.
27.	27	61	6 'a'.
28.	27	62	6 'Miters'.

THE MSS. AT WARWICK CASTLE.

1. 'these' : and so frequently, but not noted.
2. 'her'.
3. 'did make' corrected by Author to 'still make'.
4. 'of Diomedes Thrace' : and so frequently a slightly different collocation of the words : but not noted.
5. 'trophy'.
6. 'was'.
7. Originally written
      "Stirring power vpp to inequality,
      And making man as curious to be free ":
erased by the Author, and replaced by our text.
8. 'since blasted'.
9.† 'did'.
10. 'this'.
11. 'it self'.
12. At end, the first five lines of st. 27th, inserted by mistake, and erased.
13. 'man'.
14. 'throne' : but erased by the Author again.
15.† I read and interpreted 'mixt' as = mixture' : but the MS. makes a misprint of the "Remains" evident :
      "Where that well mixt and happy confluence ".
16 † 'weave'.
17.† 'rites'.
18.† 'My correction of the misprint 'more'—overlooked by Southey—is confirmed by the MS.
19.† 'So that'.
20. 'kinge'.
21. 'these'.
22. 'thorough'.
23. 'desire'.
24. 'that first transcendent' : 'first' an evident *lapsus pennæ* for 'gift'.
25. Corrected by the Author in old age from 'And' to 'Arre'.
26. 'Sibilla'.

	PAGE.	ST.	LINE.	
29.	27	63	5	' head ideas '.
30.	27	64	2	' colour '.
31.	27	65	1	' Knowing '.
32.	28	67	1	' grow '.
33.	29	69		' unwrest '.
34.	30	71	6	' And must still by their '.
35.	30	72	5	' of '.
36.	33	79	6	' swayd '.
37.	35	82	6	' times '
38.*	35	83	1	' the height ': ' the ' mis-inserted.
39.	35	83	4	' did '.
40.	35	85	2	' into '.
41.	36	87	1	' bred '.
42.	36	87	4	' colours '.
43.*	36	87	5	' Nor ': our misprint for ' not '.
44.	37	88	6	' again '.
45.*	37	89	2	' Thou ': as in 43.
46.	38	91	4	' To '.
47.	38	93	4	' go '.
48.	39	94	5	' war agree '
49.	41	99	5	' those '.
50.	41	100	1	' idle '.
51.	42	103	3	' sometimes '.
52.*	44	107	1	' Here ': our misprint.
53.*	44	108	2	' these ' : ibid.
54.*	44	108	3	' leave ' : ibid.
55.	46	112	6	' his life '.
56.	46	113	4	' of '.
57.	46	114	3	' of '.
58.	47	116	2	' kings '.
59.	47	116	5	' her '.
60.	47	117	3	' man '.
61.	48	119	3	' foundation '.
62.	48	119	6	' Tyranny '.
63.	49	122	6	' and '.
64.	49	123	3	' scepter's rights '.
65.	50	123	4	' strengths '.
66.	50	125	2	' of '.
67.	51	127	4	' nobility '.
68.	51	128	2	' represents '.
69.	51	128	3	' every '.
70.	51	129	1	' spirit '.
71.	51	129	5	' brings '.

27. 'the'
28. Originally written 'The Church': erased by Author and 'Myters' written in.
29.† 'head's ideas.'
30. 'cullour': changed by Author to 'color.'
31. '*They* knowing': but erased.
32.† 'grew'.
33. My suggested emendation of 'unwrest' is confirmed by the MS: but in st. 68th, line 2nd., the misplaced 'as' is also in the MS.
34.† 'And soe must still by miscreating'.
35. 'to'.
36. Originally 'pay'd', but erased by the Author, and 'sway'd' written in.
37.† 'crymes'.
38. 'height'
39.† 'doth'.
40. 'unto'.
41.† 'breed'
42. Originally spelled 'cullers': changed to 'colors': and this is repeated all through. The Author was evidently annoyed with his Scribe's persistence in keeping up 'culler'. Not again noted.
43. 'Not'.
44. Not in MS.
45.† 'That'.
46.† 'The'.
47.† 'come'.
48. 'war and agree'.
49. 'they'.
50. 'idlie imperious'.
51. 'sometime'.
52. 'Hence'.
53. 'such'.
54. 'yeild'.
55.† 'himself'.
56. 'a'.
57.† 'in'.
58. 'thrones'.: but erased by the Author. So too in st. 119. line 1.
59. 'their'.
60.† 'mynde'.
61. 'foundations'.

	PAGE.	ST.	LINE.	
72.	52	131	1	'the '.
73.	52	132	6	'would '.
74.*	55	138	6	'That crowns': our misprint, but a lucky accident surely.
75.*	55	140	5	'council-seats': should be spelled 'councel-seats'.
76.	59	148	5	'thus by cutting '.
77.	59	149	4	'Others '.
78.	60	151	4	'with '.
79.	61	156	4	'martial '.
80.	64	163	2	'council'.
81.	64	163	6	'let no man judge what's fit '.
82.	65	165	5	'did '.
83.	65	166	1	'precepts '.
84.	67	171	4	'fears '.
85.	67	171	5	'poize '.
86.	67	172	1	'The pain's '.
87.	68	175	3	'appearance '.
88.	68	176	5	'are '.
89.	69	178	3	'in '.
90.	69	178	5	'must'.
91.	69	178	6	'their '.
92.	70	182	4	'glean '.
93.	71	183	2	'do '.
94.	72	185	5	'the skin '.
95.	72	185	6	'in '.
96.	72	187	1	'steerage '.
97.	73	190	3	'precipice '.
98.	75	192	3	'man's '.
99.*	75	193	3	'of ': our misprint.
100.	76	196	5	'and people's '.
101.	78	202	5	'forrainer and home-bred '.
102.	78	202	6	'and '.
103.	78	203	3	'When '.
104.	79	206	6	'rite '.
105.	80	207	2	'judging '.
106.	80	208	1	'prayers '.
107.	80	208	3	'the priest out of his pride's '.
108.	80	209	1	'king '.
109.*	81	210	4	'invention ': our misprint.
110.	81	211	6	'nature '.
111.	81	212	2	'their '.
112.	82	213	1	'such '.

62. ' Originally 'iniury' : but 'tyrannie' written in by the Author.
63. ' or '.
64.† ' scepter rights '.
65. ' strength '.
66. ' in '.
67.† ' abilitie '.
68. ' represents '.
69. ' any '.
70. ' spirits '.
71.† ' beares '.
72.† ' which '.
73. ' will '.
74. ' Then crowns '.
75. ' conscience-seats '.
76.† ' And by their cutting '.
77. ' other ' : and so in page 66, st. 170, line 3.
78.† ' of '.
79.† ' marshall : as interpreted by us.
80. ' councells '.
81.† 'let man judge which is fit.'
82.† ' will '.
83. ' precept '.
84. ' fear '.
85. ' peaze '.
86. ' The pain '.
87. ' apparance '.
88. ' be '.
89. ' to '.
90.† ' may '
91. ' her '.
92.† ' gleane ' : this I fear sets aside the conjecture of ' gleam ' by my friend Mr. W. A. Wright, as before.
93. ' doth '.
94.† ' the tender skin '.
95. ' to '.
96. ' stirrage '.
97. ' preiudice '.
98. ' kinges '.
99.† ' to '.
100.† ' and the people's '.
101.† ' forrayners and home-borne '.
102.† ' or '.

	PAGE.	ST.	LINE.	
113.	82	214	6	'purchases'.
114.	83	217	4	'mankind'.
115.	83	218	3	'raiśd'.
116.*	85	**223**	5	'shall'.
117.	87	227	6	'what'.
118.	88	230	3	'and'.
119.	88	230	6	'yet keeps outward'.
120.	89	234	6	'them'.
121.	90	236	5	'will'.
122.	90	238	1	'that'.
123.	92	240	4	'By'.
124.	93	244	1	'divided'.
125.	93	244	4	'those'.
126.	94	247	1	'For though perhaps'.
127.	96	251	2	'intend'.
128.*	96	252	6	'must'.
129.	97	255	1	'if'.
130.	98	257	1	'of all our'.
131.	99	261	6	'not'.
132.	99	262	6	'command'.
133.	100	264	2	'large'.
134.	101	265	3	'law'.
135.	102	270	1	'For'.
136.	102	270	2	'double'.
137.	102	271	**5**	'ill'.
138.	103	273	4	'upon judges or pleader's'.
139.	103	274	1	'besides'.
140.	105	278	3	'Then bind..........of their'.
141.	105	279	4	'vote'.
142.	106	284	2	'never governs'.
143.	107	286	4	'good will'.
144.	108	288	5	'medium'.
145.	108	289	5	'friends'.
146.	109	291	4	'the'.
147.*	109	292	1	'Parliament'.
148.*	109	293	3	'hearts'.
149.	110	295	3	'force or practice'.
150.	110	297	2	'Sheriff's'.
151.	110	297	3	'shapes'.
152.	111	300	3	'subjects''. (bis)
153.	112	302	2	'do'.
154.	113	307	3	'By'.
155.	115	311	6	'fruits'.

103.† ' Whence '.
104. ' Spelled ' right ' : corrected by the Author.
105.† ' guidinge ' = guiding.
106. ' prayer '.
107.† ' the high-priest out of pride's '.
108. ' kinges '.
109. ' inventions '.
110. ' Originally ' dutie ' but changed to ' nature ' by the Author.
111.† ' her '.
112. ' like '.
113.† ' purchasers '.
114. Originally ' her mynde ' but written ' mankinde ' by the Author.
115.† ' raise '.
116. ' should '.
117. ' which '.
118. ' or '
119. ' keeps the '.
120.† ' him '.
121. ' Originally ' would ' : but written ' will ' by the Author.
122.† ' this '
123.† ' As '.
124.† ' So in MS., confirming my correction of ' Remains '.
125. ' such '.
126.† ' And though perchance '.
127. Originally ' extend ' : but written ' intend ' by the Author.
128. deleted.
129.† ' though '.
130.† ' indeed of '.
131.† ' noe '.
132. ' comaunds '.
133.† ' longe '.
134. ' lawes '.
135.† ' And '.
136.† ' doubtfull '.
137.† ' all .'
138. ' upon the judges and pleader's '.
139.† So : thus confirming our emendation.
140. ' Then againe bind it ' : ' of their ' deleted.
141† ' rote '.

	PAGE.	ST.	LINE.	
156.	115	312	6	' from '.
157.	116	314	2	' person '.
158.*	116	315	3	' and '.
159.	116	315	4	' Help '.
160.	117	317	3	' States '.
161.	119	322	3	' uniformity '.
162.	119	323	6	' chain'd '.
163.	119	324	2	' the '.
164.	121	330	2	' according '.
165.	122	331	1	' consent of disagreeing '.
166.	122	332	2	' A secret '.
167.	122	333	4	' princes '.
168.	123	334	6	' Gave her above all states '.
169.	126	343	2	' creators '.
170.*	126	346	2	' this '.
171.	127	348	3	' shire '.
172.	127	348	3	' grief '.
173.	130	355	4	' the '.
174.	132	361	1	' mankind's '.
175.	132	363	2	' her '.
176.	133	363	4	' her '.
177.	133	365	3	' through '.
178.	134	369	1	' that each '.
179.	136	374	3	' skill'd '.
180.	136	375	2	' complexions '.
181.	137	376	5-6	' gold ' and ' sold '.
182.	137	377	2	' exchequer '.
183.	137	377	5	' martial '.
184.	137	377	6	' the '.
185.	138	380	4	' now '.
186.	139	383	1	' Hanse's '.
187.	139	383	4	' with '.
188.	140	387	1	' for '.
189.	141	389	4	' are '.
190.	141	390	1	' the '.
191.	142	393	2	' With less hurt '.
192.	143	395	5	' seen '.
193.	143	396	4	' punishment '.
194.*	143	396	5	' As '.
195.	145	401	1	' the '
196.	145	401	2	' Albian '
197.	146	403	2	' interpoling '
198.	146	403	6	' forrainers '.

142. Originally ' skill commands not ' : but erased by the Author for text.
143. ' And ill'
144. ' medico ' : *sic* but qy. ' medio '.
145. 'friend'.
146. ' this'.
147. ' Parliaments '.
148. ' arts' : originally written 'harts' : but 'h' erased by the Author.
149. ' witty practise '.
150 ' Sheeves '.
151. ' shrapes ', [*sic*]: and line 6th originally written ' regalitie', but 'the royalitie' inserted by the Author.
152. ' subject ' (*bis*).
153. ' soone '.
154. ' But '
155. ' fruit '.
156. ' by '.
157. ' persons '.
158. ' the '.
159. ' Helpes '.
160. ' State ' : a *lapsus* as the companion rhyme is ' advocates ' : but Lord Brooke and his contemporaries use singular and plural very irregularly.
161. ' uniformites '.
162. ' enchain'd '
163. ' these '
164. ' concordinge '.
165. Originally ' yet of discordinge' : Author changes to text.
166. Originally ' A pretious secreate prove in Tyraine' : Author inserts 'pretious' and inserts 'to kings' as in text.
167.† Originally ' tyrants ' but erased by Author for ' princes '. Perhaps ' tyrants ' is preferable.
168. Originally ' Over all states gaue her ' but Author changes to text.
169. ' creator '.
170. ' their'.
171. ' shere '.
172. ' greifs '.
173. ' her'.

	PAGE.	ST.	LINE.	
199.	148	409	2	' her '.
200.	150	415	5	' Mars, his '.
201.	151	420	2	' forrain '.
202.	152	423	5	' for '.
203.	153	424	4	' frame '.
204.	152	424	6	'and '.
205.	153	425	2	' or the '.
206.	154	426	3	' in '.
207.	154	427	4	' tomb '.
208.	155	430	1	' martial '.
209.	156	433	5	' sinew-like '.
210.	157	434	6	' otherwise '.
211.	157	435	5	' pressing through '.
212.	159	441	6	' make '.
213.	160	443	3	' where '.
214.	160	443	4	' rage '.
215.	160	444	1	' that '.
216.	161	447	1	' excess '.
217.	162	450	1	' was '.
218.	162	451	3	' the '.
219.	163	453	1	' of the '.
220.	163	454	4	' proper stage '.
221.*	164	457	3	' Art '.
222.	165	459	4	' or '.
223.	165	460	2	' alter'd '.
224.	167	465	5	' their '.
225.	169	470	4	' the '.
226.	169	471	5	' Istmus '.
227.	170	474	1	' Achai '
228.	171	475	6	' excel'd '.
229.	177	496	3	' common liking '.
230.	179	500	3	' the '.
231.	180	503	3	' reputation '.
232.	180	505	6	' the '.
233.	180	506	1	' the '.
234.	181	506	3	' all '.
235.	181	506	4	' unto '.
236.	181	508	5	'through '.
237.	181	509	3	' plac'd '.
238.	182	511	5	' the '.
239.	183	512	5	' Not '.
240.	184	515	6	' less far off '.
241.*	185	519	5	' what '.

174.   Originally 'man's'; Author writes in ' man-kind's'.
175.   ' that'.
176.   Originally ' the': Author writes ' her'.
177.   ' thorough '.
178.   Originally ' every': Author writes as in text
179.   ' skill'.
180.   ' complexion'
181.   ' gould' and ' sould'.
182.   ' checker'.
183.* ' marshall'.
184.   ' that'.
185.   ' or '.
186.   'Hanses''.
187.   ' by'.
188.   ' forth'.
189.† ' ore' (= material) : besides rhyming with ' poor'
         the meaning seems better.
190.   ' this'.
191.   Originally ' Safelie upon ' : but Author writes as in
         text.
192.   ' synne'. (?)
193.   ' punishments'.
194.   ' of'.
195.   ' theis'.
196.   ' Albion'.
197.† ' interloping ' : the MS. thus removes the obscurity.
198.   ' forrainer'.
199.   ' their ' ·
200.   ' Marses ': re-written by the Author ' Mars, his'.
201.   ' over'.
202.   ' of '.
203.   ' make' but erased by the Author.
204.   ' or '.
205.   ' man or '.
206   ' by'.
207·   ' tombes'.
208.   ' marshall'.
209.   Spelled ' synnow'.
210.   ' otherwayes'.
211.   ' growne from the ': and for ' on ' reads ' to'.
212.† ' makes'.
213.† ' whence '.
214.† ' age ' : a very important reading; and I should de-

	PAGE.	ST.	LINE.	
242.	186	523	2	'bounds'.
243.	186	523	6	'in'.
244.	187	526	2	'States'.
245.	188	527	6	'interrupts'.
246.	188	528	2	'States'.
247.	188	528	4	'times'.
248.	189	530	4	'And................are'.
249.	191	537	5	'the'.
250.	191	538	6	'in'.
251.	192	540	5	'Africk's'.
252.	193	543	4	'gloss'.
253.	193	544	5	'for'.
254.	193	544	6	'naught'.
255.	194	545	2	'and'.
256.	194	546	2	'slack'.
257.	194	547	5	'of'.
258.	194	548	1	'that'
259.	195	549	2	'are'.
260.	196	553	3	'when merciless'.
261.	197	557	2	'war, league or any'.
262.	198	558	1	'Or'.
263.	199	562	5	'with'.
264.	199	563	5	'Malice'.
265.	200	564	6	'that'.
266.	200	566	6	'set down'.
267.	201	568	6	'undertakings'.
268.	202	572	3	'For'.
269.	202	572	5	'chance'.
270.	206	580	2	'in'
271.*	206	581	1	'that'.
272.	207	582	4	'which'.
273.	207	584	4	'proper'.
274.	208	586	6	'inequalities'.
275.	208	587	1	'strange'.
276.	208	587	4	'aged'.
277.	209	587	6	'Under which yet Rome did an empress grow'.
278.	209	588	2	'And even before'.
279.	209	588	3	'was with'.
280.	209	588	4	'She still affecting change'.
281.	209	588	5	'Carelessly left her Government'.
282.	209	589	6	'upright by'.
283.	209	590	2	'France'.

plore that I had not the MS. earlier, were it only
for missing this. ' Rage' gives no meaning, ' Age'
as ' low-stooping' is vivid and fine. Let the
Reader please correct instantly by erasure of ' R '.

215.   ' who'.
216.†   ' success'.
217.   ' were'.
218.   ' a'.
219.†   ' not as'.
220.†   ' prop-stage'.
221.   ' Arts'.
222.   ' and'.
223.†   ' altered'.
224 †   ' of'.
225.†   ' their'.
226.†   ' Isthmus'.
227.†   ' Achaia'.
228.†   ' exilde' : another admirable correction of the ' Remains' text, to be specially attended to by the Reader.
229.   Originally ' commonly kinges': changed to our
text by the Author..
230.   ' at'.
231.   ' estimation'.
232.†   ' her'.
233.†   ' this'.
234.   deleted.
235   ' with'.
236.†   ' thorough'.
237.   ' plaste' : corrected by Author as in text.
238.†   ' that'.
239.   ' Noe': and st. 513, line 1, ' not' for ' no' : and so
page 208, st. 585, line 1, ' not' for ' no'.
240.   ' not so far'.
241.†   ' which'.
242.†   ' grounds': also to be specially corrected.
243.†   ' to'.
244.   ' State'.
245.   ' interrupt'.
246.†   ' Fates': let the Reader accept this.
247.   ' rests'.
248.†   ' As............be'.
249.   ' their'.
250.   ' to'.

358   TEXT OF 1670.

	PAGE.	ST.	LINE.	
284.	210	591	6	'that'.
285.	211	593	6	'stainèd her'
286.	211	595	3	'policy'.
287.	212	599	2	'to'.
288.	213	600	6	'had'.
289.	213	602	1	'to'.
290.	214	603	5	'Aristocracies'.
291.	215	608	1	'of'.
292.	218	615	2	'Any averr that Rome's'.
293.	218	615	4	'into'.
294.	219	615	6	'and......Asia.'
295.	219	616	2	'the'.
296.	221	622	5	'and'.
297.	222	626	2	'of'.
298.	222	627	6	'For'.
299.	223	628	1	'Or'.
300.	223	630	1	'the'.
301.	224	633	1	'Nor'.
302.	225	634	6	'a'.
303.	225	635	2	'the'.
304.	225	foot note.		
305.	226	637	1	'Who'.
306.	226	639	2	'do'.
307.	228	642	3	'courses'
308.	229	644	6	'own'.
309.	229	645	3	'and'.
310.	229	645	6	'State'.
311.	229	646	1	'suffrages'.
312.	230	646	6	'passion'
313.	230	648	1	'such may be found'.
314.	231	649	6	'else at least'.
315.	231	650	6	'a'.
316.	232	653	2	'alike'.
317.	232	653	3	'the'.
318.	233	657	6	'tares'.
319.	234	659	6	'Which'.
320.	235	663	2	'for'.
321.	235	664	6	'Or'.
322.	239	1	1	'make'.
323.	240	4	6	'did'.
324.	243	12	1	'finely'.
325.	243	12	4	'we'.
326.	243	13	5	'that'

251.† ' Africk is '.
252.† 'glass'.
253. ' of '.
254.† 'nought' : a better rhyme for ' thought '.
255. ' or '.
256.† ' slake ': a better rhyme for ' awake '.
257. ' for '.
258. ' as '.
259. 'be '.
260. ' where '.
261. 'war, practise, league, or contribution'?
262.† ' For'.
263. ' by '.
264. 'The sinne ' : but erased by the Author, and written
       as in text.
265. 'the'.
266 ' more fit': but erased by the Author, and written
       as in text.
267. ' undertaking ': and so page 203, st. 575, line 6
       ' understands ' for ' understand '.
268.† ' Which '.
269.† ' change ' : the Reader will correct.
270. ' with '.
271.† 'which '.
272.† ' this'.
273. 'better '.
274. ' inequaltie '.
275. 'fainte': but erased by the Author and written as
       in text.
276. ' feeble' but as in 264.
277. ' Under which infant Rome was like to grow ". Sic :
       but as in 264.
278. ' Neither was that ' : but as in 264.
279. ' amongst': but as in 264.
280. " But she again changed forms " : but as in 264.
281. ' And left th' republique ': but as in 264.
282. 'by grace of': but as in 264.
283.† 'trance ': another all-important correction which
       removes the difficulty conjecturally met by us.
       Let the Reader accept it.
284. ' who '.
285.† ' stained her fame' : this word 'fame' supplies the
       lacking syllable and makes ' stained ' a monosllable.

	PAGE.	ST.	LINE.	
327.	244	17	1	'this'.
328.*	245	19	5	'all they'.
329.	247	25	2	'and'.
330.	248	27	1	'when spiritual'.
331.	248	27	2	'the'.
332.	248	23	1	'this fear['s]'.
333.	248	28	3	'But'.
334.	249	30	1	'likewise'.
335.	249	32	1	'sure in all kinds'.
336.	250	33	6	'fit.'.
337.	250	35	6	'have'
338.	251	36	3	'Religion seems'
339.	252	41	4	'thy'.
340.	253	44	1	'find'.
341.	253	44	3	'to'.
342.	254	46	6	'For'.
343.	255	47	5	'life'.
344.	255	48	2	'imperfection dies.'
345.	256	51	4	'things'.
346.	256	52	6	'prayers'.
347.	257	55	6	'their'.
348.	258	58	1	'the'.
349.	258	58	4	'life'.
350.	259	60	4	'miracles'.
351.	259	61	1	'But unto sinners' hearts'.
352.	259	61	3	'Fitteth'.
353.*	260	62	2	'and'.
354.	260	63	4	'nor life nor letter.'
355.	261	67	3	'curst'.
356.	262	68	2	'by'.
357.	263	70	6	'on'.
358.	263	72	5	'fruits'.
359.	264	73	3	'quite'.
360.	264	74	6	'worst'.
361.	264	75	3	'What'.
362.	265	78	2	'stools'.
363.	266	79	4	'and'.
364.	266	80	1	'thy'.
365.	267	81	6	'or ill they be'.
366.*	267	82	1	'of
367.	267	83	6	'ne'r had any'.
368.	267	84	2	'number'.
369.	268	85	6	'would'.

286.† ' polity '.
287.† ' at '.: Reader will accept this.
288.   ' have ' after ' pow'r ' : but as in 264.
289.   ' with '.
290.   ' Aristocraties ' : and so throughout, and with ' democ-
         racy ' and ' policy ' but not further noted.
291.   ' in '.
292.   ' He would averr that their ' : but as in 264.
293.† ' to '.
294.   ' Europe ': ' and ' deleted : but as in 264.
295.† ' their ' : and so page 220, st. 621, line 2.
296.† ' or '.
297.   ' in '.
298.† ' Fate ' : a very important reading, which the
         Reader will accept.
299.   ' But ' : as in 264.
300.† ' this '.
301. † ' Neither ' and ' that ' erased.
302.   ' his '.
303.   ' their ' : and so page 230 st. 648, line 3.
304.† ' Julian in Cæsar. 6 ' :
305.   ' Whom '.
306.† ' did '.
307.   ' councells '.
308.† ' home '.
309.   ' or ',
310.† ' States '.
811.   Originally written ' suffrings ', but corrected.
312.   ' by spleen ' but erased.
313.   ' they stand upright ' *ibid.*
314.† ' at the .'
315.   ' the '.
316.† ' as '.
317.† ' these '.
318.   ' teares ' but corrected by the Author
319.† ' What '.
320.   ' from ' but corrected by the Author.
321†.   ' For '.
322.† ' makes ' : and page 244, st. 16, line 3, ' make ' for
         ' makes '.
323.† ' do '.
324.† ' firmlie '.
325.   ' it '.
326.   ' as '.

	PAGE.	ST.	LINE.	
370.	261	86	4	' hath '.
371.	268	87	1	' the '.
372.	269	87	6	' His '.
373.	269	88	3	' rightfulness '.
374.*	269	89	5	' whose '.
375.	270	91	6	' such '.
376.	270	92	5	' hopes '.
377.	271	95	1	' which "
378.	271	95	6	' rests '.
379.	272	96	5	' and '.
380.	272	96	6	' Our '.
381.	273	100	4	' their '.
382.	273	102	1	' yet '.
383.	275	106	2	' the '.
384.	275	107	5	' of '.
385.	275	108	1	' the '.
386.	275	108	4	' laws '.
387.	277	113	2	' As '.
388.	277	113	5	' the '.
389.	278	114	6	'joy . . . thou '.

OUR VOLUME IInd FROM THE FOLIO OF 1633.

390.	8	9	4	' tunes '.
391.	9	10	3	' respect '.
392.	9	10	5	' For '.
393.	10	12	4	' intromission '.
394.	11	14	5	' But—from stainèd '.
395.	14	22	2	' scientiall '.
396.	15	24	4	' it '.
397.	22	41	5	' alwayes '.
398.	24	47	4	' obiect '.
399.	25	49	5	' other '.
400.	26	53	2	' humor '.
401.	27	54	2	' dimme '.
402.	30	62	6	' offend his '.
403.	31	66	2	' iudge '.
404.	32	68	6	' dreamers '.
405.	33	71	6	' chance '.
406.	33	72	2	' all '.

327.† 'thus' : an important correction.
328.† ' all what they '.   Cf. st. 443.
329.† ' or '.
330.† ' when our spiritual '.
331.† ' this'.
332.† 'they fear': this clears up the obscurity, and the
      Reader will please accept.
333.   ' Yet '.
334.   ' besides '.
335.† ' For in all these kinds '.
336.† ' fill' : another important correction clearing up the
      meaning, and to be accepted by the Reader.
337.   ' with' : a very inferior reading which will not be
      adopted.
338 † ' reason seemeth '.
339.   ' this '.
340.† ' feele'.
341.† ' unto '.
342.† ' To '.
343.† ' in life' : and page 256, st. 53, line 4. ' to ' for ' in '.
344.   ' imperfections die': and so page 258, st. 56, line 2,
      ' imperfection' for ' imperfections '.
345.† 'thoughtes'.
346.   ' prayer '.
347.   ' that '
348.   ' that'.
349,† 'fleshe' : a noticeable reading, but neither is very
      clear.
350.† ' miracle '.
351.   ' But to the harte of sinne '.
352.† ' Filleth ' : and cf. 346.
353.† ' but '.
354.   ' nor letter or not life ' : noticeable but obscure.
355.† ' nurst': the Reader will please accept.
356.   ' from '.
357.   ' in '.
358.   ' fruit '.
359.   ' first '.
360.   ' weake ' : not a good change.
361.† ' But '.
362.† ' Schooles '.
363.† ' or '.
364.   ' the .

	PAGE.	ST.	LINE.	
407.	37	80	3	'part'.
408.	37	82	4	'they make'.
409.	41	94	1	'the'.
410.	42	97	4	'principall'.
411.	42	97	10	'must'.
412.	46	108	4	'many'.
413.	51	120	5	'which'.
414.	51	121	6	'doing'.
415.	53	125	5	'his'.
416.	54	129	4	'Where'.
417.	57	137	3	'will'.
418.	60	145	1	'to be knowne'.
419.	60	145	5	'deeming'
420.	60	145		after line 5.
421.	60	145	7	'And'.
422.	61	148		'heights'.
423.	69	7	3	'wayes.'.
424.	70	7	4	'lose'.
425.	70	9	3	'And'.
426.	72	13	4	'this'.
427.	73	16	6	'or'.
428.	73	17	4	'what'.
429.	74	20	4	'natures..........restraine'.
430.	76	26	4	'lacking'.
431.	79	34	4	'build......imaginations'.
432.	86	51	2	'that pride'.
433.	87	54	6	'naught'.
434.	88	56	2	'Time's'.
435	94	71	3	'man-nature'.
436.	96	75	4	'needs'.
437.	96	76	2	'Vertue'.
438.	97	79	4	'buried'.
439.	103	1	3	'worke'.
440.	103	1	5	'proues'.
441.	104	4	2	'and'.
442.	108	13	3	'And'.
443.	112	26	4	'this'.
444.	115	34	5	'Let'.
445.*	118	42	4	misprinted 'Motality' for 'mortality.
446.	118	43	1	'War'.
447.	119	45	4	'no'.
448.	124	55	4	'of'.

365. ' and evill be '.
366.† ' one '.
367. ' had never '.
368. ' wisdome '.
369. ' could '.
370. ' did '.
371. ' at '.
372.† ' His owne '.
373.† ' righteousnesse '.
374. ' where '.
375. ' that '.
376. ' hope '.
377. ' who '.
378. ' lies ' but erased.
379. ' doth '.
380 . ' The '.
381.† ' her '.
382 . ' not '.
383. ' that '.
384.† ' in '
385.† ' their '.
386. ' rules ' : ' laws   erased by the Author.
387.† ' And '.
388.† ' those '.
389.† ' joyes ' : ' thou ' deleted.

THE MSS. AT WARWICK CASTLE.

390† ' tones '.
391† ' reflect ' : a valuable correction, which the Reader
        will accept.
392† ' But '.
393.† ' intromissions '
394.† ' But as ', which clears up a difficulty.
395† I am sorry that the MS. does not confirm Archdeacon
        Hare's emendation here. It also reads ' scientifi-
        call '.
396.† ' yet : an important reading.
397.† ' allayes : this removes an obscurity.
398. ' obiects '.

PAGE	ST.	LINE.	
449.	1.5	59	3	'is'.
450.	125	60	3	'will'.
451.	126	63	3	'but'.

OUR VOLUME IIId. FROM THE TEXT OF THE FOLIO OF 1633*

PAGE. LINE.

452.	13	Sonnet VI: the next is headed No. VI.
553.	15	1 'by its mouving'.
454.	16	4 'make'.
455.	20	8 of Sonnet XIII, 'boy's play'.
456.	21	5 'ran from'.
457.	21	2 of Sonnet XIV., 'cloth'd'.
458.	21	14 *ibid*, 'In Myra onely to be permanent.'
459.	22 and 24	'playing'......'decaying'.
560.	22	14 'which yet all louers beare'.
461.	24	5-6 :

"Angells enioy the heauens' inward quires
Starre gazers only multiply desires".

462.	25	2 of Sonnet XIX, 'Cælia's'.
463.	25	10 *ibid*, 'faded'.
464.	26	7 'Since'.
465.	27	2 'halfe-fast'.
466.	32	3 of Sonnet XXVII, 'laist'.
467.	35	1 'sweares'.
468.	35	5 'Venture'.
469.	37	11 'thy arrowes'.
470.	37	13 'once..........sworne'.
471.	37	14 'thou straight brau'st this good fellowe'.

the horne'.

472.	39	5 'The'.
473.	39	6 'white'.
474.*	40	1 'The': and in line 3.

---

* Our Vol. IIId. was printed off before getting the Warwick Castle MSS: and hence I have not been able to incorporate into our text such better readings as perhaps otherwise I should have done. But a number were so interesting that I cancelled the necessary leaves and reprinted in order to include them. These, as well as all the others, are carefully enumerated in these Notes in their places. G.

399. 'others'.
400. 'humors'.
401.† Unlike No. 395, Archdeacon Hare's emendation is here confirmed by the Author's 'dimm', not 'diuine'.
402. 'else hurt': but erased for the text.
403. 'deeme'.
404. 'arts doe': but erased for the text.
405.† 'choise'.
406. Originally 'at : but corrected by the Author, as in text.
407. Originally 'place': but corrected by the Author, as in text.
408. 'would' before 'they', but marked for erasure.
409. Originally 'to', but corrected by the Author.
410. Originally 'principle': but corrected by the Author.
411. The misprint 'most' confirmed by a *lapsus*.
412.† 'windy'.
413.† 'with'.
414. 'doings'.
415. 'ye' = the.
416. Originally 'That' : but corrected by the Author.
417. Not in MS.
418.† 'but to know': a good reading, as it supplies the proper rhyme with 'bestow'.
419.† 'doings'
420.† The MS. here has an entire line not in the folio of 1633,
      "Some to be knowne, and vanity is this".
421.† 'But'.
422.† 'lights'
423 Originally 'praise': but corrected by the Author as in text.
424. 'shed', but corrected by the Author as in text.
425.† 'As'.
426. The misprint 'his' inadvertently given in the MS.
427. 'nor'.
428. 'that' and cf. 338. Though removed by the MS. here, it is found there.
429. 'nature.............restraines'.
430. 'maintane': erased by Author.
431.† 'ground.............magnanimous' : the latter supplies the proper rhyme with 'to vs' : but 'ground' is erased by the Author for text.

	PAGE.	LINE.	
475.	41	2	of Sonnet xxxvi, 'who'.
476.	41	3	'vice'.
477.	41	6	'weakenesse'.
478.	43	6	'cause'.
479.	45	1	'flame'.
480.	45	2	'in downe'.
481.	45	5	'runnes'.
482.	45	9	'While'.
483.	45	10	'is prou'd'.
484.	46	7	'But'.
485.	46	1	of Sonnet xl, 'his'.
486.	47	3	'loue'.
487.	48	8	'that scorns thee, shall'.
488.	50	4	'alone'.
489.	53	19	'starues'.
490.	52	22	'Beauty tyes'.
491.	54	3	'Presence'.
492.	58	15	'And on her backe-side fine silke did bestow'
493.	59	6	'of Sonnet lii, 'the'.
494.	60	18	'the'.
495.	63	3	'conquers by close'.
496.	63	7	'and'.
497.	63	10	'his'.
498.	64	6	of Sonnet lxvi, 'hire'.
499.	64	12	'I'.
500.	64	16	'As harme our'.
501.	65	8	(See opposite in 501.)
502	68	3	'To mourne for thoughts by her worth's ouerthrowne.'
503.	70	6	'enioynèd are to please'.
504.	73	12	'succession'.
505.	74	2	of Sonnet lxiii, 'Art'.
506.	75	6	'ouer'
507.	77	5	'enriching vs'.
508.	78	1	'through'.
509.	78	9	'For'
510.	78	10	'So that man being but mere hypocrisie'.
511.	78	13	'the'
512.	78	21	'strange'.
513.	79	1	'a new-form'd'.
514.	79	3	'What then'.
515.	79	3	'fast'.
516.	79	7	of Sonnet lxvii, 'loueth it selfe'.

432.† 'that for'.
433.† 'nought'.
434. 'Sinnes' : apparently, but doubtful.
435.† 'man's nature' : this clears an obscurity and relieves
  Southey of a misprint, albeit the folio *is* 'man-
  nature'.
436. 'seeks' : but corrected by the Author as in text.
437. 'Vertues'.
438. 'ruin'd' : but erased.
439. 'make'
440.† 'improues'.
441.† 'an'.
442.† 'As'.
443.† 'the'.
444.† 'Lets '.
445. 'mortality'.
446. 'Warres'.
447.† 'not' : this makes all clear, the 'not' coming in before 'then' and so cancels the ['no '] conjecturally
  supplied.
448.† 'to'.
449. Not in MS.
450. 'would'.
451. 'all'.

THE MSS. AT WARWICK CASTLE.

452. This Sonnet is not in the MS.
453 † 'moving it self'.
454.† 'makes'.
455. 'practise' : but corrected by the Auther as in text.
456. So originally spelled 'rann' : but thus, st'rd =
  strayed, written over by Author.
457.† 'loth'd' : a valuable correction.
458. ' In Myra's worth to lyve and dy content' written
  over the text by the Author : but '*stet*' placed
  beside the original.
459. 'play'....'decay'.
460. Originally 'which louers yett must beare' : over it
  'yet all louers' and erased 'this man '.
461. Originally,

Y

PAGE. LINE.

517. 80   8 ' desire'.
518. 80   5 of Sonnet lxviii ' dues'.
519. 80   6 *ibid*, ' that '.
520. 82   5 ' my loue '
521. 84   7 ' womenkinde'.
522. 84   10 ' talke'.
523. 85   8 ' of Sonnet lxxiii, ' makes '
524. 87   7 ' true Loue'.
525. 88   sonnet lxxv.
526. 91   17 ' In those men whom Chance disgraceth '.
527. 91   18 ' As in those she higher placeth '.
528. 93   4 ' dead loue '.
529. 93   14 ' the'.
530. 94   19 ' and '
531. 98   Sonnet lxxviii.
532. 100   6 ' rates '.
533. 100   12 ' Which glow-worme-like, by shining show
             'tis night '.
534. 101   5 ' Tempt man to throw '.
5 5. 101   7 ' To soare, not in his owne, but eagle's
             wings '.
536. 101   8 ' which they see '.
537. 101   9 ' And let fall those strengths which make
             all States great '.
538. 101   10 ' By free truths chang'd to seruile fiatterie '.
539. 101   11 ' men ' : and lir e 12 ' tyrants '.
540. 102   11 ' Which '.
541. 102   1 ' of Sonnet lxxxi, ' Cleare '.
542. 102   7 ' loue all constant grounds '.
543. 103   3 ' An actiue Power '.
544. 103   4 ' For though in Nature's waine these guests
             come forth '.
545. 103   5 ' Can place or stampe make currant ought
             but worth '.
546. 104   4 ' bodies ' . . . . . . ' soules '.
547. 105   13 ' but make '.
548. 106   6 ' and nothing else receiue '.
549. 107   5 ' thoughts '.
550. 107   6 ' worth '.
551. 108   4 ' no '.
552. 108   5 ' ioy '
553. 108   12 ' new '.
554. 109   11 ' Nor '.

" Angelles enioy the heauens inward throne
Star-gazers by vaine prophecies are knowne."

The Author changes in the first line 'throne' into 'quires':
and to correspond with this writes in the second line 'only
multiply desyres'—both as in text. But previously he
had written only to erase these variations, 'but skie vanities are knowne' and 'by vanyty are knowen'.

462. Cala's,' as in the folio, but corrected by us in text.
463. 'falne then': but erased by the Author.
464. 'For' but corrected to 'since' by the Author.
465.† 'fac'st'.
466. 'laid'st'.
467.† 'sweare'.
468. 'Hazard'.
469. 'and'.
470. Originally 'half' but corrected to 'once': and
        'close' written before 'yoke' and 'once' before
        'sworne', removed.
471. Originally 'Thou threatnest that good fellowe wth
        the horne': but altered to the text.
472. 'These'.
473. 'soft': but erased by the Author.
474. 'Thy' (bis): the former 'the' the latter 'thy' in
        folio : our misprint in the latter.
475. 'that': but erased by the Author.
476. 'sinnes': ibid.
477.† 'weakenesses': this removes the somewhat awkward
        trisyllable.
478.† 'case'.
479.† 'fame': probably the preferable word.
480. 'downe in'.
481. 'comes'.
482. 'Yet' and 'Till': but both erased by the Author.
483. 'find it proue': ibid.
484. 'And': ibid.
485. 'the'.
486. 'loues'.
487. 'Myra shall scorne thee and': originally as in text,
        but changed to this.
488. 'only'.
489. 'sterves'.
490.† 'beautie's tyes'.
491. 'Pleasure'. See our note, and cf. four lines back.
        Both in the folio and MS. there seems a lapsus.

PAGE. LINE.

555. 111 6 'Behold the mappe of death-like life exil'd from louely blisse'.

556. 111 10 'And as in shadowes of curst death, a prospect of despaire'.

557. 112 2 'Forlone'.

558. 113 5 of Sonnet lxxxvi, 'goddesse'.

559. 115 2 of Sonnet lxxxviii, 'his'.

560.* 115 11-12 should be placed in a little from the previous lines as in the first stanza.

561. 116 10 'and all these types depart'.

562. 117 4 of Sonnet xci, 'Nature finds both'.

563. 118 4 'princes'.

564. 118 6 'people'.

565. 118 6 'of Sonnet xcii, 'should gouerne it'.

566. 118 9 *ibid*, 'her'.

567. 118 10 *ibid*, 'him'... 'he was'.

568. 118 11-12 *ibid*: 'Yet still a slaue, dimm'd by mist of of a crowne'.
Lest he should see, what riseth, what puls downe'.

569. 119 6 'We thus deciau'd'.

570. 119 3 of Sonnet xciii, 'influence'.

571.* 119 5 'these black', should have been spelled with 'e'.

572. 119 6 'onely in the wealth which Hope findes out.'

573. 120 6 'fooles'.

574. 120 6 of Sonnet xciv, 'scorned it.'.

575. 121 6 'We know'.

576. 121 3 of Sonnet xcv, 'with little'.

577. 121 6 'best'.

578. 122 3 'earthy'

579. 123 8 'and therefore beares'.

580. 123 2 of Sonnet xcvii, 'shall'.

581. 124 9 'while'.

582. 124 13 'Yet'.

583. 124 14 'fiery'.

584. 124 17 'In which confused sphere'.

585. 124 25 'By which true mappe'.

586. 125 2 'of finale humanity'.

587. 125 9 'that'.

588. 127 5 'mine'.

589. 128 10 'doome'.

590. 128 11 'humane'.

492. Originally 'And on her backe fine silke hee did be-
       stowe': 'syde' written in and 'satten did'
       written but erased, with '*stet*' beneath.
493. 'his' : but erased by the Author.
494. 'thee' : so that the MS. comfirms the folio of 1633 :
       but I must still think with Dr. Hannah that this is
       a *lapsus.*
495. 'conquers best by close': originally 'conceaul'd'
       but erased by Author.
496. 'As' : *ibid.*
497. 'her'.
498.† 'heyre' = heir : a valuable reading.
499. Erased.
500. 'As doe harme sences': 'doe' erased and 'our' in-
       serted as in text.
501.† After this the following 24 lines occur in the MS :
           "Shaddowing it with curious art,
            Nettes of sullen golden haire :
            Mars am I, and may not part,
            Till that I be taken there.
            Therewᵗʰ all I heard a sound
            Made of all the partes of loue,
            Wᶜʰ did feirce delight and wound :
            Planetts with such musicke move.
            Those ioyes drewe desires neare
            The heauens blusht, the white shew'd redd,
            Such redd as in skyes appeare
            When Sol parts from Thetis' bedd.
            Then vnto my self I said
            Surely I Apollo am,
            Yonder is the glorious maide
            Which men doe Aurora name,
            Who for pryde she hath in mee
            Blushing forth desire and feare
            While she would haue no man see,
            Makes the world know I am there.
            I resolue to play my sonne,
            And misguide my chariott fire :
            And the skye to overcome,
            And enflame with my desire :
       Line 11 has 'the skyes' but 'the' erased, and line 17
       'ioy' for 'pryde' but the latter written over the other.
       This hitherto unpublished considerable addition is too

PAGE.   LINE.

591.   128   18 ' and '.
592.   130   1 and 3, ' darkenesse' and ' confusednesse '.
593.   130   6 'Which but expressions be of inward
             euils'.
594.   131   3 ' true '.
595.   131   19 ' For '.
596.   131   21 ' That '.
597.   131   24 ' within them is '.
598.   132   7 ' no sooner '.
599.   132   9 ' But straight he '........' to '.
600.   132   15 ' confusions '.
601.   133   4 ' Is there '.
602.   133   15 ' my '.
603.   135   3 ' So man was led '.
604.   135   4 ' hee '.
605.   135   5 ' trust......serpents, who learn'd.
606.   135   6 ' Knew '.
607.   135   7 ' Which crafty '.
608.   135   12 ' nowe it is '.
609.   136   4 ' flesh '.
610.   136   9 ' fleshly '.
611.   136   2 of Sonnet cv., ' make '.
612.   136   6 ' And racketh .'
613.   137   7 of Sonnet cvi., ' beare '.
614.   137   8 ' shippe ' : spelled simply ' ship' in folio.
615.   137   13 ' mind '.
616.   138   6 ' and against both '.
617.   138   7 ' hauing '.
618.   138   7 of Sonnet cvii., ' Hates Reason's '.
619.   139   1 ' all his vices ',
620.   139   2 ' true worth '.
621.   139   4 ' deeper '.
622.   139   3 of Sonnet cviii., 'And makes her on an
             asse '.
623.   139   5 ' Inspire '.
624.   139   14 ' but '.
625.   139   16 ' Makes gilded curbs '.
626.   140   9 ' seedes '.
627.   140   10 ' self-wit '.
628.   140   11 ' inconstant '.
629.   140   14 thence ',
630.   140   16 ' while lawes, oathes ',
631.   141   2 ' Man's faith abus'd '.

important to be left out : but it had been better if the
Author had *not* ' given reynes to his conceipt '.

502. Originally, ' To mourne for those her worths made
woe begone ' : changed to text, having ' by beauty
for ' her worths ' but erased. In the previous line
for ' puts ' the MS. reads ' weares '.

503. So in the MS : but originally those powers to please ' :
erased.

504. ' strangers '.

505.† ' Arts '.

506. ' ever '.

507. ' enriching nature ' : but ' nature ' erased by the
Author.

508.† ' thorough '.

509. ' Where ' : but erased.

510. So in the MS : but ' state ' inserted and erased after
' man ' and ' but ' and ' meere ' and ' being ' written
and erased.

511.† ' their '

512. ' new ' : but erased by the Author.

513. So in the MS : but originally ' againe an image ' :
corrected by Author.

514. ' Then what ' : *ibid.*

515. ' fac't '.

516. ' it selfe loueth ' : but altered as in text by the Author.

517.† ' desires '.

518. ' Dewes '.

519.† ' the '.

520. ' beautie ' : but altered by the Author to text.

521. ' womankinde '.

522.† ' take '.

523. ' make '.

524.† ' true ' : not in the MS.

525.† This forms part of the preceding Sonnet, reading on
thus, from line 7, (page 88) :
How fatall are blinde Cupid's waies,
Where Endimion's poore hope is &c.:
' hope ' an important correction.

526. Originally ' In those whom chance hath disgraced '
but corrected as in text by the Author.

527. Originally ' As in men in her thrones placed ' : *ibid.*

528. Originally ' fell a '.

529. ' his '.

PAGE.	LINE.	
632.	141	3 'stirs up .
633.	142	16 ' vaste. '
634.	143	1—6.
635.	143	11 ' Jesus '.
636.	143	11 ' yeeld '.
637.	159	12 In folio ' Mate .
638.	162	4 ' sillinesse '.
639.	162	8 ' that '.
640.	163	15 ' mischiefe '.
641.	165	4 ' ye '.
642.	167	2 ' cast ' in folio.
643.	168	12 'pittie' in folio.
644.	168	19 ' Euer ' and line 20 ' scope '.
645.	169	13 ' With '.
646.	170	23 ' forget'.
647.	171	19 ' Respect '.
648.	176	16 ' on '.
649.	181	5 ' chance '.
650.	181	9 ' Our'.
651.	184	5 ' on '.
652.	185	17 ' are '.
653.	189	12 ' these '.
654.	197	5 ' way '.
655.	200	14 'for the instrument '.
656.	201	16 ' Hala '........
657.	202	5 Alaham......
658.	213	16 ' princes '.
659.	213	22 ' showe'.
660.	214	3 ' [The] harsh spirit hates them that do not hate '.
661.	215	4 ' speake '.
662.	221	7 ' foyle '.
663.	222	19 ' which '
664.	222	22 ' threed '
665.	224	18 ' giue'.
666.	227	22 ' temptations ' : and so p 239, line 12, ' for tunes ' is ' fortune ' : p 242, line 12, ' besides ' is ' beside' : p 243, ' suspects ' is ' suspect ' in the MS. So others not worth-while recording.
667.	232	6 ' the '.
668.	234	13 ' feare or '.
669.	243	9 ' suspects '.
670.	251	13 ' crests '.

530. Not in the MS : and we have accepted the removal of ' and '.

531. See Introductory Note prefixed to these various read-ings from the MSS. for details on this Sonnet which is interlined and changed in a remarkable way.

532.† ' rate '.

533. This vivid line in the MS has undergone various changes : originally it runs, ' Where shyne they doe by hiding of the light ' : another interlined version is 'And lyke glowe worms shyne more bright to shew 'tis night ' with separate words filled in and erased so as to be illegible. Then comes our text.

534. ' Make man first throwe' : but changed to text by the Author.

535. Originally 'To sore the higher vpp on [illegible] wings' : ' princes ' written over the illegible word. All save ' on ' for 'in' changed to our text by Author.

536. Originally *sic* : but ' of supremacie ' placed above, only to be erased and '*stet*' placed against the former

537. Originally ' Let fall those strengths which make the 'publique great ' : ' those ' changed to ' this strength ' : ' make ' to ' should' ' 'publique' to ' monarchs' : but all erased for the text.

538. Originally ' Transforming truth and right to flatterie ' a great number of words written in and erased : and the text substituted in the end.

539. ' they ', ' princes' : erased and as in text. Below—as shewn in Facsimile is written 'this Song stands' a line having been drawn across the whole. See, our Introductory Note to this Description of the MSS.

540. ' And ' : but erased.

541. ' Thyne ' : erased.

542. Originally ' prayse sadd reall grounds' : but erased for text.

543. ' As pow'r supreame ' : *ibid.*

544. Originally ' For as in Nature's wealth they are brought forth ' and again ' power brings them forth ' and other erased words : *ibid.*

z

	PAGE.	LINE.	
671.	252	8	'phantom'd'.
672.	252	11	'miracle'.
673.	256	11	'to[o]'.
674.	256	14	'my'.
675.*	266	8	'labyrinth'.
676.	267	17	'and'.
677.	269	1	'silly'.
678.*	270	19	'the billowes'.
679.	272	12	'eke'.
680.	281	4	'with'.
681.	284	13	'rod'.
682.	295		Speakers' Names.
683.	297	14.	
684.	298	1	'broken'.
685.	298	11	'would desire to beare':
686.	298	12	'd squiet.
687.	298	14 and 2 0.	
688.	299	6	'Time's present'.
689.	300	3	'guilt'. See Note Vol. III. p 468, No. 52: but the MS. gives 'good': and so the MS. reads 'least' as in Note No. 54 *ibid.*
690.	302	2	'for me'.
691.	303	17	'oft'.
692.	303	18	'strong'.
693.	304	15	'to'
694.*	308	23	'Vpon'.
695	310	7	'which'.
696.	310	17	'Empire'.
697.	313	9	's'.
698.	323	9	'doubts'.
699.	324	10	'humor'.
700.	327	16	'estates'.
701.	328	15	'danger'.
702.	329	4	'keies'.
703.	332	17	'home'.
704.	334	14	'by hate'.
705.	337	17	'spites'.
706.	339	14	'this.
707.	344	13	'decided'.
708.	346	21	'and'.
709.	347	9	'your'.
710.	361	5	'mother's'.
711.*	363	12	'and'.

545. Originally 'Soe be they currant but in supreame worth' : *ibid.*
546. Order inadvertently reversed : but corrected by Author.
547. 'they be' but erased.
548 Originally 'and to her passion cleave' and again 'her darke decrees receave' : but erased by text.
549.† 'hopes' perhaps preferable.
550.† I am unexpectedly confirmed in my rejection of the emendation 'wrath' made in the text, in the "Courtly Poets", by the MS. which reads plainly 'worth'. See our foot-note, page 107.
551. 'yett'.
552. 'ioyes'.
553. 'the' : but erased by text.
554 † 'Now'.
555. Originally 'Behold the mapp of heavy life..........
 wonted' : for behold' is written 'then see' : but again erased and the text given.
556. Originally, 'And in the shadowes of my death, my prospect my despaire : altered to our text.
557.† 'forlorne'.
558. 'true goddesse', but 'true' erased.
559. 'this'.
560. So in MS. also.
561. Originally 'and all the rest' and 'these workes' : but changed to text.
562. 'Nature yet finds honour'.
563. 'powers' : but changed for text by the Author.
564. 'men may' : *ibid.*
565. 'giues life to it' : *ibid.*
566. 'this' : *ibid.*
567. 'vs'....'wee were' : *ibid.*
568.† 'These lines must have proved unusually troublesome to the Author, as they are confusingly interlineated. Originally they run,
 'Yet still but slaues rais'd by a tyrant crowne
 That we may hardlie see what pulls it downe'.
Over the first line is written as in our text : the second line, with words written and erased and re-written, seems to have been left a-while thus : 'Least he should seeke to see what pulls it downe' and again 'what reyseth, what pulls it downe' and finally as in text.

	PAGE.	LINE.	
712.	366	1	' ell '
713.	366	3	' in '
714.	375	14	' are '
715	381	8	' diuills '.
716.	384	13	' rebellion '
717.	384	18	' and '.
718.	388	22	' fashion '
719.	391	6	' the '.
720.*	394	22	' that '.
721.	399	5	' rumor '.
722.	403	21 and 25	' gods ' and ' the gods '.
723.	404	1	' Furies runne '.
724.	406	8	' strake '.
725.*	410	4	' gods make '......' their '.
726.	415	3	' dissolution '·
727.	416		Chorvs Sarcedotvm.

569. ' When thus deceau'd ' : but chang'd to our text by the Author, save that ' deceau'd ' is in the MS. properly spelled.

570. ' secret power ' : but erased by Author for our text.

571. ' hidden ' : *ibid*.

572. More prosaically this line ran originally, ' Rich but in wealth wch they hope to finde out ' : *ibid*.

573. ' beasts ' : *ibid*.

574. 'laugh at it ' : *ibid*.

575. ' Hee knowes '.

576. ' he hauinge ' : corrected as in text by Author.

577. ' first ' : *ibid* : lines 5-6 written in old-age handwriting.

578.† ' each ' a good correction.

579. ' and so beares image of ' : but the text returned to by the Author and ' *stet* ' written under it.

580. ' may ' : but as in text by the Author.

581. ' Now ' : *ibid*.

582. ' But '.

583. ' spetious '.

584. ' Now in this spheare confused ' : but as in text by the Author.

585. ' Yet ' written and erased.

586. ' of our humanitie ' and ' his humanitie ' and ' evill ' or ? ' still free '.

587. ' which ' : but erased.

588. ' my '.

589.† ' downe ' : a valuable correction.

590.† My emendation is again confirmed by the MS. here.

591. ' not : and so in corresponding of next stanza : but inasmuch as the MS. has scraped out ' not ' in the previous and written in, ' and ', it seems clear the thing has been inadvertently omitted in the other two places.

592. ' darkenesses ' and ' confusednesses '.

593. ' Originally, ' Expressions, as I said, of inward evilles' : altered to our text by the Author.

594. ' brave '.

595. ' Now ' : erased by Author.

596. ' Where ' : *ibid*.

597. ' within them sure is feare and art ' : *ibid*.

598.† ' when hee had '.

599.† ' Hee straightwais......for ' ' for ' altered to ' to '.

600.† ' remorses '.

601.† 'Yett is there'.
602. 'the': altered by Author to our text.
603. 'Soe were wee for'ct': *ibid.*
604.† 'man'·
605. 'creditt ... soules, wch haue': partially erased.
606. 'Knowne'.
607. 'And by this': erased by the Author.
608. 'nowe find': *ibid.*
609. 'selfe': *ibid.*
610. 'humane': *ibid.*
611. 'makes'.
612. 'And so are those harts' and again 'and stores vpp':
       changed to our text by the Author.
613. 'blowe'.
614. 'shape': this is an evident *lapsus.*
615. 'hartes': no rhyme with 'wind' and therefore a
       lapsus.
616. Originally 'And so no strength but in it selfe alone'
       changed to our text, but 'therefore' written and
       erased for 'against'.
617. 'wch hathe': erased by the Author.
618. 'Hateth All [word illegible]: *ibid.*
619. 'guiltinesse to': *ibid.*
620. 'goodnes': *ibid.*
621. 'deep'.
622. 'And on an asse, in triumph makes her': *ibid.*
623. 'Inspires': next line inserted in old-age handwriting.
624. 'for': erased by the Author.
625. 'Make power's guilded curbes': *ibid.*
626. 'things': *ibid.*
627.† 'selfe-nesse': *ibid.*
628.† 'vnconstant'.
629. 'soe': altered by Author to text.
630. 'lawes and oathes', the 'for' being prefixed later.
631. 'Which faith abus'd' and in a later hand 'That
       vision falyd': changed to our text.
632. 'Shee stirs fame'.
633. 'Not in MS.
634. 'Not in the M.S.
635. 'Iesu'.
636. 'give'.
637.† 'Hate'. This clears up a hopelessly obscure line,
       and I have gladly accepted it.

628. Spelled 'seelinesse'.
639. 'whuch'.
640. 'mischiefes'.
641. 'you'.
642.† 'rust': a valuable correction which gives a rhyme
　　　with 'trust' and a clear meaning: therefore ac-
　　　cepted.
643.† 'pettie': *ibid*
944.† 'Euen'....'scopes': these adopted.
645.† 'which'.
646. 'forgatte'.
647.† 'Respects'.
648. 'in'.
649.† 'change'.
650. 'The': but erased by Author.
651. 'in'.
652. 'art'.
653. 'this'.
654.† 'wayes'.
655.† 'for instruments'.
656. Given to Alaham in MS.
657.† Belongs to Alaham by No. 656 : and so confirms our
　　　emendation.
658.† *Sic* and thus confirms our emendation.
659.† 'showes'.
660.† 'Harsh spirit hates them that do not hate with it' :
　　　which makes all clear.
661. 'speaks'.
662. Originally 'fayle' : altered to 'foyle'.
663. 'that' : erased.
664 'thinge': *ibid*.
665.† 'gaue'.
666.† 'temptation'.
667.† 'my'.
668. 'feare nor': and so 'nor' for 'or' elsewhere, but
　　　not noted.
669.† 'suspect'.
670.† 'crustes' : Query = crusts or plaster, the reference
　　　being to the well-known allusion (albeit here
　　　anachronistic) to the sculptor that carved his own
　　　name on the living rock, his lord's on the mere
　　　coating or crust. This being so makes Pharos
　　　not = Pharoahs but = the light-house or pharos.

671. 'phantasm'd' : 'phantome' in pencil.
672. ' miracle '.
673† ' too ' : and so confirms our emendation : and so in last line ' to ' should have been ' too '.
674. Not in MS.
675. 'labyrinthes '
676.† ' woe ' : a valuable correction of the folio.
677. Spelled ' seelie ' : and so elsewhere. It may be noted that ' yeeld ' is spelled ' yeld ' in the MS. : and in other forms.
678. ' those '.
679. Not in MS. : deeds and seeds. spelled with ' es '.
680. ' in '.
681. ' rue ' : this supplies a rhyme with ' two ', but the meaning is obscured. Qy = rule ?
682. The MS. adds ' Preist '.
683. Not in the MS
684. ' broke '.
685. ' worldes desires to beare ' :
686. ' desire '.
687. Not in the MS.
688. See Note in Vol. III, No. 47. After all the MS. corrects both, by reading ' Time present's children'. Cf. Index of words under ' Time ', and by a re-print leaf I have adopted the MS reading.
689. None of these preferable.
690. The MS furnishes this correction of a perplexing reading in the folio and quarto viz., ' forme '. The leaf has been re-printed in order to give it.
691. ' often '.
692. ' like ' : but erased.
693. ' by '.
694. ' Unto'.
695. ' what '.
696. ' Empires '.
697. ' his '.
698. ' doubt ':
699. ' honor ' : see Vol III, Note 91, p 471 : the MS confirms ' honor '.
700. ' estate '.
701. ' dangers'.
702. ' wayes ' : see Vol III, Note 107, p 472 : the MS confirms ' keies ' as the reading ? and so in Note 110 *ibid*, reads ' worlds repine '.

703.† 'honie': this word is so good that I have had this leaf also re-printed in order to introduce it.

704. See Vol. III, Note No. 132, p 474: the MS. reads 'and': so in Note 133, 'the' not ·thy': Note 139, 'might' not 'night': Note 145, 'itselfe' not 'herselfe': Note 147, 'presumes vncall'd': not · vncalled presumes': Note 155, 'mistes' not 'spites': Note 163, 'the' not 'this': the MS. does not seem in these preferable to the printed text.

705. 'mistes'.

706. 'the'.

707†. 'derided': a good reading.

708. 'all'.

709† .'our': a good reading.

710. 'woman's'. See Vol· III. Note 198, p 483.

711. 'or'.

712.† 'elfe': perhaps a preferable reading.

713. 'of'.

714. 'be'.

715. 'evill's': the folio reads thus also, but I silently corrected the evident misprint and *lapsus*.

716. 'rebellious': See Vol. III. Note 265, p 489.

717. Not in MS. But see Vol. III, Note 254, p 489.

718. 'fashion'.

719. Not in MS.

720. 'which'.

721. 'rumors'. See Vol. III. Note 265, p 489.

722. 'God' and 'That God'. See Vol. III. Note 306, p 492.

723. 'Furie runnes': probably this is the correct reading

724. 'stroke'.

725. 'God makes'......his': See Vol. III. Note 326, p 494.

726. 'desolation'. See Vol. III. Note 341, p 495.

727. Not in the MS.

Indices.

I. INDEX OF THINGS AND THOUGHTS = SUBJECTS.

The principle acted upon in the preparation of this portion of the Indices, was, as before, to select *things* and *thoughts*, rather than mere *words*. I have aimed to include the two former under headings most likely to suggest themselves, and with as varied and minute distribution as possible. I have also sought to express each as completely as might be, usually by a single word. But the consulter of these Indices is reminded that an Index differs from a Concordance. G.

A.

Abbies, i. 200.

A B C, ii. 97.

Absence, iii. 405.

Abuse and use, i. 97, 249.

Abuse, i, 175.

Act, divine thought an, iii. 328.

Actions, i. 64, 107; noble, i. 214; ii. 234.

Activeness, i. 20.

Accusations excusing treason, iii. 167-168.

Addition to 'Cælica', iv. 473 (No. 541.)

Additional MSS., [B. Museum] I. xxxii, lv, lxvi, xci

Advantage, i 106, 162.

'Advertisement' of 'Remains' I. 3-4.

Adversity, i. 215.

Advocates, no, i. 104.

Affection, iii. 206, 209.

Affections, blind, i. 244; supplanted, ii. 75; brittle, iii. 353.

Affinity, i. 16.

Affliction, i. 274; iii. 413.

Age, i. 47, 86: old, ii. 82; iii. 130, 308, 309: golden, iii. 51: iv. 236: brazen, iii, 52, iv. 238: guilt, iii. 52; iv. 355-6—a valuable correction.

Agonies, iii. 267.

Agrarian laws, ii. 92.

Aid, i. 187.

Air, infected, i. 48, muddy, 203; spirits, iii. 165.

Alaham, tragedy of, iii. 155, 288; Langbaine on, ii, 156; speakers on, iii. 157.

Atheists, iii. 35, 159.

Alchymie, ii. 21.
Alcoran, i. 79.
All, for one, i. 28,
Alliance, i. 163,
Ambassadors, i. 163.
Ambition, i. 59, 179, 184, 188, 189 : iii. 216 : female, 196 : base, iii. 413.
Anarchy, i. 14, 35, 127, 233 : iii. 388,
Anchorites, i. 215.
Angels, i. 240 ; evil, iii. 339, 359 ; fall of, iii. 389.
Anger, i. 109.
Anglo-Poetica, I. x.
Antiquity, i. 85.
Aphorisms, i. 99.
Apostles, i. 260, 265.
Apostrophe, i. 231 ; ii. 26, 33, 87, 99 ; iii. 18, 276.
Applause, i., 177.
Arcadia, I. xx.
Archers, iii. 25.
Arguments, ii. 38.
Aristocracy, i. 206 *et seqq*, 214, 316.
Arithmetic, ii., 50
Ark, i. 164, 271, 277.
Arm and exercise in peace, i. 190, 198.
Armada, I. xxxi, lii : iv. 205.
Armies-land, i. 148.
Armor, i. 189.
Arms in Trinity oriel-window, I, xxix; of the Church, i. 80, 83.
Art and Arts, i. 5, 6, 22, 51, 63, 121, 134, 135, 136, 140, 141, 156, 169, 185, 241, 249, 275 : ii. 13, 15, 19, 21, 32, 35, 44, 52, 57, 105.
Artisans, i. 140.
Ashes, i. 202.

Aspire, aspirers, i. 29, 61 : iii, 200, 207, 409.
Assaults, iv. 259.
Assemblies, i. 108 (See ' *Parliament* ').
Astrologer, iii. 222.
Astronomy, ii. 50.
Audits, i 187.
Augurs, ii. 85 ; iii. 120.
Auld-lang--syne, ii. 142.
Authority and care, i. 8, absolute, i. 15, 131, webs. of i. 22, audits of, i. 52. lights of, i. 55, beauty of, i. 62; shadows of, i. 166 : ii 44 : not by blood, iii, 184, 379.
Authors, one or two, ii. 36.
Avarice, i. 82, 100, 103.
Awe, i. 116, 184, 248.
Axe, iii. 231, 315, 479 (note 72).

B.

Babels, ii. 61.
Backsliding,i. 263.
Ballance, of power &c., i. 71, 77, 184, 192 : iv. 62, 90, 102.
Banishment, i. 213.
Bankrupts, ii. 90.
Banners, i. 188.
Baptism, ii. 39.
Bar, i. 76.
Barbarism, i. 170, 223.
Barons, i. 126.
Barter, i. 142.
Baseness, i 83, 84.
Basshas, disgraced iii. 168 *et seqq.*
Battles-sea, i. 204.
Beacons, i. 162.
Beasts, i. 17 : birds and, i.

49, 69 : wild and tame, i. 128, 182, 183 : vertues of ii. 105. iii. 457.

Beauty, iii. 11, 12, 15 16 ; faded, iii 16 ; gentle, 22, 34, 43, 53,84.

Bee, i. 118.

Better and betters, i. 122 ; ii 58.

'Beseech', i. 48.

Bible, i. 80 : ii. 23.

Biographia Brittannica, (17 57) i xii-xiii, xix. xxxviii, xxxix,lvii,lxxii-iii,lxxxiii. -iv, lxxxvi, xcv-ix : iii. 496, (note 352.)

Birth, i. 17 : second, i. 250 ; base, iii. 283, 436.

Bishops, married, i. 87.

Blanks, i. 21.

Blind, iii. 38, 255, 258, 268.

Blood, i. 17 : letting, i. 146.

Boats, i. 168.

Bodleian Library, I. xvii.

Body, ii. 42 : tomb to soul, ii. 62.

Bondage, i. 10, 81 : iii. 420.

Books, i. 228, 261 : ii. 20, 35 : iii. 77, 317.

Bought, worth i. 124.

Bounds, i. 193.

Boy and boys, iii. 73.

Brass, i. 11.

Brazen, age. iv. 238.

Brave men, iii. 208.

Bridges, i. 168.

British Bibliographer, i. xci.

British Museum, I. xvii.

Broils-home, i. 189.

Broken, wayes iii. 437.

Buck, sent to Mrs. Hickes, i. lix-lx.

Buildings, ii 52.

Bullion, i. 122, 140, 14,2 146, 162 : ii. 53.

Burroughs, i. 109.

C

Calculation, i. 6,7.

Calendar of State Papers iv. 316 et seqq.

Camel, i. 259.

Camp, iii. 307, 308.

Cancelled pages, I. xii-xiii, xcvii-viii.

Capitals, i. xi.

Care, and authority i. 8, 41, 105.

Cathedrals, i. 115 ; chairs of, i. 270.

Cautions, against weak extremities, i. 44-57, 167.

Celibacy, i. 87

Censure, i. 88 ; (See Index of Words) ; Church, ii. 41.

Chain, i. 239 ; eternall, ii. 55.

Chaos, second, i. 253.

Chance, i. 17, 19, 20, 40, 51, 85, 107,176, 178, 181, 202, 229, 232, 233, 253 ; ii. 29. iii, 14-15, 25, 179,362,363.

Charge, i. 166.

Child and nurse, iii. 70.

Children, i. 65, 166 ; God's, ii. 31, 204 ; iii. 242, 337, 338, 446, 447.

Choice, happy, i. 50 ; free, i. 110, 152, 225.

Chorus, of good spirits, iii. 188-195 ; of people, iii. 270 et seqq ; of converts to Mahometisme, iii. 389 et seqq.

Chosen, i. 263.

Christian and Turk, i. 204 ; Churches, i. 204.

Christians, divisions of, ii. 127.

Church, i. 56, 74, 87, 91, 176, 195, 198 ; outward, i. 260, 276 ; invisible, i. 260, 261 ; both, i. 268 ; in England, i. 271 ; ii. 36 ; iii. 174-175 ; and State, iii. 390, 392, 393.

Cinthia, a song of, ii. 137-139 ; another, ii. 139-140.

Circles, iii. 347.

Citizens, i. 182.

Clergy, age of, i. 87 ; papal, i. 199.

Clime, i. 157 ; forrain, i. 190.

Cloister, i. 164.

Cloth, i. 143.

Cloud, pillar of, i. 22 ; clouds, i. 57, 125.

Cob-webs, law's, i. 8, of wit, i. 172 ; Art's, ii. 44, contradiction's, ii. 59.

Cockatrice, i. 62 ; iii. 384.

Coin, i. 163, 176.

Collation of MSS. iv. 343 et seqq.

Colonies, i. 178, 180, 181 ; iii. 314.

Colour, i. 192.

' Come again ', iii. 71.

Comets, i. 58 ; iii. 313.

Comitia, i. 230.

Commanded, more than man can do, i. 265.

Commerce, of, i. 132-153 ; of delight, i. 142, 176.

Committee, what, iv. 315.

Commonwealth, i. 183.

Comparison, iii. 400.

Complaint, i. 77.

Comprehend, iii. 312.

Concealment, iii. 439, 440.

Conceit, iii. 220.

Conclave, i. 230.

Condemnation, i. 243.

Conditioned, in conception of God, i. 241, 272, 273.

Confession, i, 196 ; iii. 217, 220.

Confusion, i. 46, 56, 75.

Confusions, i. 229, 233 ; iii, 444.

Conquest, i. 115, 178, 179.

Conquests-after, i. 219.

Conscience, i. 18, 21, 79, 83, 91, 93, 107, 110, 119, 193, 194 ; freedom (spurious), i. 197, 243, 244, 258 ; ii. 40, 82 ; iii. 127, 281 ; spies of, iv. 240.

Consent, i. 115 ; of Nations, i. 242.

Conspiracy, iii. 334 : conspire, iii. 374.

Constraint, i. 77, 177.

Consuls, i. 188, 209, 229 ;

Consummation, i. 156.

Contemplative, i. 173.

Contempt, of laws, i. 40, 129 ; iii. 376.

Content, i. 144 ; iii. 353.

Contraries, iii. 370.

Conventions, i. 108 (See Parliament).

Corruption, i. 61, 71, 243, 250 ; ii. 77 ; iii 227.

Cottage, guarded, ii. 41.

Councils, monarchal, i. 23, 55 ; held, i. 176 ; divine, i. 266.

Counsellors, iii. 317.

Counsels, ii. 38.

Courses, i. 228.
Course-set, i. 178.
Courage, i. 188 ; ii. 106. iii. 36.
Courts, i. 6, 55, 105.
Coward-soule, iii. 164.
Craft. i. 11, 12, 35, 106, 109, 139, 162, 245.
Crafty not wise, ii. 53.
Craven, a wretch, iii. 263.
Creation, i. 85, 126, 127, 144, 166, 253, 254, 267.
Credit, i. 140, 141.
Creeds, i. 58.
Crooked, i. 72.
Crowns, i. 46, 55, 73, 114, 115, 154, 186; rights, i. 187, ambition after, iii. 173 ; all in all, iii. 425.
Crudity, i. 118.
Cruelty, iii 232, 264 *et segg.*
Crusades, ii. 110.
Cuckoes, i. 139.
Cures, i. 47.
Curse, ii. 24 : iii, 270.
Curtesie, i. 126.
Curtizan, ii. 35.
Custome, i. 27, 143, 145, 157, 251.

D.

Damn, i. 199.
Darkness-self, i. 45 ; Egyptian, ii. 6 ; iii. 140; gulph of, iii. 428.
Dead, men, iii. 329, 449.
Deafness, i. 242.
Death, iii. 445, 446, 462.
Decay, i. 144-145.
Deceit, i. 12, 68, 81, 165; ii. 7.
Decorum, i. 200.

Dedicatory-epistle to Wright and Clark, I. iii-v ; a good-mannered custom, I. iii.
Deeds, not words, iii. 360 ; ill, iii. 384, 412
Defection, i. 269.
Defence, i. 186.
Deformity, i. 51.
Degree, i. 121, 176.
Deitie, i. 187, 231.
Delays, law's, i. 103 ; iii. 332, 341.
Delicacy, i. 204.
Delights, ii. 32 ; iii. 50 ; and disasters, iii. 360,
Deliverance, iii. 127.
Demagogues, i. 226.
Democracy, i. 215, 216 *et seqq* ; 218, 219, 235, 226; 228.
Demonstration, ii. 15.
Deposing, i. 194.
Depths, of despair, iii. 128.
Descending, meek, i. 6.
Descent, i. 67, 84 ; national, i. 178.
Description of the Manuscripts at Warwick Castle, iv. 331,*et seqq.*
Desire, i. 20. 50 ; iii. 19, 450, iv. 243 : mad, iii. 26, 410, 459.
Desmesnes, i. 158, 159, 160, 225.
Desolation, i. 278; iii. 157.
Despair, i. 257 ; iii. 372.
Destiny, iii. 45.
Devill, ii. 54, 113, 114; iv. 248.
Devotion, ii. 29.
Dew, i. 29.
Dialogue, of good and evil sports,

Dice, i. 69.
Dictator. i. 215.
Diet i. 157.
Dig, i. 160.
Dignity, solitary regal, iii. 297 ; attendance adds, iii. 305.
Discipline, i. 13, 88, 116, 175, 190, 197, 203 ; ii. 39, 41.
Discontent, i. 13, 70, 130, 202.
Discords, i. 121, 204.
Disease, i 23, 44, 47, 48, 57, 202, 222, 225.
Disgrace, and grace, i. 8, 167.
Dishonour, i. 162.
Disorder, i. 158.
Disprayse of a courtly life, iv. 227-8.
Disproportion, ii. 70.
Dissentions, i. 72. 131.
Distinction, i. 19.
Distraction, iii. 195, 213, 301.
Distributing, i. 144.
Divinity-school, i. 261.
Division, i. 12, 92, 134 ; iv. 238.
Divorce, death only, iv. 234.
Doctrine, i 56.
Doctrine, i. 200.
Do, ii. 59.
' Dog fair' = lady-love, iii. 10
Doing, i. 151, 175, 260 : ill, ii. 77.
Dotage, iii. 354 ; iv. 243.
Doubt, i. 241 ; iii. 164, 174, 206, 301, 420.
Dove, sacred, i. 25.
Downe, iii. 358, 359.

Downfalls, i. 41.
Dreams, i. 174 ; of Time, i. 221.
Drone, i. 136, 153.
Dropsy, iii. 319, 333.
Duels, i. 130, 131 ; iv. 268.
Duty and duties, i. 74, 99, 93, 222 ; ii. 58 ; iii. 125, 446.

E,

Earth, the, i. 133, 154 ; perishing ii. 120, 121, ; foolish, ii. 22-23 ; self-derived suffering, iii. 114.
Echo, ii. 49, 100
Editing, what it costs, I. iii-iv ; integrity in, I. x.
Education, i. 249.
Elder-born, iii. 181 ; second to, iii. 181.
Elect, i. 273, 276
Election, i. 17, 225, 253, 254, 258.
Elements, i. 154, 184.
Elephants, i. 173.
Eloquence, ii. 47 ; iii. 120.
Emperors and empire, i. 113, 182, 183, 187, 225 ; rise and fall, ii. 117.
Emploiment, i. 9.
Emulation, i. 155.
Endowments, i. 83.
Ends and means, iii. 175.
Enemies, i. 182.
Enjoying, mutual, iv. 239.
Envy, i. 11.
Epitaph on and by Lord Brooke, correctly interpreted, I. lxxxix, ; epitaph-libel, I. xcix-c.

Equal, free, i. 42; stil'd, i. 217; equals, i. 106, 122.

Equality, i. 16, 128, 141, 161, 177.

Equivocation, i. 65, 161.

Error, i. 7, 23, 28, 35, 42, 63, 98, 164, 165, 186, 256; ii. 37, 38, 41, 56, 59, 62, 99

Essay on Poetry of Lord Brooke, I. xvi; II, x-xci; characterised, v-vi; mindful of material more than workmanship, vi; Milton-Philipps on, vi; Mrs. Cooper on, *ibid*; persistence of study needed, vii; 'margent-notes' viii; Henry More, viii-ix; shallow misjudgments, by Hallam,&c., x-xiii; the critic's incapacity, xi-xiv; lucidity not all, xiv-xv, yet cloudiness of words not largeness of thought, xiv; negligence of form *v* thought xv; over-regard to form, xv-xvi; tragedies of Alaham and Mustapha, and Antonie and Cleopatra, xv-xvi; faults to be overlooked, xvi; Lamb, xvi-xvii; SirWilliam Hamilton, xvii-xviii; the mass of his thought, xviii-xxvi; quotations, *ibid*; index of subjects, xix; widest subjects, xix; 'metaphysical school', xix-xx; selah, xx; man's destiny, xxi-xxii; thraldom, xxii; ' body a tomb'. xxiv; modern poets, xxv-xxvi;

quantity of thought, xxvi; the wisdom and nobleness of his opinions, xxvi-xxxiv; restless thinkers, spider and bee, xxvi; transparent Christianliness, xxvii; greatness must rest on goodness, quotations, xxvii *et seqq*; Sidney, xxxi; sympathies with 'the people', xxxi; progress, xxxi; the Puritans, xxxi-ii; manly indignation, xxxii-xxxiii; falseness and baseness, xxxiii; patriot, xxxiii; xxxiv; vitality of counsels, xxxiv-lviii; permanent worth, xxxiv; Law, with quotations, xxxv *et seqq*; monarchs, with quotations, xxxviii *et seqq*; church-authorities, with quotations, xl *et seqq*; a Christian man, xliii; priest-craft, xliii-xliv; quotations, xliv *et seqq*; political verdicts, with quotations, xlvii *et seqq*; duels xlvii-xlviii; free-trade, xlviii-xlix; aphoristic truths, numerous quotations, xlix *et seqq*; *the realness of his poetic gift*, lviii-xci; depth and delicacy, lviii; " Cælica ", with quotations, lix *et seqq*; Farr, mistakes of, lxviii; pointed sayings, with quotations: Dr. Hannah on Brooke and Dyer, lxxi *et seqq*; Brooke and Spenser, lxxiii; Coleridge, odd misquotation of, lxxiv ; Shakespearean bits, lxxvii *et seqq* ; lxxxiv, *et seqq* ; Miltonic bits, lxxxvii *et seqq* ; fine modesty, xc ; quotation from Henry Ellison, xc-xci.

Essence, i. 72.

Eternal, Breast. ii. 55-56.

Eternity, i. 77 ; iii. 178, 365 *et seqq.*

Eunuchs, iii. 402-3.

Everlasting, ground, i. 17.

Evil, i. 162, 264 ; deeds and name, iii. 353 ; keep from iv. 236.

Exactions, i. 225.

Example, i. 239 ; iii. 165, 180 : examples-throne, i. 106, 181.

Excesse, i 20, 29, 33, 34, 77, 157, 161, 166, 186, 200, 222, 224, 232 ; ii. 31 ; iii. 208-9, 319, 396.

Exchange, i. 138, 141, 150, 163 ; ii. 104.

Exchequers, i. 55.

Execution, by fire, iii. 277, *et seqq.*

Exilde, iv. 357 (No. 220) : a good reading.

Expeditions, iv. 202.

Expense, i. 156, 165, 167.

Extreames, iii. 356.

Extremities, cautions against weak, i. 44-57, 75, 231.

Eyes, iii. 12, 13, 17, 21, 22 23, 32, 40, 48, 412.

F.

Fables, 160, 1 1, 227.

Facsimiles of Lord Brooke's handwriting, I. xvii ; iv. xi.

Faction, i. 54, 55, 69, 70, 85 127, 165, 195, 211, 214 iii. 34.

Faith, i. 64, 65, 107 ; loss of, i. 139 ; false, i. 196 ; Christian, i. 197, 253, 257, 262, 265, 271, 273, 277 ; ii. 37, 97 ; iii. 136.

Fall, man's, ii. 19, 25, 112.

Fall, rise and, i. 42, 43 ; of princes, i. 197.

Fallen, man, i. 240-1, 252 ; iii. 134.

False lights, i. 106.

Fame, i. 51, 52, 62, 117, 123 ; 173, 179 ; ii. 70 ; and Honour, inquisition of, ii. 65-100 ; overthrown, evil of, ii. 76 *et seqq* ; source of, ii. 84 ; true, ii. 94 ; definition of, ii. 95, 96 ; worship of, is idolatry, ii. 96 ; what, iii. 119, 137-138, 214-215.

Familiar things, iii. 61.

Fancy, ii. 8.

Far off, i. 183.

Fate, i. 38, 44, 45, 46, 188, = iv. 357 No. 246, 189, 222 ; ii. 75, 115, 360, 387,

Father, a royal, wretched, iii 255 ; asking of his son, iii. 305 *et seqq.*

Favor, i. 54, 120.

Favors, princes, iii. 170.

Fear and hope, i. 22, 38, 126, 184, 196, 245, 246, 248, 278 ; iii. 219 ; iv. 264.

Fenns, i. 160.

Fence, i. 142.

Fees, i. 116.

Fence, i. 142.
Feud, i. 131.
Fever, i. 26.
Fine-money, i. 125.
Finite, infinite, i. 52; ii. 37;
man's faculties, iii. 382.
Fire, common, i. 45, 278 ; a
good servant, ii. 93; en-
chaunted, iii. 433.
Flattery, i. 10 ; iii. 213.
Fleece, golden, i. 137.
Flesh and blood, i. 250, 251,
263, 276 ; iii. 125.
Flight, ii. 383.
Flock, little, i. 276.
Flowers, of Time, iii. 252.
Folio of 1633, title-page of,
ii. 3.
Fooles, ii. 20, 22.
Force, i. 35, 64, 106, 110,
176, 177; iii. 386.
Forecastings, iii. 426-7.
Forgiving, i. 253.
Form, i. 41, 56, 88, 269.
Forms, i. 169.
Fortifications, i. 189.
Fortune, i. 122, 230.
Foundation, i. 233 ; ii. 61.
Frailty, i. 13, 24, 38, 56, 91,
106.
France, iv. 359 (No. 283):
important correction.
Fraud, i. 140.
Freedom, i. 23, 41, 75.
Freedoms, i. 228.
Free-justice, i, 125.
Friends, many, iii. 137-8.
Friendship, fearful, iii. 232.
Frugality, i. 157, 166.
Fuel, i. 226.
Funeral, iii. 245-6.

Furies, chorus of, iii. 221-
227.
Fury, iii. 204, 408, 452.

G

Gages, i. 145, 151.
Gain, i. 9, 136.
Gains, i. 181.
Geometrie, ii. 18, 19, 50.
Giants and pygmies, i. 11.
Gives, forgives, i. 15.
Glass, iii. 47 ; iii. 115.
Glass-looking, iii. 323.
Glories, borrow'd, i. 107 ;
cheap, i. 109, 186.
Glory, ii. 6, 69, 70, 71, 76,
81 : iii. 207, 243, 244.
Glow-wormes, iii. 100.
God variously regarded, i.
24 ; fear lowers, i. 246 ;
false or sense, ii. 23 ;
heathen, iii. 39, 98.
Godhead, papal, i. 26
Gods, kings worshipped as,
i. 6 ; gone from earth, i.
11; feign'd, i. 32, 84, 119,
129, 132, 134 ; tyrants
not, i. 234; man, i. 240 ;
Greek, ii. 109.
Golden, days, i. 5, 11; age,
iv, 236.
Good, dealing, i. 6 ; seeming,
i. 14; real, 192; men i.
228, 230, ; the, i. 243 ; supernatural, i. 256 ; and
evil, ii. 44 ; lose, ii. 62 ;
iii. 338
Good-fellowes, iii. 37.
Goodness, i. 12, 256, 268 ;
II. xxvii et seqq. 53, 98.
Goodwill, iii. 386, 448.

Government, grudge against,
i. 13 ; monarchall and aris-
tocratical, i. 196 ; art of,
iv. 237.

Governors, i. 117.

Grace and disgrace, i. 8, 240,
242, 250, 253.

Grain, sowing, i. 132.

Grammar, ii. 20, 45.

Grants, royal, I. li ; ii. 64.

Grape, i. 133.

Grass, i. 182.

Gray-head, iii. 56.

Great, the, i. 125.

Greatnesse, i. 7, 88, 107, 126;
ii. xxvii, 107 ; love of, iii·
207.

Griefs, i. 6 ; iii. 50.

Growings, i. 222,

Growth, of States, i, 222.

Guilt, ii. 27.

H

Habits, i. 252.

Hair, iii. 67.

Handicraft, i. 132.

Happy, vnhappy, ii. 105.

Hard, not great, ii. 19.

Hardness, i. 204.

Harmony, i. 93, 121 ; iii.
396.

Harm-self, i. 177.

Harshness, iii. 214.

Hate, i. 214; ii. 60 ; iii.
200, 205.

Havens, i. 169.

Hazard, i. 41, 67, 194, 200.

Head, of the Church, i. 195.

Health, of State, i. 105, 112 ;
everlasting, i. 194 ; body's,
ii. 43.

Hearts, united, i. 5 ; large,

i. 10 ; hard, i. 13 ; man's,
i. 183; the, i. 244, 271 ;
double, iii. 79 ; altar of
loue, iii. 80, 81 ; wicked,
442-3, 447, God sees the,
iii. 462 ; great, iii. 421.

Heaven and Heavens, i. 7,
198 ; ii. 17 ; deafe, iii.
434; star-bearing, iii. 441.

Heights and depths, iii. 322.

Helicon, English, (1600) i.
ix, l.

Hell, i. 182, 198 ; woes of,
portrayed, iii. 156, et seqq;
emissaries of, iii. 163-4 ;
in man, iii. 207 ; no light
in, iii. 231 ; of thought no ?
iii. 413.

Heretics, i. 194.

History-Lecture, i. lxxxvi.

Holiness, i. 248.

Holy Land, ii. 110.

Honour, i. 10 83 ; ii. 67 ; iii.
462 ; undeserved, i. 124 ;
brittle iii. 124 ; our, iii.
430, 462 ; iv. 267.

Hope and Fear, i, 22, 194,
245.

Hopes, bad, iii. 176-7.

Horror-self, i. 246 ; iii. 204.

Horse, i. 182.

House-keeping, i. 166.

Human, nature, i. 44.

Humanity, i. 17 ; wearisome
condition of, iii. 416.

Humilltie, ii. 79 ; iii.246.

Humours, i. 30, 68, 106,
115, 117, 161, 184, 226,
228, 247 ; iii. 302, 354 ;
iv. 257.

Husband, and wife talking,
iii. 197 et seqq ; odious
name, iii. 203 ; authorities

of, iv. 241, 245 ; master mind of, iv. 244-5 ; please, iv. 248 et seqq ; master, mend or please, iv. 253.
Husbands. ill, 221.
Hypocrisie, i. 91, 199, 245, 248, 249, 252 ; ii. 37.

I.

Ideas, refined ii. 75.
Idle, i. 20, 77.
Idolatry, i. 245, 268 ; ii. 99.
Idoll, iii. 358.
Idols i. 28, 90, 93, 199, 241, 267.
Ignorance, i. 24, 170, 239 ; ii. 7, 28.
Ill, real, i. 14 ; doing i. 68 ; ruins good, ii. 76 ; far off, iii. 190, 213, 214, 216, 355 ; in vaine iii. 412.
Ill, name i. 185 ; deeds i. 222 ; shame of ii. 77.
Illumination, i. 266.
Illusions, ii. 67.
Image, divine and devil's, ii. 112.
Images, divine, i. 125 ; ii. 62.
Imagination, ii. 9 et seqq.
Imbargo, i. 147.
Immortal, mortal iii. 318.
Imperfection, man's ii. 7.
Impositions, i. 112, 167.
Impossibilities, iii. 428.
Impossible, iii. 163, 175, 338.
Impotence, man's ii. 7.
Impressions of God, i. 242-3
Incarnation, i. 255.
Incense, i. 143.
Inconstancy, i. 24 ; iii. 79, 5.
Incroaching, i. 193.

Indecision, iii. 210.
Indigence, i. 225.
Induction, ii. 11.
Industry, i 17, 140, 146, 149, 156.
Inequality, i. 12, 14, 122, 178, ii. 71.
Infamy, i. 158.
Infancy, i. 161.
Infant i. 256.
Infection. i. 70, 105, 252.
Infidelity, i. 239.
Infinite, i. 22, 77, 258 ; ii. 98.
Injustice, i. 32.
Insight, i. 165.
Instruments, i. 165 ; iii. 341.
Intemperance, ii. 75.
Interlineations of MSS. iv. 337-8.
Interruptions of intended adventure, i. xxiii; et seqq.
Invention, i. 85.
Io pæan, i. 171.
Irreverence, i. 56.
Island-states, i. 147.
Italics, i. xi.
Ixion, ii. 6.

J.

Jealousie, i. 50, 110.
Judges, i. 103, 104, 159, 211,
Just, be i. 67, 213.
Justice, common i. 103-4 ; vile i. 159 ; personified i. 246.

K.

Keep-down, i 232.
Keys, i. 80.
Kindnesse, more than iii. 371

Kisses, iii. 57.
Kings, boundless i. 13-14 ; types of excellence, i. 167 ; ultra i. 183 ; counsel for, i. 200; grateful, iii. 41 ; become a king, iii. 227 ; of men, but not of self, iii. 370.
Know v read, ii. 43.
Knowledge, i. 229 239 ; of God, i. 243 ; ii 5-6, 59 ; ends of, ii. 60 ; vain, ii. 63 ; a burden, ii. 421.
Known, ii 60.
Knows, i. 111.

L.

Labour, i, 153.
Labourers, i. 258.
Ladder, Jacob's ii. 96.
Ladders, iii. 400.
Lady-love, iii. 9-10, 11, 14, 24.
Language, students of, I. xi.
Latitudes, i. 89.
Laughing, ii. 60.
Laws, of i. 92-118. 8, 40, 88 ; divine and human i. 93; described i. 94 ; universal, i. 97 ; of God, i. 98 ; outward, i. 98 ; in common language i. 99; better none, than kept as mystery, i. 100-101 ; clear i. 101 : varying administration of. i. 104-5 ; often changed i. 105; subiects, i. 106, 181 ; by men's voices, i. 225 ; God's, and man's, i, 275 276 ; obedience to ii. 40, 59 ; books

of ii. 113 ; obey God's not make serve us, ii. 129 ; God rules by, iii. 315, 331 ; monarchall, iii. 380 ; unwritten, iv. 235.
Leaders, i. 190.
Leading and following, iii. 165.
Leagues, i. 168.
Learning, treatie of humane, ii. 5-63, 22, 30, 33.
Lecturers, iv. 47.
Legists, i. 102.
Less, i. 185.
Letter, to an honourable Lady, iv. 231-299 ; to Varney, iv. 301-9 ; various Letters to and from Lord Brooke, iv. 313 et seqq.
Levity, i. 124.
Libertines, i. 200.
Liberty i. 71, 97, 233, 110 ; show of, iii. 178 ; iii. 420.
Licet si libet, i. 26.
Lie, i. 261.
Life, i. 119, 199; good, i. 200, 244, 276 ; long-liv'd, i. 228 ; human, ii. 67 ; iii. 447, 454.
Lightning, iii. 435.
Light, of nature i. 94.
Lights, false i. 106, 112.
Liking, common i. 177.
Line, right ii. 19.
Literature, early i. xi.
Little, things i. 111 ; iii. 317.
Liturgies, i. 101.
Liuing, the, iii. 274.
Loans-money, I. lvii-viii.
Logike, ii. 45.
Lookers on, I. lxxvi.
Lot, i. 104, 229.

Love, i. 29, 112, 167, 184, 257, 273; ii. 83; iii. 9, 10, 11, 12, 13, 16-17, 17-18, 24-25, 27-29, 35, *et alibi* : it seems needless to record the numerous occurrencese of 'love' seeing the whole set of 'Cælica' sonnets, is dedicated thereto, and present the ever-varying aspects of the passion; dead iii. 81-2; abandoned iii. 84; woe of, iii. 104-112 : a spunge, iii. 209; secret iii. 210; God covets man's, iii. 295; blind, iii. 419.

Lovers, i. 260.

Loyalty, i. 13.

Lucke, ill, iii. 434.

Luxury, i. 151.

M.

Madmen, ii. 32.

Madness, iii, 460.

Magick, i. 246.

Magike word, ii. 17.

Magistrate, iii. 138.

Magistrates, age of, i. 86, 87,

Magnanimity, ii. 71.

Magnificence, i. 185; brave, i. 123.

Maid and flowers, iii. 121.

Majesty, frugal, i. 123; iii. 471 (note 87).

Malice, i. 199 ; iii. 122, 186

Man, prince of earth, i. 241 : unfallen, i. 255.

Mankinde, iii. 352.

Manners, i. 157.

Manufactures, i. 149.

Manuscripts of Lord Brooke's Writings, I. ix-x, xi-xii ; of Mustapha, Life of Sidney and Letter to Varney, I. xi-xii; description of at Warwick Castle, iv. 331 *et seqq.*

Many, 23 ; too, i. 124.

Mariners, i. 149.

Mark, i. 251.

Marriage, an unhapy : advices to the Lady, iv. 231-299.

Marriage, Spanish, I. lxxvvii ; bad, i. 25.

Marryed, having a worthy lady &c., ii. 140-143.

Marts, of place, i. 103, 139, 146, 149.

Martyr-deaths, iii. 277 *et seqq*, 479 (note 176.)

Meadow, i. 159.

Mediums, i. 76.

Melibœus, old, song courting his nymph, ii. 137.

Members, i. 184.

Memorial - Introduction, I. xiv : xix-c.

Memory, immortal, i. 7 ; ii. 11 *et seqq* ;

Men, loved by women, iii. 208.

Mens adepta, i. 251.

Merchandise, ill, ii. 90.

Merchants, i. 150, 163.

Mercies, iii. 340, 382, 449.

Mercury, i. 154.

Merit, i. 54, 83, 116, 120.

Merits, ii. 38.

Messengers of heaven, i. 200.

Method, iii. 74.

Might, i. 23, 24, 29, 30, 39, 47, 70, 75, 76, 105, 106, 186 ; ii. 22.

Milk, i. 49.

Mind, of man, i. 5, 183, 184 ; supreme, iii. 350.

Mines, i. 132.

Ministers-under, i. 50.

Mints, i. 164.

Minor Poems, ii. 131-147 ; sources of, ii. 133.

Minute, i. 152.

Miracles, i. 259, 267 ; false, iii. 415.

Mischance, i. 31, 67.

Mischiefe, iii, 187, 375, 384, 425, 438, 441.

Misdoing, i. 67.

Misery, iii. 470 (note 87),

Misforming, i. 151.

Misfortune and vice, i. 38 ; iii. 447.

Misgovernment, i. 31 ; iii, 46 .-2.

Misprison, i. 193.

Mistery, i. 184.

Mistresse, iv. 242.

Mists, false, i. 38.

Miters, i. 27, 79, 80, 81, 83, 248.

Mob, in fury, iii. 403-6.

Moderation, iv. 260.

Modernisation of text shunned, x-xi.

Monarchy, treatise of. i. 5-235 ; of the beginning of, i. 5-20 ; Declination of to violence, i. 21-33 : French i. 105; no true, i. 183 ; excellency of, compared with aristocracy, i. 206-216 ; compared with Democracy, i. 217 *et seqq* ;

continuance of, i. 222, 223 ; compared with Aristocracy and Democracy, jovntly, i. 228-235 ; imperial, i. 234.

Monarchies, the four, i. 182.

Mongers-word, i. 104.

Moncks, i. 83, 174; iii. 30, 136.

Monopolies, i. 145.

Monsters, iii. 333, 424, 476 (note 158).

Monuments, i. 169, 182 ; noiseless, I. xx.

Moralities, i. 199 ; finer, iv. 18.

Mortalitie, ii. 42, 120.

Mothers, iii. 361, 362, 413 459.

Mottects, I. xci.

Mould, throne or subject's i. 15

Moulds, ii. 24, 27 ; iii. 371.

Movers, i. 185.

Multiplicity, i. 215, 218, 231.

Multitude blind, i. 217, 218. iv. 295.

Munition, i. 189.

Murder, of Lord Brooke, I. xcv-xcix ; iii. 211-12, 230, *et seqq*; pretended, iii. 233 ; mistaken, iii. 284-5,

Muses, i. 171, 173.

Music, ii. 18, 47, 49.

Mustapha, surreptitiously published, I. ix; MS. of, I. xi, l, lxxxvii ; a tragedy, iii. 289-417 ; Appendix ii. 419-463 ; speakers in, iii. 241 ; MS. of, iii. 291; noble death of, iii. 403.

Mutiny, ii. 153 ; iv. 260.

Mysteries, curious, ii. 38 ; iii. 115-116.
Mystery, i. 265.

N.

Name, glorious, i. 78 ; only ii. 95.
Naturalisation, i. lxi.
Nature, not lawes or arts, i. 5 ; religion not, i. 21 ; perverted, i. 76 ; laws of, i. 97, 107 ; majesty of, i. 121 ; distressed, i. 240 ; not God's, i. 241 ; grace not, i. 250 ; to act, ii. 16 ; science from, ii. 55 ; study ii. 62 ; matter, ii. 104 ; a great book, iii. 77-8, ; forsake not. iii. 416 ; contradictory, iii. 417.
Navies, i. 148, 203, 204, 205 ; iv. 60.
Necessity, iii. 235, 385.
Need, ii. 104.
Neglect, i. 188.
Negligence, i. 24.
Neighing v music, ii. 8.
Nets, legal, i. 111 ; iii. 315.
Neuters, i. 195.
New, i. 29 ; man, i. 169.
Night, iii. 129.
Nobility, of 119-131, 122 ; iii. 118, 119.
Nobleness i. 120.
N omnal and real, i. 174.
Notes and Queries i. xvi ii. 18.
Nothings, ii. 95.
Notions, ii. 11, 12.
Novelty, i. 206 ; iii. 363.
Number, i. 63, 267 ; iii. 373, 485 (Note 212).

Nurseries, i. 13, 150, 152, 170.
Nursery, nature's, iii. 255.
Nurses, i. 49; sea, i. 162 ; change of, ii. 36.

O

Oak, 421, 422.
Oath, i. 65, 107.
Obedience, i. 70, 166, 167, 255, 263, 269, 273, 278 ; ii. 31, 58; iii. 352, iv. 277 et seqq ; iv. 284 et seqq.
Obscurity, iii. 69.
Occasion, i. 115, 176, 187.
Occupations, i. 153.
Ocean, ii. 42.
Oddes, ii. 71.
Oligarchal, tyranny, i. 228.
Oligarchy, i. 36.
Olives, i. 133.
Omens, iii. 298.
Omnipotence, i. 122.
One, king and people, i. 5 ; all for, i. 28, 58, side, i. 71 ; way, i. 109.
Opinion i. 18, 19, 38, 83, 85, 241, 255, 271 ; ii. 28, 40, 87.
Opposites, i. 72.
Oppression, i. 32, 74, 159.
Optimates, i. 228.
Oracles, consulted, iii. 165-6.
Order, i. 6, 14, 40, 56, 102, 115, 157, 179, 233 ; ii. 41, 70.
Ordinance, i. 189.
Ornaments, ii. 48.
Orthography, of MSS. iv. 337-8
Ostentation, ii. 80.
Ostracisme, i. 213.

Ostridge, i. 142.
Ourselves, study, ii. 62.
Outward, i. 98.
Overdoing, i 77.
Over-greatness, i. 126.
Oversight, i. 24.
' Owne my ' iii. 242.

P

Painter, i. 51.
Painting, iil. 30.
Paradise of Dainty Devices
  (1576) I. ix; ii. 140; of
  love, iii. 44. 45.
Paradox, i. 234.
Pardons, i. 112.
Parity, i 121.
Parliament, i. 28, 55, 108,
  109, 112, 113, 158, 159;
  Lord Brooke in, iv. 313 et
  seqq; privileges of, iv.
  315-316; Lord Brooke in,
  iv. 313, et seqq.
Parricide, iii 173, 269-270,
  330, 340.
Passion-governed, i. 230 ;
  tares of, 233 ; personified,
  i. 251.
Passions, i. 23, 72, 75, 97,
  109; iii. 354.
Past, i. 181.
Patience, iii. 54.
Pawns, i. 146.
Peace, of i. 168-185, 185,
  186, 192, 278; inward, ii.
  78 ; harvest of ii. 103;
  blessings of ii. 103, 104 ;
  iii. 140 ;
Pedigrees, I. xx.
Pen and sword, i. 174.
Penalties, i. 111.
Penitence, iii. 185.

People, the, i. 31, 81, 111,
  128, 152, 159, 160, 177,
  190 ; ii. 84, 93; iii. 270 et
  seqq, 352, 403-404,
Perfection, i. 47, 51, 263 ,
  new i. 253.
Perfidie, i. 65.
Perjury, i. 65. 66.
Periods of States, i. 222.
Perplexity, i. 15.
Persuasion, i. 177.
Pestilence, i. 70.
Philosophie, ii. 17, 20, 42
Phœnix, i. 36.
Phœnix, Nest (1593), I. ix,
  1; fire, i, 36, 252 ; the, iii,
  419.
Phrases, popular, iii. 325.
Physician, i. 44.
Physicke, ii. 42.
Pictures, ii. 9,
Pillars, i. 156, 176.
Place, i. 16, 54, 103, 117;
  worth, ii. 91.
P'agues, I. lix ; 12.
Planets, iii. 444.
Plate, security of, I. lix.
Playing-music, ii. 9.
Plea, i. 104.
Pleasure, ii. 88.
Plebescite, iii. 178.
Pledges, i. 107.
Plenty, i. 156.
Plot revealed, iii. 186 et seqq,
  216-217.
Ploughing, i. 69.
Poet and Poets, i. 231 ; ii.
  47, 49.
Poetic symbols, iv. 242.
Poison, iii. 283.
Policie, iii. 46.
Policy-self, i. 176, 180.
Politick, i. 245 ; ii. 43.

Polypus, ii. 87.

Pomp, i. 163.

Poor. i. 8, 100.'103, 105, 125.

Pope, I. lxxxi, 26, 80-81, 89, 126. 194.

Popery, crimes of, i, 26, 83, 164, 193, 194, 198 ; ii. 109, 128.

Portents, iii. 180, 369.

Ports, i. 146.

Possibility, iii.' 244.

Posthumous, Lord Brooke's writings, I. xx.

Poverty. i. 151.

Power, how maintained, i. 6, 10 ; degenerated, i. 12 ; bounded, i. 19 ; *ultra*, i. 24 ; reputation of i. 34 ; feeble, i. 40. 51 ; lasting, based on worth, i. 43 ; end of. i. 74 ; mould of, i. 107 ; absolute, i. 185 ; royal, i. 187 ; pope's temporal, i. 194 ; children of, ii. 44 ; wicked, ii. 53.

Practice, i. 195, 229 ; ii. 32 ; false i. 65, 117 ; iii. 303.

Prayer, in unknown tongue, i. 101 ; with doing, i. 260.

Precedents, I. lxx.

Precepts, i. 118, 239 ; ii. 32.

Prejudice, i. 185.

Prerogatives, i. 115, 161 ; iii. 176, 437.

Present, i. 181.

Pride, i. 83, 151, 195, 267 ; iii. 45 ; spiritual, ii. 79, 106.

Priesthood, i. 100 ; iii. 246.

Priesthood-high i. 270.

Priests, i. 164 ; false, i. 262 ; chorus of Mahomedan, iii. 343 *et seqq*.

Princes, iii. 56-57.

Privation, i. 14.

Problems, postponed till hereafter, i. 265.

Processes, length of i. 103.

Profit, i. 165.

Promoter. i. 164.

Prophets, false, iii. 216.

Proportion. i. 141.

Prose Writings of Lord Brooke : account of IV. v-xii ; Life of Sidney, IV. v-ix, 1-229 : Letter to an honourable Lady, IV. ix : 231-299 ; Letter to Varney, IV. ix-x : 301-309 ; Speech for Bacon, IV. x : 311 *et seqq* ; Description of the Manuscripts at War- wick Castle, IV. xi, 331, *et seqq*.

Prosperity, i. 41, 151, 168, 185.

Protection, i. 192 ; ii. 42.

Proverb, i. 225.

Providence, i. 184.

Provinces, i. 164.

Pulpit, i, 76, 115, 200.

Punishments, i. 186 ; iii. 435 ; small i. 19.

Purity, i. 255.

Q.

Questions, wrangling, i. 86, 242.

Quirks, of law, i. 161.

Quotation, marks, i. xi.

⁎ But with reference to these it is to be noted that they nowhere appear in the Warwick Castle MSS. G.

404 INDEX.

R

Rage, iii. 239, 264 *et seqq;*
356, 431, 483, (note 193).
Rain, iii. 438.
Rainbow, i. 18.
Rank, over-valued iii. 120.
Real and nominal, i. 174.
Reason, i. 35, 93, 119, 135,
174, 175, 233, 239; ii. 12,
16, 37; iii. 21, 22, 424.
Rebellion, ii. 112.
Rebellions, iii. 384, 462.
Rebel, i. 158.
Records, keeper of I. lv.
Reeds, i. 127.
Refining, iii. 255.
Refuge, i. 189.
Refugees, iv. 168.
Regality, i. 178.
Regard, i. 166
Regeneration, i. 253, 266;
not of baptism merely, ii.
39; paine of, ii. 63; di-
vine, iii. 125.
Rejection-love, iii. 75, 76, 86-
97.
Relief, i. 153.
Religion, treatise of, sup-
posed suppression of, I. xiii,
xcv-ix, 237-275; founda-
tion, i. 78; conscience in i.
119, 193, 242, 243; not the
cancelled pages of folio, i.
238; (See Note at end of
this index) false, i. 245;
true, i. 250, 254; fashioned
to War, ii. 109;
Remaines, I. ix; title-page
of, i. 2.
Remedies, iii. 360.
Remorse, iii. 184-5, 211, 217,
280-1 401, 487, (note 239).

Remorses, i. 241, 244.
Rents, 156, 167.
Repentance, iii. 19.
Repining, iii. 255.
Reprobate, i. 266.
Republick, i 5, 209, 214.
Reputation, i. 14, 124, 201,
219.
Reservedness, i. 73.
Resistance, iii. 328.
Respect, i. 222; iii. 131.
Rest, i. 231.
Restorers, I. xi.
Resurrection, i. 7.
Retirement from duty, i. 44,
45.
Retreat, i. 117.
Revenge, i. 203; iii. 174,
200, 201, 202, 235, 239,
240 *et seqq;* 274, *et seqq*;
hideous, iii. 281 *et seqq*;
378, 411.
Revenue, of crown, i. 154-
167, 158.
Revenues, i. 167, 202.
Reverence, i. 122, 124, 156.
Revolution, iii. 81.
Reward, i. 116.
Rewards, iii. 118, 298.
Rhetoric and Rhetoricians,
ii. 20, 46.
Rich, not good, i. 137.
Riches, 141, 152.
Riddles, of State, i. 40.
Right and Rights, super-
stitious, i. 18; inferior, i.
27; native, i. 176, 177;
the, ii. 59; beyond, iii.
220.
Rights-throne, i. 184, 186,
187.
Ring, marriage i. 257.
Riot, i. 160, 162.

Rise and fall. i. 42, 43.
Rite, i. 79.
Rites, church ii. 49 ; super-
stitious, iii. 391.
Rocks, ii. 58 ; iii. 422, 473,
(note 125) iv. 278.
ii. 63 ; divine, iii. 125.
Rod, iii. 40, 59, 447.
Royalties, i. 130.
Ruin, i. 49, 168, 179, 183 ;
works of, ii. 112, 113 ; iii.
201, 452.
Rule, i. 47, 51, 118.
Rules, few and good, i. 6,
58.
Rumour, iii 260.
Rupture, i. 194.

S

Sabbath-day, i. 112.
Sacerdotum, Chorus, iii. 416-
417.
Sacrament. iii. 264.
Sailors, i. 149.
Saint, iii. 35.
Saints, i. 199.
Salt, ii. 20.
Saltnesse, iii. 219.
Sanctification, i. 253.
Savage, lands, i. 178.
Sauce, ii. 48.
Saylers, iii. 27.
Scandal, i. 199.
Scepter, fear-thundring i. 7 ;
made less, i. 8 ; bankrupt,
i. 62.
Scepters, i. 27, 95, 248 ; iii.
99, 131, 398.
Schismes, ii. 38.
Schoolmen, i. 37.
Schools, i. 272.
Science, i. 173.

Sciences and Arts, ii. 13, 21 ;
neglect of, ii. 29, 35.
Scorne, iii. 202, 375.
Scriptures, Holy, i. 258, 269.
Sea, i. 203 ; ii. 16 ; iii. 465.
Seas, i. 148.
Secrecy, iii. 186.
Secrets, ii. 61.
Sects, i. 85, 250, 267 ; iii.
170.
Security, i. 117, 188 ; ii. 41.
Sedition, i. 114; ii. 120.
Seed, i. 155 ; heavenly, i.
261.
Seeming, i. 249.
Self, iii. 173.
Selfenesse, i. 182.
Selfishness-non, i. 254.
Self-love, i. 76.
Senate and senators, i. 113,
220, 229.
Sense, i. 27, 240, 243 ;
doubtful and double, i.
102 ; ii. 7 et seqq ; 23 ;
iii. 195, 213.
Sensual, i. 240.
Seminaries, i. 194.
Separation, i. 193.
Serve, not possess, ii. 50.
Servile, i. 107, 115.
Serpents, ii. 97.
Shadows, i. 10, 42, 200, 235,
244 ; sunset, iii. 74.
Shame. i. 83 ; ii. 77 ; iii.
178, 432.
Shapes, i. 233.
Shepheard's sorrow for his
Phœbe's disdaine, ii. 135-
136.
Sheriffs, of Scotland i. 110,
127.
Shews, i. 17.
Ships, i. 133, 134, 145, 149,

Shipwrights, iv 199.
Sicke, iii. 550.
Siege, i. 189.
Silk, i. 133, 147.
Silver, i. 154.
Sincerity, i. 104.
Sn i. 56, 87. 140, 239, 243
    259, 260, 277 ; ii. 98 ; iii.
    132 ; origin of iii 132-5.
Skill, i 140.
Slaves, i. 6, 61, 107, 125,
    152, 182, 196, 198, 224,
    241
Snow, i. 82 ; iii. 405.
Sloth, i. 38, 156.
Society-ocean, iii. 320.
Soliloqv, iii. 227 *et seqq.*
Solitariness, iii. 179.
Sonnets, misnumbered, I,
    xlvi; in Cælica cx ; the
    word, iii. 8.
Sophistication, i 89 ; ii. 54.
Sophistries, i. 196.
Sorrow, i. 278.
Soul, i. 81 ; ii. 25.
South, i 158.
Soveraignty, i. 109, 112.
    197.
Sparks. iii. 261, 453.
Speak, not but live, i. 199.
Speech feed our, i. 111, 112 ;
    for Bacon, I. xiv; iv. 311
    et seqq.
Spelling, old, I. iii
Spheres, ambition's iii.
    216.
Spider, i. 118 : iii. 319.
Spies, i. 55.
Spite, i. 34; iii. 185, 196,
    240.
Spirits, good and evil, iii.
    13, 188-195, 247 *et seqq.*
Spoiler, i. 189.

Spy, i. 164.
'Squirrel', I. xxxiii.
Stamp, i. 122.
Standard, wisedome's i. 11.
Staples, i. 137, 141, 147, 158.
Star-divines, i. 246 ; iii. 102.
Stars, blazing i. 42 ; hierar-
    chy of i. 120 ; the, ii. 16 ;
    iii. 12, 102 186, 444.
State, a i. 176 and 177.
States, neighbour i. 192 ;
    degrees of, ii. 118.
State-Trials, iv. 313.
Stews, i. 160.
Step-mother, i. 125 ; iii.
    382, 394.
Sticks, iii. 424, 425, 433.
Stile, i. 118, 174.
Stooping-low i. 160.
Stones, rowling i. 207.
'Stony-ways ', i. 261.
Stories, i. 179.
Storms, i. 203 ; iii. 4, 11.
Story, before times of, i. 5.
Straights, i. 22.
Strangers, i. 152.
Stream and ocean, iii. 337.
Strength, i. 36.
Strives, i. 179.
Strong, the iii. 206.
Stumbling, i. 201.
Style, ii. 48.
Subject and subjects, i. 106,
    123, 131.
Subjection, i. 13 ; iii. 119.
Submission-over i. 24.
Subsides, i. 202.
Subsidy, i. 112.
Success, bad and base, iii.
    227, 274. *et seqq.*
Succession, i. 107, 178 ; iii.
    308.
Succors, i. 202.

Sudden, falls, iii. 338.
Suffer, i. 24.
Suffrages, i. 229.
Sun, i. 29 ; ii. 12.
Sunset. iii. 89.
Superiors and inferiors, i. 254.
Superstition, i. 78, 81, 143, 195, 196, 245, 246 ; iii. 238.
Suppress, i. 151.
Supremacy, papal, I. lxxxi, regal, 68, 69, 89, 194, 195, 198.
Surplus, i. 150.
Surprize, i. 189.
Suspected, iii. 181-2, 305.
Suspition, iii. 351, 358.
' Sweetness, reserved ', i. 6.
Sword, i. 80; and pen, i. 174, 187.
Symbols, iii. 376-377.
Sympathie, ii. 72.
Synodie, i. 114.
Synods, ii. 38.

T

Tares, i, 233,
Taxes, i. 112, 158, 159, 202.
Tears, I. xxx, 80 ; iii. 237, 462.
Tediousnesse, i, 206.
Ten commandments, ii. 40.
Tennis, iv. 65.
Terror, i. 74 ; iv. 270, et seqq.
Temperance, i, 161.
Tempt, i. 272, 278 ; no more, iii. 448.
Temptations, i. 117, 239 ; iv. 259-60.
Thanks, exorbitant, i. 6.

Theefe and Theeues, iii. 37, 42-46.
Things, endless, boundless, heavenly. i, 248, 278,
Thirty, the, i. 54.
Thief, i. 153
Thoughts, iii. 333.
Threatening, iv. 272 et seqq.
Three, i, 210,
Thrones, over-exalted, i. 6 ; as now are, i. 16 : seeming infinite, i. 18 ; strong, i. 28 ; idols, i. 28 ; supports of, i 55, 235 ; ii. 69.
Thunder, iii. 426, 435.
Time, i. 10, 31, 36, 56, 84, 168, 175 ; vices of, i. 59 ; study, ii. 62 ; chorus of, iii 104, 362 et seqq ; healing iii. 210 ; as a serpent-circle, iii. 366 ; decaying iii. 366 ; limits of, iii. 367 ; vision of iii. 369-70.
Titles, i. 103, 123, 124, 178 ; golden, iii. 384.
Tomb, i. 252.
Tombs, not treasures, i. 145.
Tongues, i. 248, 261.
Tools, ii. 44.
Torrents, i. 185 ; not streams, ii. 76.
Touchstone, i 66.
Tournament, i. xl.
Toys, i. 48, 65, 142, 143.
Trades, i. 137, : free i. 138, 147.
Traffic, various, i. 139, 140, 1431, 46 ; of man's will, i. 248.
Transmutation, i. 140.
Transubstantiation, ii. 45.
Treachery, female iii. 196, 202-3, 207, 230 et seqq.

Treason spurious i. 95 ; and murder intended, iii. 165.
Treaty, i. 146.
Tree, iii. 67.
Tribes, Roman i. 13.
Tribunes, i. 209, 220, 226, 229.
Trinity, i. 264.
Triumphs, i. 182.
Trivial, i. 157.
Trophies. i. 175
True, truth, i. 85, 256.
Trumpet, ii. 82
Trust, in words, i. 191 ; iii. 296.
Truth, i. 259, 260 ; ii. 14, 39, 99 ; iii. 167, 331.
Tumult. i, 189.
Twins, i. 145, 183.
Tyrants, of weak-minded, i. 34-43 ; active and unactive, i. 37 ; strong, i. 58-74 ; not gods, i. 234 ; submission to, i. 247.
Tyranny, i. 23, 29, 31, 33, 34, 48, 61, 106, 113 ; ii. 111

U

Understanding, i. 92 ; ii. 9, 10, 11 et seqq.
Unhappy, iii. 208.
Union, i. 230.
Unity, i. 85, 121, 183, 204, 233, 240.
Unkindnesse. iii. 72.
Unprosperity, i. 158, 189, 203.
Unthankfulnesse, iii, 182.
Untrue, to God 2 83.
Uprightness, iv. 286-287.
Use, i. 106, 177 ; ii. 32 ; iii. 354.

Usurpation, i. 30, 52.
Unworthiness, i. 51.

V

Vagrant. i. 153.
Vanity, i. 46, 138, 141, 142, 174. 235, 252 ; ii. 29, 53.
Vapours, iii. 74.
Variety, i. 157.
Venting, i. 138, 149.
Venture, iii. 35 (misprinted 53).
Verbalists, i. 18.
Ve tue, ii. 90 ; temple of Fame, ii. 96 ; a grace, iii. 33.
Vertues, i. 60, 242, 250 ; divine, ii. 97.
Vice and vices, i. 8, 35, 36, 38, 40, 42, 59, 60, 61, 62, 73, 151, 202, 223, 242, 263, 412 ; ii. 105 ; iii. 318.
Vicissitudes, i. 188 ; ii. 117, 118.
Violence, i. 21-33 ; ii. 112, 263, 412.
Viper, i, 227.
Virgins, sacred, i. 65 ; a virgin of Eternity, iii 422, 423.
Virgula, diuina, iii. 119.
Visions, of treason. iii. 172, 173 ; of honor, iii. 280 ; idle, iii. 314.
Vows, i. 270; iii. 76, 2 64,

W.

War, of, i. 113, 186-205 ; (misprinted 250) 188, 191, 203, 204 ; ii. 28

Want, i. 157.

Wantonness, i. 222,

Wares, i. 164.

Warres,treatise of,ii. 28,101-129; horror of, ii. 105; desolation by, ii. 106; fruit of. ii. 108; false names of, ii. 110; people suffer by, ii. 111; a hell, ii. 113; God in, ii. 111, 115, 118; ends in, ii. 115, 116, 117, 119; causes of, ii. 116, 117, 119: civil, ii. 117; over-ruled, ii. 121, 122; of God and of man, ii. 122; sacred, ii. 123; of glory, ii. 123, 124; regarded by Christians, ii. 125; by the world, ii. 126; to be abhorred, ii. 129; States given to, iii. 140-141.

Water, i. 49.

Wax, i. 49; iii. 323, 352; changed to steel, i. 177.

Weeds, i. 95; iii. 163, 223, 319.

Wealth, of States, i. 10, 152, 156, 157, 185, 218; iii. 384.

Weak minds, i 48, 49.

Weakness, i. 36-37, 51.

Weather, good, ii. 67.

Well doing, i. 203.

Well, ii. 59.

Weeping, ii. 60.

Wheat, iii. 46.

Wife, a tool, iii. 177-178; unfaithfulness of, iii. 183; base, iii. 195-197; a, iii. 281; privileges of a iv. 241; subject iv. 261; restraints, iv. 273; separation, iv. 275; obedience, iv. 277 et seqq; discipline, iv. 290 et seqq.

Will, of tyrants, i. 19; boundless, i. 19; dominant, i. 25; law turned to, i. 41; powerful, i. 79; withstand, i. 94, 115; raigns, i. 234.

Winning one, iv. 292; the world, iv. 293 et seqq.

Winds, iii. 270.

Wings, i. 199.

Wisdom, i. 184: of the world and God's, i. 272; godlesse, ii. 61; divine, ii. 63.

Wisedome, i. 11, 18, 179.

Wit, i. 41, 64, 106, 164, 188, 247; II. vi.

Within, true, i. 199; i. 250, 272.

Without, i. 246, 262.

Woe, i. 27; ii. 60.

Woes, threatened. iii. 180.

Wooing, iii. 27-29.

Wolf, ii. 120.

Woman, iii. 9-10; iii. 285, 288.

Worms, i. 203.

Worse and worst, i. 201; ii. 53.

World, i. 21, 278; ii. 31; in not of the, ii. 54; fame and, ii. 94; woman's, iii. 48.

Word-sellers, ii. 17, 46.

Words, i. 248; best, ii. 47, 58; mystery of. iii. 380. 156, 157, 185, 218.

Worship, i. 239, 244.

Works, public. i. 169.

Worth, i. 17, 36, 40, 43, 75, 122; i. 175, 181, 213, 229

Wounds, i. 72.
Wounded i. 202.
Wrath, king's, iii. 425, 426.
Writs, i. 65.
Writing, i. 175.
Wrong. i. 104.
Wrongs-love, iii. 50-51.
Wrinckle, iii. 221.

Y.

Year, i. 100 ; Julian &c., i. 100.

Youth, i. 64, 86, 87; iii 130.

Z.

Zeal, i. 10.
Zenith, of power, i. 18.
Zodiack.i. 121.
Zones, i. 76.

NOTE.—The following is an entry in Sir Henry Herbert's Journal as Licenser : " Received from Henry Seyle for allowinge a booke of my verses of my Lord Brook's, entitled Religion, Human Learning, Warr and Honor, this 17th of October, 1632; in money £1 4s." It would thus seem that after all ' Of Religion ' was intended to occupy (in part at least) the cancelled pages. Malone's Shakespeare by Boswell (Vol. iii. 231) to which I am indebted for this entry. ascribes the cancelling " Of Religion " to the " order, probably of Archbishop Laud " : but see Vol. I., viii, 238 *et alibi*. G.

II. INDEX OF NAMES, PERSONS, AND PLACES.

Impersonations or personifications (exclusive of those necessarily given in the Index of Things and Thoughts) are included herein. G.

A.

Abel and Cain. i. 267.
Absence, iii. 20, 21, 52, 53, 54.
Achaia, i. 170, 191 : iv. 357, (Note 227)
Acheron, iii. 158.
Achma, i. 191.
Adam, i. 262, 264, 266, 272 ; iii. 316 ; and Eve, i. 20.
Adams, Thomas ii. 98 ; iii. 470.
Ægusa, i. 191.
Aelian, ii. 14, 80.
Æolus, i. 33 ; iii. 316.
Æsculapius, iii. 82.
Æsop, i. 123, 235 ; ii. 92 : iii. 101 , iv. 245.
Ætolians, i. 192.
Affection, iii. 40.
Africa, i. 191, 192, 219.
Africanus, Scipio i. 123.
Agamemnon iii. 229.
Agrarian. i. 220.
Aix, i. 105.
Alabama, I. xxxii.
Alarick, i. 244.
Albion, 126, 145, 190.
Alcester, I. xxi.
Alcibiades, i 212.
Alcyone, i. 207.
Aleppo, i. 145.
Alexander, i. 56 ; ii. 14.
Alexandrine library, ii 85.

Alios, i. 169.
Allia, i, 224.
Allibone, II. x-xii.
Alpes, i. 105 ; iv. 47.
Altamaha, 1. xxxii.
Alva, i. 42.
Ambition, iii. 327.
Amphialus, iv. 18.
Amphiction, Synodic i. 114.
Anteros, iii. 82.
Antonie and Cleopatra, iv. 155-156, 281.
Antonio, don, iv. 75.
Anjou, I. xl.
Anthela, i. 114.
Anthony, i. 226.
Appian way, i. 169.
Appius. Claudius, i. 96,209.
Apollo, i. 171, 210 ; iii. 82 ; iv. 77.
Arches, iv. 187.
Archimedes, iv. 245
Aretine, ii. 89.
Argus, iii. 28.
Aristides, i. 213 ; ii. 84 ; iv. 283.
Aristotle ii 69.
Artenesia, ii. 68.
Arundel, I. xl.
Ashmole, MSS. I. xix.
Ashton, Mr. I. xxv-vi.
Asia, i. 78, 124, 192, 219.
Asiaticus, i. 124.
Assem, iii. 229.
Astolpho, iii. 39.

Astræa, i. 93.

Ateas, ii, 8.

Athenæus, ii. 14, 80.

Athens, i. 96, 104, 148, 157, 170, 180, 210, 212, 215, 218; ii. 20, iv. 191. (See under Minotaur).

Atlas, iii. 55.

Attyla, i. 224.

Auernus, iii. 861, 429.

Augustine, i. 261 ; ii. 29.

Augustus, i. 95. 169, 226.

Austria, i. 41; Don John of, iv. 35-36.

Authority, iii. 100.

Avon, i. xx.

Axil, iv. 121.

B.

Babel, i. 198 ; iii. 45 ; tower of, iv. 247.

Babylon, i. 185.

Bacon, I. iii ; speech for, I. xiv ; iv. 327-329 et seqq ; letters to and from, I. xiv-xv, lvii, lxiii-lxix, lxix-lxx ; ' apophthegem-es ' of, lxx ; friendship with, lxxxiii ; quoted I. 86 ; ii. 5, 8. 10, 13, 17, 20, 21, 22 36, 40. 48, 55, 74, 79, 89, 90, 122, 211; IV. x, 311 et seqq.

Bacchus, i. 132.

Bactria, i. 93.

Baker, I. lxxxvi.

Bancroft, Archbishop, I. xxix.

Baptista, I. liv.

Barbarie, i. 137.

Basilius, iv. 18.

Basylt, Simon, i. liv.

Battus, i. 66,

Batory, Stephen, iv. 83.

Beauchamps, family and lands, I. xx, xxi, xxii.

Beaumont, Sir John, ii. 56.

Belgia, i. 42.

Bermuda, iii, 68.

Berti, Dom. iv. 322 et seqq.

Blake, I. lii.

Bodenham, I. l.

Boiardo, iii. 39.

Bolton, Edmund. iii. 291.

Bordeaux, i. 105.

Bourne, xxiv.

Boyes, J. F. i. 87, 112.

Braybroke, Lord, iv. 22 81.

Bridges, Sir Egerton, xxiv ; IV. vii.

Britwell, Library of, I. xc.

Bright, MSS. sale, I. ix-x iv. 333.

Bright, John, II. xlxii et seqq.

Brooke, Lord, published no-thing considerable him-sel, I. ix; MSS. of his Writings, ix-x, xi-xii ; our's, first collective edi-tion ; x ; text reproduced in integrity, x-xi ; unpub-lished Letter of, xiv-xv ; duty of his present repre-sentatives, xv-xvi ; an-cestry of, xix et seqq ; Brook-home, seat of, xx ; Robert. lord, xxi ; married Elizabeth, daughter and co-heir of Lord Beau-champ, xxi ; daughter, Elizabeth, xxi ; married to Sir Fulke Greville, xxi ; love-story, xxi-xxii ; (foot-note) grandfather of our

Lord Brooke, xxii; parent of, xxii; birth and birth-place, xxii; sister Margaret, xxii-xxiii; meaning of name 'Fulk', xxiii, related to Sidney, xxiii-iv birth-date a memorable, epoch, xxiv-v, at school in Shrewsbury with Sidney, xxv *et seqq*; register entry, xxvi; school-fellow of Sidney, xxvii-viii; university career, obscure, xxviii; entered at Jesus College, Cambridge, xxviii: *not* in Trinity, xxviii-ix; connection with Trinity, xxix-xxx; origin of Trinity tradition, xxx; at Oxford, xxxi; Brooke and Sidney visit each other at Oxford and Cambridge, xxxi; intended adventures with Sidney, xxxii *et seqq*; hindered by Elizabeth, xxxiii, *et seqq*; kept at home, xxxvii *et seqq*; correspondence unpublished, xxxvii; rose to eminent employments, xxxvii; introduced to Court, xxxviii; office in Wales, xxxviii - xxxix; letter of Sidney in favour of, xxxix; clerk of the signet, xxxix; secretary of Principality of Wales, xli; letter to Walsingham shewing 'straits', xli *et seqq*; unmarried, *not* of choice, xlii; romance of love in " Cælica" xlii. *et seqq ;* reality of love-

passion in Cælica, xliii-vii; like Phineas Fletcher, xlvii-viii; death of Sidney, a life-long sorrow; xlix; books left to, xlix; poetic studies, xlix-li; complaints against li. royal grants to li-ii; knighted li; treasurer of the Wars, lii; treasurer of marine causes, lii; rear-admiral, lii; official letter to, liii-iv; letter to Hickes, lv - lvi; handwriting, lvi; short letter to Sir Robert Cotton, lvi; Wedgnock granted to him, lvii; pecuniary straits, lvii; hitherto unpublished letters, lvii-lxiii, letter to Earl of Salisbury on the Gunpowder Plot, lxii-lxiii; letters to and from Bacon, xiv, xv, lvii, lxiii-lxix; speeches of in Parliament, lxix - lxx ; ' Robin Goodfellow ' lxx; character of, by Naunton, lxx - lxxi: accession of James, lxxii ; created knight of the Bath, lxxii ; grant of Warwick Castle, lxxii; Biographia Britannica on his position, lxxii-lxxiii ; James, warm friend, lxxii-lxxiv; gentleman of Bedchamber, lxxiv ; created Lord Brooke, lxxiv ; family-papers, much wished, lxxiv - lxxv ; letter on Spanish Marriage, lxxv-lxxvii; letter on Palatinate, lxxvii-lxxxii ; counsellor of State under Charles, Ist., lxxxiii; relations to illustrious contemporaries, lxxxiii -viii ; friendship with Sidney, lxxxiii ; Bacon, lxxxiii ; Camden, lxxxiii-lxxxiv; Speed lxxxv; Dorislaus, History - chair, lxxxv-lxxxvi; Overall, lxxxvi ; poets, lxxxvi - lxxxvii ; Lok, lxxxvii ; murdered, lxxxviii ; monumental-inscription, lxxxix ; mourning song, xc ; defamed, xci-xcii, xcix-c ; appeal to present representatives, xcii - xciii ; portraits of xciii ; Essay on Poetry of, II. v-xci ; (See under Essay in Index I.) Writings, &c , described in Life of Sidney, iv. 146 et seqq ; early incidents in his Life, hindrances by Elizabeth, 146 et seqq ; Tragedies and Treatises, 150 et seqq ; old age 151-152 ; Declination of Monarchy, 152 et seqq ; other Treatises, 154-155 et seqq ; ('Antonie and Cleopatra) destroyed, 155-156 ;) Earl of Essex, 157 et seqq ; recollections of Elizabeth, 162 et seqq ; her regard to Religion 178 et seqq ; her home-government, 183 et seqq ; reasons for not writing Life of Elizabeth, 214 etseqq ; the surviving Tragedies 220 et seqq ; de-

sign of life of Sidney, 224 ; Appendix to Life of Sidney, 225 et seqq ; speech for Bacon, 311 et seqq ; in Parliament, 313, 316 et seqq ; Letters in Calendars of State Papers, 316 et seqq.

Brooke, Lord Robert, I. xii, xv-xvi, lxxiv, xc-xcvii ; IV. xi.

Brooke, Christopher, I. xxx.

Brooke, Dr. Samuel, I. xiii, xiv, xxx.

Brookes, living, I. xvi.

Broke, de Willoughbys, I. xx.

Bootes, i. 121.

Brown, Sir William, iv. 123.

Browne, Wm ii. 17, 89.

Browne, Mr. iv. 228

Browning, Robert, II. xxvi.

Bruce, John, iv. 322 et alibi.

Bruno, Giordano, iv. 323-325.

Brutus, i. 29 ; iv. 261.

Buch, I. lxiii.

Buchurst [sic] I. liv; iv. 324.

Burke, peerage of, I. xix, xxii.

Buckingham, I. lxxv-lxxxii.

Burton, Robert, I. xc.

Busyre, i. 9.

Butrech, Peter, iv. 3.

C.

Cælia, iii. 25.

Cælica, i. xliii et seqq ; quotation from, I. xliv et seqq ; in cx sonnets, iii 7-154 ; it seems needless to

state the many occurrences
of the name.
Cæsar, I. 29, 60, 173,232,225.
Cain and Abel, i. 267.
Caine. iii. 169 (and all through
Alaham : not noted)
Cairo, i. 80, 145.
Caius, i. 9.
Calchas, iii. 229.
Caligula, i. 31, 161.
Caliph, i. 80.
Cam. river, I. xxxi.
Camillus, i. 214; ii. 84.
Cambridge, I. xxviii (See
under *Brooke, Jesus, Trin-
ity*.) annals of by Cooper,
I. xxxi.
Camden, Wm., I. xx, xxii,
xxiii. lxxxiii-lxxxv.
Campbell, ii xviii, xxvi, li.
Cambyses i. 25.
Canna. i. 213.
Caracalla, mother, of, i. 26.
Carter, I. lxxxvi.
Carthage, i. 123, 162, 214,
221.
Carthigenians, i. 191 ; iv.
285.
Caspian Sea, ii. 33.
Cassimires, iv. 147.
Cassiopea, i. 120.
Cassius, i. 29.
Castile, iv. 115.
Castor and Pollux. i. 18, 134.
Catherine, de Medicis, I. xl
Cato, i. 46.
Caution, i. 251.
Cecyll, I. liv.
Ceres, i. 92, 132.
Chalmers, Alex., I. xxiv.
Chambers, i. 25.
Chance, i. 178, 211 ; iii. 63,
100, 164, 165, 166, 197,
234, 365.

Change, i. 185 ; iii. 36, 48-
49, 71, 379.
Charon, iv. 264.
Charles 1st, I. li. lxxxiii.
Charles V.. i. 64.
Chatham, I. iiii.
Cheops. i. 170,
Chersiphron, ii. 93.
Chester, Colonel, I. xvi.
Chilo. i. 226.
Christ, i. 240, 257, 262, 263,
265. 269 ; iii. 117.
Cicero, i. 213 ; iv. 7, 153.
Cicero. M. T. a tragedy, *not*
by Lord Brooke, I. xiii,
220.
Circe, iv. 193, 258.
Clark, W. G. M.A., I. iii-v.
Claudius, i. 39.
Cleombrotus. ii. 68.
Cobbet, iv. 313.
Cobden, Richard, ii. xlvii.
Coke. iv. 329.
Codrus, i. 210.
Colchis, i. 10.
Cole, MSS of, I. xxxii.
Coleridge. ii. lxxxiv, 128.
Collins, Arthur, I. xix,
xxvi, xxix, lii, lxii, xcvii.
Collier, ii. 133 : iii. 61; iv.
225.
Cooper, Mrs. ii. vi-vii.
Confusion, i. 210, 250.
Conquest. i. 178, 189.
Constantine, i. 190, 226.
Constantinople, i. 145, 223 ;
iv. 211.
Corbet, Bishop, i. lxxxvi; iii.
298-4.
Corinth, i. 169.
Corrie, Dr., I. xxviii.
Corrupt Reason, iii. 221 *et
seqq*.
Corruption, i. 257.

Corser, Rev. Thomas M.A.
I. x, xii ; ii. 133.
Cotton MSS. 1. lvi.
Craft, iii. 167, 221 et seqq.
Cranmer, I. xxx.
Creet, i. 170.
Crewe, Lord iv. 228.
Croesus, ii. 117.
Crossley, James IV. xii.
Cudworth, ii. 51.
Cumberland, iv. 206.
Cupid, iii. 19, 20, 24. 25, 26,
    27, 28, 31, 32-34, 35, 37,
    38, 39, 40 et alibi : it would
    serve no end to note the
    abounding occurrences of
    the love-god in Cælica
Cybele, i. 26.
Cyclops, i. 129.
Cynthia, I. xliii ; iii. 23, 24,
    55, 56, 62. 63-64 : a night
    vision of, iii. 64-66 : Cf. iv.
    373 (No. 501.)
Cyprus, i. 221.

D.

Danae, iii. 39.
Dante, II. xxi,v.
D' Ewes, Sir Symonds, I.
    lxix ; iv. 313 et seqq.
D'Israeli, I. xii.
Danger, iii. 256.
Daniel, i. 182.
Daniel, Samuel 1. lxxxvi.
    31 ; ii. 115 ; iii. 292-293.
Danuby, i. 189.
Davenant, Sir William I.
    lxxxvii-viii.
David, i. 263, 270.
Davies, John of Hereford,
    I. lxxxvii ; ii. 210 ; iii.
    219, 290-291 ; iv. 272.

Davies, Sir John iii. 55.
Davies, of Hereford II. x.
Davidson, iv. 225.
Deathe, iii. 158 336.
Deity, ii. 14' 15.
Delphos, iii. 184.
Demades, ii 14.
Demetrius, ii. 93.
Demosthenes, i. 212 ; ii. 14,
    90.
Democritus, ii. 89 ; iv. 289.
Denmark, iv. 84.
Derby, earl of i. 1.
Desire, iii. 19, 23, 28, 40, 47
    49, 63, 87, 137, 197.
Devotion, iii. 277.
Diana, i. 121 ; iii. 55 ; iv.
    242.
Dijon, i. 105.
Diogenes, ii. 89.
Diomedes, i, 9.
Dionysius, i. 114 ; ii. 118.
Disorder, i. 62. 94.
Discontent, i. 207, 212.
Dixon, Hepworth, i. lxix.
Domitian, i. 45
Donne. (Dr.) II. x. 26.
Dorians, i. 180
Dowland, ii. 133 ; iii. 61.
Drake, Sir Francis, I. xxiv ;
    IV. vii, 71, et seqq.
Druids, i. 81.
Dugdale, Sir William I. xix.
    xxxix, xli, lii, lvii, lxxii.
    lxxiv, xcvi.
Dunkerers, iv. 203.
Dutch. Treaty i. 1
Dyer, Sir Edward. I. xlviii ;
    imitates ord Brooke, I.
    xlviii ; in Sidney's Will.
    I. xlix ; ii. 134 ; iii. 104 ;
    a Fancy by, iii. 145-150 ;
    iv. 147.

E.

Eastern cities, i. 144.
Edmundson, I. xxix.
Edmington, [= Edmonton]
    I. lxi.
Edwardes, ii. 140.
Edward VI., I. xxv.
Egypt, i. 137, 142, 172, 592,
    274, 277.
Elis, i. 90.
Elias, i. 253.
Elizabeth, I. xxxiii, xxxviii ;
    her greatness asserted, I.
    xxxviii ; Anjou and, I. xl ;
    dead, I. 1 ; economy in
    reign of, I. liii ; Bacon
    and, I. lxiv-lxv, lxx,
    lxxvii, 147 ; undertakings
    of, i. 204, 205 ; iii. 103 ;
    iv. 30 et seqq, 49 et seqq,
    94 et seqq, 162 et seqq ;
    and Essex, iv. 176 ; and
    all through Life of Sid-
    ney, not further noted.
Endymion, iii. 24, 55, 88 ;
    iv. 242.
England, i. 118.
Enoch, i. 253.
Envy, iii. 238, 434.
Epicurus, ii. 88.
Erigone, i. 120.
Error, i. 232 ; iii. 393.
Eros, iii. 82.
Essex, I. lxiv, lxviii-lxix ; iv.
    157 et seqq., 208.
Esau and Jacob, i. 266.
Eternall, iii. 225, 268-269.
Euarchus, iv. 17.
Europe, i. 137.
Europa, iii. 39, 62.
Euxine, i. 180.
Euphrat, i. 189.

Eurystheus, i. 8.
Eumenes, i. 192.
Eve, ii. 125.
Evill spirits, iii. 221 et seqq.
Expectation, iii. 262.
    157 et seqq ; iv. 208.

F.

Faction, iii. 181, 330.
Fairholt. i. 80.
Faithlessness, i. 68.
Fame, i. 116, 172, 251.
Farr, Edward, II. lxviii.
Feare, iii. 26, 68, 180, 300,
    332, 339, 360.
Ferrat, iv. 212.
Flanders, iv. 88 et frequenter.
Flavius, i. 100.
Fleming, I. lxvi.
Fletcher. Phineas, I. xlvii-
    xlviii, lxii, 36, 40, 67, 82,
    183, 189, 190 ; II. viii,
    45, 62. 93, 101 ; iv. 128.
Flecknoe, Richard, I. lxxxvi ;
    iii. 293.
Fletcher, Giles, i. 32.
Florus, i. 221.
Flushingers, iv. 203.
Fortescue, Sir John, I. li,
    liv, lxiv.
Fortune, i. 201 ; ii. 38, 97,
    197 ; iii. 299, 371, 452.
Fowles, Sir David, I. lvi.
France, i. 82, 155, 159 ; i.
    209 (misprint: see iv. 359
    note 253) 219 ; travels in,
    iv. 88 et frequenter ; 301
    et seqq.
Fraud, iii. 357.
Frobisher, I. xxxii.
Froude, I. xxxviii.
Frugality, iii. 317.

Fulk or Fulke, meaning of, I. xxiii.
Fulvius, i. 172.

G.

Galba, i. 39.
Galienus, i. 54.
Gamage, IV. ix, 229-230.
Gascoigne, iv. 64.
Gaule, John, II. xii-xiii.
Gauls, i. 224.
Geneva, I. lxxxi.
Gentiles, i. 268, 269.
George, Dr., I, lxxxvi.
Gerion, i. 9.
Germany, i. 126, 155.
Germans, i. 190, 219; iv. 83 et frequenter.
Gifford, Rev. John, IV. viii.
Gilbert, Sir Humphrey, I. xxxiii.
Gladstone, W. E., I. li, lxxv
God, ii. 57, 62; conditioned conception,of, ii. 241; unknowne, iii. 142-143.
Golding, Arthur, I. v.
Gorgon, iii. 49.
Goswell, William, iv. 301.
Goths, i. 190, 191.
Greece, i. 171; ii. 105.
Gregorie, Arthur, i. liv.
Greeks, i. 35, 137; iii. 344; iv, 61.
Greiv-ill, iii. 112.
Grenoble, i. 105.
Grevil, Sir Edward, of Milcote, I. xxi, xci; John, I. xxi.
Greville, Fulk (See under Brooke, Lord), author of "Maxims", I. xvi.
Greville, Fulke and Robert,

I. xxii; Sir Fulk died in 1606, I. xxii.
Groniland, iv. 199.
Guise, Duke of, iv. 56.

H.

Hailes, lord, iv. 13.
Hakluyt, I. xxxiii.
Hala, iii. 161 (one of the chief female characters in Alaham : not noted as so frequent and easily traced, iii. 161.
Hall, John, I. xx.
Hallam, II. x, xviii.
Hamilton, Sir William II. xvii-xviii.
Halliwell, i. 31, 70, 146; ii. 133.
Hannah, Dr. I. xvi, xxx, xlviii; ii. lxxi-ii, lxxiii, 48, 134; iii. 60, 104, 107, 110.
Hannibal, i. 123,
Hanse's i. 139.
Hare, Archdeacon ii. 14, 27,
Harleian, MSS. I. xlii. lxxxiii.
Harington, Sir John iii. 39.
Harvey, John Esq., IV. vii.
Haywood, I. lxxxviii; defence of I. xci.
Hazlitt, W. C. xii. c. ii. 17, 32, 89; iv. 64.
Heaven, i. 198.
Heidelberge, I. lxxxi.
Helena, iv. 18.
Helens, of Troy ii. 16.
Heli, iii. 165; (and through Alaham : no noted.
Hell, i. 198.
Henry III. and IV., iv. 148.

Henry IV. i. 155.
Henry, VII. I xxi.
Hephestion, i. 61.
Heraclitus, ii. 89 ;iv. 289.
Herbert, George I. xxii ; iii. 129.
Herbert, Henry Sir, iii. 283, 497 (note 359).
Hercules, i. 9, 120, 171, 172.
Herostratus, ii. 93.
Hermes, i. 251.
Herrick, ii. 22.
Herringman, Henry, i. 2, 4.
Hesperides, ii. 51.
Hicks, and subsequently S r Michael, I lv.-vi, lxxv.
Hippolytus, iv. 242.
Holland or Netherlanders, iv. 58 et seqq ; 88 et seqq, 142 et seqq.
Hollander, i. 143, 144.
Hollock, Count, iv. 125-126; 132 et alibi.
Holmes, I. lxxxvi.
Holofernes, iv. 210.
Homer, ii. 55, 85 ; iii. 229 ; iv. 7, 101.
Honour, iii. 47.
Hope, iii. 89.
Horace, ii. 48.
Horror, i. 82 ; iii. 235.
Hume, iv. 276.
Hungary, i. 155.
Hunnes, , i. 190.
Hunnis, William I. xciii.
Hunter, I. xxvi.
Huth, I. c.

I.

Icarus, iii. 391.
Icalousie, iii. 28, 402.
India, i. 137, 204.

Inequality, i. 212 ; iv. 10.
Innocence, i. 171 ; iii. 325, 328.
I o, iii. 18.
Iob, iv. 271.
Ionian colonies, i 180.
Inquisitions, i. 196.
Isis, iii. 139.
Isocrates, i 213.
Irus, ii. 117.
Israel, i. 260, 262, 269, 277.
Ister, i. 170.
Italy, i. 82, 180, 224 ; iv. 85.
Iudith, iv. 210.
Ixion, iii. 42 ; iv. 242.

J.

Jacob and Esau, i. 266; ii. 124, 128.
James Ist., Five years of not by lord Brooke, I. xiii-xiv ; MS. of, I. xiv ; portrayed, I. l, movements of I. lx-lxi ; accession of I, lxxii ; warm friend to Lord Brooke, I. lxxiii-iv ; iv. 35.
James, Dr. I. lv.
Janus, i. 188.
Jason, i. 10.
Jesuits, iv. 26.
Jesus College, Cambridge, I. xxviii-ix.
Jethro, ii. 91.
Jonson, Ben I. xlii ; ii. 56 iv. 9.
Jove. i. 89, 90, 96, 135, 171 231.
Joy, true, iii. 37.
Julian, i. 226.
Julius, i. 226.

Juno, i. 9 ; iii. 18, 49, 62 ;
    iv. 285.
Jupiter, i. 7, 66, 133 ; iii. 62.
Justice, I. 7, 56, 65, 103,120,
    214, 220.

K.

Kennedy, Dr. I. xxvi.
Knackwood, I. li.
Keats, iv. 64.

L.

Lacedemon, i. 104,160, 180 :
    ii. 22.
Iactantius, i. 129.
Lais, ii. 93.
Lamb, II. xvi-xvii ; ii. 144 ;
    iv. xii.
Lambeth, MSS. I. lxiv, lxvi.
Lancaster, iv. 185.
Langbaine, I. xcvi ; ii. 155.
Languet, I. xxxiii.
Lansdowne MSS., I. lviii,
    lix, lx, lxi, lxii.
Laud, wrongly blamed, I.
    xii, xci.
Leda, iii. 39.
Legge, I. xxviii.
Leicester, I. xlix.
Leicester, earl of iv. 32,
    148 et alibi.
Lethe, iii. 158.
Leveson, Sir John, I. liv.
Lewis, xi. i. 159.
Lisle, viscount, I. xxiii-xxiv.
Livy, i. 172, 209, 224.
Lloyd, I. xxiv, xxvi, lxxxix.
Locrians, i. 93.
Lodge, II. lxxii.
Lok, Henry, I. lxxxvi-
    lxxxvii.

Love-self, iii. 22.
Lowe, I. lxxv.
Lucan, ii. 107.
Lucian, ii. 89.
Luctatius, i. 190.
Lust, iii. 26.
Luther, i. 82.
Lycaon, i. 32.
Lysander, i. 65.
Lycurgus, i. 93 ; ii. 84.

M.

Macedonicus, i. 124.
Macedonians, i. 61, 172.
Magellan, I. xxxiii.
Mahomet, I. 25, 79, 185, 223;
    ii. 109; iii. 136.
Mahomet (bassha) in Alaham
    iii. 166. (all through Ala-
    ham : not noted).
Malet, Michael i. 4.
Malice iii. 221 ; et seqq ; 378,
Malone, i. xii ; ii. 113.
Mamertines, i. 221.
Manicheans, iii. 116.
Marathon, i. 213.
Marcus, i. 226.
Marius, ii. 88.
Marlowe, I. xxv, 71.
Mars, i. 171, 172, 173, 188,
    190, 201 ; iii. 20, 396, 489.
    (note 260).
Mary, iv. 50.
Masanissa, i. 192.
Mauors, Mamers, ii. 107 ; iii.
    61, 73. (See also under
    Mars.)
Mausolus, ii. 68.
McDonald, Dr. ii, 70 ; cur-
    ious blunder of ii. 113.
Mecha, i. 185.
Melanthe, I. xxx.
Menædemus, ii. 20.

Mendoza, I. xlix ; iv. 36.
Menecrates, ii. 80.
Mercury, i. 135.
Merit and Worth, iv. 249.
Merlin, iii. 29, 30.
Metellus, ii. 84.
Midas, i. 8, 78, 160.
Milton, I. iii. xv, 73 ; II. vi. viii, xxvi ; ii. 9, 18 ; iii. 53, 100, 101 ; iii. 475 (note 140) iv. 59.
Mimus, ii. 113.
Minos, i. 7.
Minotaur, iii. 109.
Misfortune, iii. 460.
Mississippi, I. xxxii.
Momus, i. 96 ; ii. 113.
Moore, Thomas ii. xxv,
More, Henry, II. viii ix, x, xviii.
Morris, William I. 10.
Moscovite, iv. 86.
Moses, ii. 91.
Moss, Dr. I. xxvi.
Motley, I. xxxvii, xl, corrected I. xli.
Motte, la iv. 122.
Murder, iii. 336.
Muscovian, i. 147.
Myra, and Mira, I. xliii-iv ; iii. 15, 20, 21, 22 ; 27, 29 31, 32, 33, 35, 36, 38, 40, 41, et alibi. It seems needless to note the abounding occurrences of the name of Lord Brooke's lady-love in the Sonnets.
Myraphill, I. xliii ; iii. 85

N.

Naples, i. 126 ; iv. 100.
Narcissus, i. 8.

Nassau, Wm. of, prince of Orange, iv. 23 et seqq.
Naunton, I. xxxi ; character of Lord Brooke, by, I. lxx-lxxi.
Navarre, Henry of, iv. 35.
Naxians, i. 132.
Nemesis, ii. 37 ; iii 364.
Neptune, iii. 67, 341.
Nereids, i. 231.
Nero, i. 31, 45, 61, 95, 124.
Nestor, iv. 7.
Netherlanders, i. 149.
Netherlands, I. lxxviii.
Nevilles, i. xxii, xxix.
Newhaven, iv. 166.
Nicias, i. 212 ; iv. 283.
Nimrod, ii. 108.
Nombre de Dios, iv. 117.
Norris, Sir John, iv. 206.
Northumberland, John duke of, I. lvii.
Nothing, iii. 366.
Notingham, I. liv.
Nylus, i. 172.

O.

Obedience, iii. 319.
Occasion, i. 63, 365, 407.
Octauiua, iv. 281.
Olympus, i. 7, 34.
Omar, i. 224.
Omnipotence, i. 186 ; one, i. 242.
Opinion, iii. 102, 122, 123, 135, 460.
Orestes, i. 32.
Orion, i. 121.
Ormus, ghost of one of the kings of, iii. 156 et seqq.
Otho, i. 31, 59.
Ottoman, i. 114.

Ovid, i. 32, 207 : ii. 16, 107.
Oxford, earl of, I. x ; university of, i. xxxi : lord, ii. 144 ; university library, MS. iv. 301.

P.

Paeonius, ii. 93.
Poland, i. 82, 125, 126.
Palatinate, letter on, I. xv, lxxvii-lxxxii.
Pales, i. 154.
Pallas, i. 8, 133.
Pandora, i. 114.
Pantheus, i. 32.
Paris, i. 106.
Parnassus, i. 173.
Paul, St. i. 80, 264.
Paulet, iv. 185.
Pausanins, i. 114.
Pavley, John, I. xx.
Pawson, John, I. xx.
Peacham, I. lxix.
Peck, I. xcvi.
Peerson, Martin, I. xc.
Pelius, iii. 48.
Pembroke, earl of, iii. 145.
Pepys, iv. 228.
Perseus, i. 120, 124.
Persians, I. xxxv.
Pertinax, i. 60.
Peter, St. i. 80.
Peter's pence, i. 198.
Phædra, iv. 242.
Pharaoh, i. 262 ; ii. 91.
Pharos, i. 261.
Philautus, iv. 283.
Philip, I. xlix, 137 ; ii. 80.
Philip and Mary, iv. 50.
Phillips, *Theatrum Poetarum*, I. xiii, xxx ; II. vi.
Philocell, iii. 89.

Philopæmen, i. 191.
Phœbe, iv. 242.
Phœbus, i. 26, 159, 155 ; iii. 71, 74.
Phœnix Nest, ii. 143-144.
Phormio, iv. 153.
Phrygia, i. 78.
Piræus, i. 157.
Pittie, iii. 62, 87.
Pittie-selfe, iii. 15.
Place, iii. 99.
Plato, ii. 48,55, 85.
Pleasure, iii. 123.
Plutarch, i. 224 ; ii. 8, 48, 90 ; iii. 110.
Polacke, iv. 184.
Pollux and Castor, i. 18, 134.
Polyphemus, iv. 101.
Politeuphia, i. 129, 257.
Polybius, i. 221.
Pomona, i. 154.
Pomp, i. 199.
Pope, the, i. 255 ; iv. 167 *et frequenter*.
Pope (poet) II. xxx.
Power, i. 181, 182, 224, 271, 275 ; iii. 277.
Presence, iii. 53.
Pride, iii. 221 ; *et seqq.*
Priscus, i. 45.
Priuation, iii. 158.
Probability, iii. 135.
Procustes, i. 107 ; iii. 303.
Prometheus, i, 119.
Protection, i. 186.
Proteus, ii. 88.
Ptolomæus, i. 221.
Pulman, I. xcix.
Punick, war, i. 191, 221.
Purgatory, i. 198.
Pygmalion, ii. 16.
Pythagoras, iv. 190.

Q.

Quarles, Francis, II. lxvi, 113.
Quintin, St., iv. 50.

R.

Rage, iii. 187, 240-241, 357, 381, 402.
Raleigh, I. xxiv.
Ramage, Dr., I. xvi ; ii. 48.
Randolph, I. xxviii.
Rawley, Dr. I. lxviii, lxxxiv.
Rehoboam, i. 64
Reputation, I. 62, 68.
Rhadamanthus, i. 7.
Rhene, i. 189.
Rhodes, i. 170.
Rich Lady, IV. ix.
Rimbault, Dr., I. xvi; ii. 133.
Roderigo, i. 121.
Rogers, Samuel, II. xxv.
Romans, i 36, 112, 180, 181, 192, 204 ; ii. 96, 105.
Rome, I. lxxvii, 35, 82, 96, 100, 113, 123, 169, 170, 172, 180. 181, 188, 189, 208, 209, 210, 213, 214, 218, 219, 220. 223, 230, 270, 271 ; ii. 22, 117, 136 ; iv. 45 *et seqq* ; 285.
Rone, I. 105.
Rossa, dying speech of, iii. 410-414.
Rudyard, I. xxx ; iii. 145.
Rumor, iii. 45, 51, 59, 399.
Rutilius, ii. 284.

S.

Sabeans, i. 143.

Sabine, i. 219.
Sacharissa, iv. 2.
Salisbury, earl of 1. lx.
Salmoneus, i. 90.
Salomon, i. 62, 270 ; ii. 57.
Samos, i. 212.
Sampson, ii. 75.
Saracens, i. 142, 191, 219.
Sathan, iii. 26-27.
Saturn, i. 34.
Satyr, iii. 27, 124.
Savage, Richard, I. xv.
Saxony, duke of iv. 11.
Schneidewin, II. 90.
Scipio, i. 214 ; ii. 84.
Scirpalus, iv. 61.
Scoggin, iii. 57, 58.
Scott, Sir Walter, deplorable royalism of I. xci.
Scotland, i. 127.
Scythians, i. 190.
Seleucus, i. 93.
Sence, i 175, 232.
Seneca, i. 45 ; ii. 85, 86.
Seville, iv. 92.
Sextus Pompeius, iv. 61.
Shakespeare, the Cambridge characterized, I. iii-iv ; I. xxv, xciii ; i. 8, 20, 47, 73, 130, 163, II. xv, xxii, lxxviii ; ii. 8, 9, 11, 12, 18, 19, 25, 28, 34, 36, 39. 40, 46. 70, 74, 97, 98, 117, 128 ; iii. 8, 49, 51 ; IV. x, 10, 281.
Shame, iii. 87.
Shrewsbury, school at I. xxv.
Sibbes, ii. 25, 74 ; iii. 245.
Sicil, i. 132
Sidney, Life of Sir Philip : never before rightly put before the world, I. xi-

xii ; IV. v-xii ; Cambridge
MS of, IV. v, vii ; its purpose, IV. v, vi ; related
to Lord Brooke, I. xxiii-
iv ; lives of, I, xxiv;
contemporary, I. xxiv ;
letter of Sir Henry Sidney
to his son, I. xxvi *et seqq* ;
at school with Lord
Brooke, I. xxvii-xxviii;
(See under Brooke, Lord)
letter in favor of Lord
Brooke, I. xxxix ; at
tournament, I. xl ; marr-
iage, I. xlii ; death, I.
xlix ; will, 1. 1 ; Boston,
life of, II. x ; elegy on
death of, II. 143-147 ;
introductory Note to Life
of, IV. v-xii ; purpose
of 'Life', vi ; friendship
of, and Greville, and
Dyer, vi, 225-229; MS.
from John Harvey, Esq.,
vii-viii ; title-page of Life
of Sidney, xiii ; Epistle-
dedicatory, 1-3 ; past
memories, 5 ; retired
thoughts, 5, 6 ; " Defence
of Poesie ", 6 ; deep love
to, 7; blood, 7 - 9 ; Sir
Henry Sidney, 8 ; mother,
8, 9 ; remarkable youth,
9, 10 ; early gravity, 10 ;
Languet, 10-14 *et alibi* ;
letters of, 13 ; purposed
no book-monuments, 15 ;
teaching of Arcadia, 15
et seqq ; ordered destruc-
tion of, 20 ; might have
left noble books, 21 ; loved
by all, 21-22; testimonies
to greatness of, 23 *et seqq* ;

Prince of Orange, opinions
of, 25 *et seqq* ; earl of
Leicester, 32, 33 ; Sir
Francis Walsingham, 33-
34 ; James, I., 35 ; Henry
of Navarre, Don John of
Austria, 35-36 ; Mendoza,
36 ; a model of worth, 37;
renowned abroad, 37 ;
his example, 38 ; a true
Christian, 39 - 40 ; pre-
mature death, 40 : envy
of 41 ; never a magis-
trate or in great office, 42,
et seqq; yet a potential
life, 44 ; negotiator 45 *et
seqq ;* Germany, 45, *et
seqq ;* treaty, 47 ; marriage of Elizabeth, with
Duke of Aniou, negotia-
tions on 49 *et seqq ;* Phillip
50 *et seqq ;* change of Religion &c., 54 *et seqq ;* prophetic anticipations con-
cerning Holland or the
Netherlanders, 58 *et seqq ;*
(cf. iv. 228-229) : opposition to the marriage of Elizabeth, 63 : noble conduct
in relation to, 64 *et seqq ;*
quarrel with a nobleman,
[Earl of Oxford] 65 *et
seqq ;* bearing towards the
Queen, 69, 70 ; expedition
of Sir Francis Drake, 71
et seqq ; Lord Brooke,
associated with, 74 *et seqq ;*
interrupted by the Queen,
75 *et seqq ;* hitherto suppressed testimony to Drake,
77-78 ; estimate of Eng-
land, 79 *et seqq ;* survey
of 'forrain nations', 81

et seqq ; Henry the Third, Rome, Hanse towns, &c., &c. 81 *et seqq ;* Spain, 86 *et seqq ;* Holland's future, 88 *et seqq ;* war against Spain, 91 ; *et seqq ;* Elizabeth and Throgmorton &c., 94 *et seqq*; France, certain cities in, 97 *et seqq* ; Austria, 98 *et seqq*; alliance with France, 100 *et seqq* ; Venetians, 102 *et seqq* ; Italy 104 ; the Pope, 105 ; Elizabeth, 107-108 ; Peru and Mexico, 109 ; West Indies, 111 *et seqq* ; succession of Scottish kings, 112 ; Spain, 113 *et seqq* ; unbelieved Cassandra, 115; religion, 116 United Provinces, 117 ; enterprises abroad and associates, 118 *et seqq* ; voyage to America, 119 ; 'diverting' employment in the Low Countries, 121 *et seqq;* military experience, 121-122 *et seqq*; Gravelin, 122-123 ; Count Hollock, 125-126 ; Britaine Scipio, 128 ; Zutphen, death-wound, illness, conversations and death, 129 *et seqq*; (the 'poor soldier' and the bottle of water, 130;) groups around the death-bed and conversations, 136 *et seqq*; (*La cuisse rompue* 138) ; farewell, 140; Holland 142; *et seqq ;* final tribute, 145 ; Appendix to life of Sidney, 225 *et seqq ?* l astorall

by Sidney on himself and Greville, and Dyer, 225-28
Sidney, ii. Life of, by Lord Brooke, never before rightly put before the world, I. xi-xii ; related to Lord Brooke I. xxiii-iv ; lives of, I. xxiv ; contemporary, i. xxiv ; letter of Sir Henry to his son, I. xxvi *et seqq* ; at school, with Lord Brooke, xxvii - viii, (See under Brooke, Lord, letter in favour of Lord Brooke, I. xxxix ; at tournament, I. xl; marriage of, I. xliii. death, xlix ; will, l. 1. ' Boston' life of, II. x ;. elegy on death of, ii. 143-147
Sidney, Sir Henry I. xxv *et seqq*, xxxviii ; iv. 8
Sidney, Marie I. xxvi.
Signior, grand iv. 86.
Simon, i. 83.
Singer, ii. 18.
Sinon, iv. 122.
Siracuse, i. 212.
Sisyphus, iii. 158.
Smith, Richard, I. xcvi.
Smythe, iv. 2.
Socrates, ii. 90; iv. 7.
Solon, i. 93 ; ii. 84.
Solon's fooles ii. 90.
Sorrow, i. 270, 274; iii. 86, 371, 387.
Sotheby, I. x.
Southey, I. xi, 18, 22, 73, (*bis*) 96, 104, 107, 108, 116 118, 138, 157 160, 163 168, 179, 196, 203, 240 246, 247, 259, 262,

(*bis*) 266, 268, 271 ; esti-
mate of Lord Brooke, II.
xviii-xix ; error of, ii. 30,
42, 55, 94, 106.
Southwell,I. xlviii ; II. lxxi;
iii. 104, Dyer's Fancy
turned by, iii. 150-154.
Spain, I. lxxv-vii ; i. 82,
190, 191 ; iv. 45, 46, 86,
91 *et seqq. et alibi.*
Spartacus, i. 224.
Spedding, edition of Bacon,
I. lxiv *et alibi, passim :*
lxviii, lxix, lxx ; ii. 9).
Speed, John. I. lxxxv-vi.
Spelman, I lxxxvi.
Spencer Thomas, I. xix.
Spencer, 3d Lord, iv. 1.
Spenser, Edmund i. xxiv;
iii. 11.
Spenser, II. lxxiii.
Spicer, William I. liv.
Spirit, the i. 258, 266.
Stainton, Howard I. xxv.
Staunton, Howard I. xxv.
Steinhart, ii. 89.
Stygian, lake i. 65.
Subjection, i. 70.
Succession, iii. 168, 312, 323,
341, 349, 377, 433.
Suidas, ii. 68, 80.
Sultan, i. 80, 182, 190.
Sunderland, Countess of iv.
1-3.
Superstition, iii. 415.
Suspition, iii. 305.
Sussex, duke of iii. 290.
Sydney, Lady Dorothy, iv. 1.
Sydney, Algernon, iv. 1.
Sylla, ii. 88.
Syon, iii. 140-1.
Syria, i. 137 ; 143.
Syros, I. xxx.

Sysiphus. iv. 281.
Sytha = Scytha, ii. 9.
Sythia, i. 223.
Sweden, iv. 84.
Swiss, i. 41.
Switzer, iv. 85.

T.

Tacitus, ii. 107.
Tagus, iii. 66.
Tamerlane, i. 224.
Tanner, MSS. I. xv, lxxv,
lxxxiii.
Tanner, Robert ii. 9.
Tantalus, i. 66.
Tariff, i. 191.
Tarquin, i. 210, 219, 223.
Tartororum, chorus iii. 415
et seqq.
Taylor, Bp. Jeremy ii. 20.
Tereus, i. 32.
Tennyson, I. lxxxix ; II.
v-vi, xxvi.
Themistocles, ii. 84 ; iv. 129
Theopompus, i. 77.
Thermopylæ, i. 114.
Theseus, iii. 341.
Thessaly, i. 7.
Thetis, iii. 48.
Thief, the penitent i. 263.
Thomas, I. xix.
Thorpe, I. x.
Throgmorton, Sir Nicholas,
iv. 94.
Tiberius, i. 65.
Tillotson, iii. 496 (note 352).
Tolous, i. 105.
Trajan, i. 170, 173, 225.
Trinity College, Cambridge,
I. xxix.

Truth, i. 172 ; iii. 126.
Truth and Power i. 64, 66.
Tudors, i. xxv.
Turk, ii. 23, 127 ; iii. 117, 347.
Turkey, i. 148, 171, 203.
Turnbull, iii. 150.
Turnus, iv. 283.
Tusser, i. xvii.
Tyrannie, i. 182, 184-5, 200.
Tybris, i. 80.
Twins, i. 121.

U.

Ullyses, iv. 258.
Upupa, i, 32.

V.

Varney or Verney, I. xxiii.
Varney, Greuill, iv. 301-309.
Vaughan the Silurist, I. xc.
Velladoune, iii. 229.
Velleius, Paterculus, i. 210.
Venice, I. 1, 82, 137, 229.
Venus, i. 34, iii. 20, 6 1,82 ; iv. 285.
Vertue, i. 171, 173 ; iii. 324, 333, 334, 335, 444 ; iv. 7.
Vespasian,i. 59.
Vice, iii. 192.
Vincent, Captain St., iv. 172.
Vindex, i. 31.
Virgil. i. 207 ; ii. 86, 87 ; iv. 122.
Vitellius, i. 59.
Voltaline, I. lxxviii.
Vpnor, castle of, I. liii, liv.
Vossius, iv. 325.
Vulcan, i. 133 ; ii. 94 ; iii. 28, 61.

W.

Waddington, Dr., I. xvi.
Wales, I. xxxviii, court of Marches of, I. xxxix.
Waller, iii. 150 ; iv. 2.
Walpole, ii. xii
Walsingham, I. xxxix
Walsingham, Sir Francis, iv. 33-34, 147.
Ward, Knox, I. xix.
Warwick, earl of and Brooke, IV. x-xi. 333.
Warwick, Ambrose, earl of, Warwickshire, renowned son of, I. xxv ; worthies of, a poor book, I. lxxxviii.
Washbourne, Dr. I. xc.
Wechel, iv. 11.
Wedgnock Park, I. lvii, lix.
Westminster. iv. 187.
Westmoreland, earl of, I. xxii.
Whateley, i. 227.
William of Nassau, I xxxviii.
Willoughbys, I. xx, xxi.
Wilson, Arthur, false, I. lxxxiv-v.
Wilson, Alexander, II. lvii.
Wilson, Thomas, iv. 325.
Windsor, Lerd, I. xl.
Winstanley, I. xiii, xxx, xl.
Wisedome, i. 68 ; iii. 299.
Wither, II. lxvi, 113.
Wither, George, i. 63.
Wood, Anthony-a, I. xxiv, xxxi, xxxviii, lxxxv, lxxxvi, lxxxviii, xcvi.
Wordsworth, ii. xxvi.
Worth, i. 172, 176, 230 ; iii. 321 ; and Merit, iv. 249.

Worthiness, iii. 30 84.

Wraynham, I. lxxxiv ; iv. 313.

Wright, W. Aldis, M.A., I. iii-v. xii, xiii, xvi ; helpful throughout, I. iii, xv, xvi, xx, xxviii, xxix, xxxii, lxxxvi, 5, 70, 86, 137, ,176 232, 257 ; ii. 5, 8, 11, 15, 17, 18, 21, 36, 40, 55, 74, 76, 89, 92 ; iii. 497 ; IV. vii, 123, 211.

Wright, Thomas, i. 146 ; ii. 5.

Wrong, i. 67. 68.

X.

Xerxes, i. 148, 213.

Y.

Yelverton, Sir Henry, .I. lxxxiviv ; iv. 313.

Z.

Zeraphus, iii. 229.

Zorcaster, i. 93.

Zouch, IV. viii.

Zutphen, IV. ix. 229-230 (misprinted 'Zutpen', p. 229 title).

III. INDEX OF WORDS : NOTICEABLE AND RARE = GLOSSARIAL INDEX.

Throughout, *as a rule*, as before, we have not given grammatical forms of words. *i. e.* noun, adjective, verb, &c., are brought together. As in Fletcher and others, there will be found in this portion of the Indices excellent examples of now accepted words in their transitional state, and many, elucidative of Shakespeare and his contemporaries. In nearly every case the several references guide to explanations or illustrations, in the places. The 'various readings' from the Warwick MSS. given in Vol. IV. pp 344-388 being marked wherever noticeable with † may serve for Index thereto : but besides there will be found herein all those of special value and interest. G.

A.

Aborne, iii. 89,

Abbord, iv. 65.

Adamants, iii. 214 ; iv. 119.

Admires, ii. 99.

Aduow, iii. 233.

Aequilibrium, i. 53.

Affect, i. 10, 12, 36, 59, 88, 193, 206, 209, 232, 240, 241, 277 , ii. 79, 81, 83, 96, 114, 121 ; iii. 89, 296, 365, 411 ; iii. 465, (note 10) 484, (note 201).

Agast, iii. 380.

Age, 355-356 (No. 214.)

Alchoran, iii. 348, 387.

Alchymie, iii. 367.

Allay'd, i. 6, 58, 88, 130, 145, 256 ; ii. 17, 22, 35, 53.

Allayes, iv. 365 (No. 397.) ; alwayes = allayes.

Angel'd, iii. 415.

Annoynted, iii. 385, 387.

Apparence, i. 82 ; ii. 17 ; iv. 179.

Apparitions, i. 21 ; ii. 11 ; iii. 124.

Architectonical, iv. 21.

Aristocratie, iv. 84. 361, No. 290.

Artificial, i. 72 ; iv. 82 .

Artless, i. 39, 127 ; ii. 32 ; iii. 124.

Aspects, iii. 444.

Assassinate, i. 31.

Assiduous, i. 73, 184.

Assumpsit, iv. 163.

Aswell, i. 228.

At, iv. 351 ; No. 287.

Atomi, ii. 33, 59 ; iii. 100, 367.

Atomized, ii. 51.

Attone, i. 176.

B.

Babyes, iii. 74 ; iv. 266.

Baby-thoughts, iii. 100.
Backside, iii. 58.
Ballancing. iv. 90, 102.
Bands, iii. 381.
Banes, iv. 314.
Barbars, i. 54, 189.
Basshas, iii. 166, 312, 409,
(note 70), and all through
' Alaham' and ' Musta-
pha' : not noted.
Beam, ii. 76.
Bents, iii. 313.
Bide, i. 7,
Blaz'd, ii. 62.
Blaze. iv. 41.
Bodied, iii. 420.
Bootes, iii. 450.
Bot, iv. 75.
Bound, i. 17.
Boundlessenesse, ii. 51.
Breathed, long, i. 180.
Brickwall, iii. 368.
Bright, iii. 53,
Brook, i. 58, 158, 197 ; iii.
377.
Brookes, ii. 39.
Britaine, iv. 128.
Bruit, iii. 436.
But as, iv. 355 (No. 394).
But to know, iv. 367 (No.
418).

C.

Caddies, iii. 312, 388, 469
(note 70).
Cadmus-men, iii. 368.
Cage-birds, iii. 315).
Canker, iii. 303.
Cantonise, i. 41.
Capitolian, i. 26.
Carroach, i. 90.
Catapult, ii. 114.

Cavelling, iv. 54.
Cell-bred, iii. 347.
Censure, i. 37, 66, 95. 258 ; ii.
85 ; iii. 375, 391 ; iv. 248.
Ceraphin, iii. 45.
Champian, i. 190.
Chancelors, i, 7.
Chaos'd, ii. 27.
Characts, i. 174, ; iii. 11, 55 ;
iv. 116.
Charrets, ii. 96.
Charrev, ii. 96.
Checquer-gaine, iii.   273,
316, 470 (note 75).
Chimera's, ii. 26, 87.
Church, ii. 21.
Cinnons, iv. 111.
Citadellize, iv. 99.
Ciuillity, ii. 89.
Civility, i. 79, 179, 217 ; iii.
348.
Clip, iii. 49.
Coarse, iii. 29.
Commerce, i. 17.
Compasse, iii 75.
Competence, iii. 303, 357,
469 (note 663), 480 (note
184), iv, 142
Complexions, i. 121, 136,
154, 229 ; iii. 63, 395, 489,
(note 259).
Compositions, ii. 13.
Compremise, iii. 393, 489
(Note 258).
Conclude, iv. 67.
Concordinge, iv. 353 (note
164).
Confine, iv. 59.
Confuse, ii. 93.
Consist, i. 201 ; ii. 135.
Conversation, i. 5.
Contentation, ii. 48.
Convince, ii. 11.

Countermining, iii. 162.
Counterpane, ii. 35.
Counter-peaze, i. 50, 52, 71.
Couuters, ii. 91.
Corporation, i. 11.
Covert-baron. iv. 53.
Creation, iii 316 ; iv. 6.
Creature, iii. 376.
Creatures, i. 8.
Crased, ii. 52, 72.
Craz'd, i. 226.
Crests (= crustes), iii. 151 ;
    iv. 383, (No. 670).
Crustes, iv. 383 (note 670).
Cullour, iv. 347 (notes, 30
    and 42).
Curious, i. 12, 137, 187 ; ii.
    31, 100, 361, 426 ; iii. 50.

D.

Debilities, ii. 8, 12.
Deceipt, ii. 7, 23.
Declination, i. 13, 21, 42, 44,
    195, 271 ; ii. 18, 24, 28,
    30.
Deeping, iii. 191.
Defection, ii. 72.
Degeneration, iii. 127.
Degrees, i. 266.
Demission, i. 73.
Democrate, i. 144, 224 ; (iv.
    361 No. 290).
Denne, iii. 98.
Denizing, i. 165.
Deprave, ii. 74, 85,
Derive, i. 261.
Despaired, i. 44.
Devilly, iv. 116.
Devote, i. 183.
Diepe, iv. 213.
Dimme, ii. 27 : iv, 367, (No.
    401).

Dirge, iii. 451.
Discreation, i. 66 ; ii. 69,
    [revived by SWINBURNE
    in his noble poem on proc-
    lamation of the Republic
    in France, September,
    1870.]
Disease, i. 40, 183 ; ii. 49 ;
    iii. 331, 343, 473, (note
    118)
Disestimation, i. 25 ; ii. 74.
Disfashion, i. 98 ; iii. 351.
Disnature, ii. 74.
Dispeople, i. 182.
Disseason, i. 179.
Diverting, iv. 121.
Divisions, iv. 95.
Doing, iii. 361, 402.
Doom, i. 9, 65, 66, 93, 96,
    100, 123, 128, 147, 164,
    169, 190, 200, 201, 202,
    205, 220, 223, 240, 270 ; ii.
    59, 75, 99, 116, 117 ; iii.
    102, 124, 157, 166, 186,
    236, 282, 306, 308, 320,
    368, 391, 462 ; iv. 270.
Domination, ii. 91.
Doublet, iv. 224.
Downe, iv 381 (No. 589).
Duplicitie, iii. 366.

E.

Earth-eyd, iv. 55.
Eccho's, iii. 276.
Effeminatish, i. 188.
Ejulation, iv. 139.
Elench, ii. 21. 26.
Ell, elfe, 366 ; iv.
Elue, iv. 235.
Embase, i. 162.
Embedlam, iii. 204.
Embody, ii. 27 ; iii. 159.

Embrodered, iii. 401.
Enammell, iv. 282.
Enviless, i. 6.
Enwall, i. 91.
Equilibrium, ii. 119 ; iv. 107.
Erecting, i. 181.
Eternall, iv. 137.
Eterniz'd, iii. 416.
Excellently, iv 276.
Excentricks, i. 21.
Exchequer-men, iii. 121.
Exercises, iv. 5.
Exilde, iv. 357, (No. 228.)
Experiments, ii. 34.

F.

Factorage, i. 163.
Facts, iii. 440.
Fadome, ii. 6 ; iii. 85, 135, 340, 478 (note 169).
Faigned, iv. 6.
Fall, iv. 363, (No. 336).
Fame, iv. 359 (No. 285).
Fangledness, new i. 207.
Fantosmes, i. 39.
Fates, iv. 357 (No, 246) ; iv. 361 (No. 298).
Faultlessnesse iii. 465 (note 12)
Fear, they iv. 363, (No. 332)
Fere, ii. 142.
Finely i. 243.
Fleshe, iv. 363, (No. 349).
Fondly, i. 41 ; iii. 180, 355.
Forge-masters, ii. 107.
Forges, iii. 381.
Forme, iiii. 422.
Forked, three i. 232.
Forlorne, iv. 379 (No 557, and ibid p 372
Foster, iii. 60 ; cf. iv.
Foyle, iii 49, 221.

Freends, I. iii.
Froth, iii. 457.

G.

Gaining, i. 104.
Gastly, iv. 130.
Gaze, i. 197.
Ghesse, iii. 335.
Ghostly, i. 44.
Giddie, iii. 100, 466 (note 21).
Gilt, ii. 81 ; iii. 52, 208.
Glean, i. 70 ; iv, 349 (No. 92).
Gloss, i. 193 : See iv. 359 No. 252.
Godlesse, ii. 61.
Graunge, iii. 86.
Great, i. 39.
Guidon, iii. 376, 485 (note 213).
Guiltlesse, iii.`443, 445.
Gyves, i. 75.

H.

Hability, i. 124.
Halfe-fast. iii. 27, 79.
Hapt, iii. 88.
Hatche, iv. 12.
Haughture, iv, 36.
Heady, i. 222 ; iii. 400, 455, 490 (note 282).
Helme, iii. 428.
Heteroclite, i 226,
Heyre, iv. 373 (note 498.)
Hire, iii. 64 ; cf. iv. 373, note 498.
Hitherwards, iii. 455.
Horizons, wandring, iv. 150
Humorists, iii. 304.
Humourous, i. 130 ; iii. 304,

379, 469 (note 67) 486, (note 222).
Hyperboles, iii. 102.

I.

Idea's, ii. 33, 99 ; iii. 18.
Idols, ii, 20, 27.
Ieat, iii. 100.
Imbas'd, i. 23.
Imbound, iii. 230.
Imbrued, iii. 297, 466 (note 15).
Impart, iv. 120.
Impawn'd, iii. 395.
Imping, i. 36.
Imposthum'd. i. 203.
Imposture, line, ii. 26.
Incivility, i. 222.
Indefinite, i. 18, 221.
Indifferent, ii. 41 ; iv. 43.
Inequality, iv. 43.
Infancy, i. 254.
Infirmary, ii. 76.
Ingenuity, i. 7.
Ingenuous, i. 135, 152, 167 ; ii. 69.
Ingenuously, iv. 5, 8, 13, (and so frequently : but not further noted).
Inhabilitie, i. 189.
Inned, iv. 186.
Instrumentall, ii. 44 (not 'instruments all ').
Intend, i. 96.
Intented, v. 82.
Intents, iii. 330.
Interpoling, i. 146 = iv. 355 (No. 197).
Intromission, ii. 10.

J.

Jubiles, i. 75

K.

Kcies, iii. 329. 472 (note 107)·
Kingships, i. 198.
Knowledges, iii. 389.

L.

Labarinth, I. lxxviii ; ii. 67.
Lamiæ, iv. 64.
Leager, i. 163.
Legall, i. 162.
Letts, i. 257 ; ii. 140 ; iii. 15, 171, 218, 221, 337, 357, 475 (note 153) 493 (note 317.)
Level, i. 85, 235 ; ii. 37.
Life-forsaken, iii. 390.
Lightnesse, iii. 357.
List, i. 25, 186, 233 ; iii. 364, 484 (note 200.)
Liuerie, iii. 33.
Long-breathed, iv. 45.
Looking-glasse, iii. 71.
Loose, i. 22,
Loth'd, iv. 369 (note 457).
Lottarie, iii. 344.
Lurke, iii. 180, 462.
Lust, i. 158 ; ii. 58.

M.

Main, i. 47 ; iv. 97.
Man-nature, ii. 94.
Manumised, iv. 169.
Margents, iii. 317.
Marre-right, iii 259
Marshall, iv ; 349 (No 79.)
Martial, i. 61.
Mean, i. 16.
Mears, i. 169.
Meer, i. 211 ; ii. 34, 40.
Meeres, iv. 211.

434INDEX.

Merchantable, i. 83.
Merciless, i. 196.
Mercurists, iii. 73.
Metall, iv 255
Minute, i. 195, 201, 222, 233.
Misaduenture, iii. 429
Miscomplaints, iii. 357.
Misconster, iii 400.
Miscreating, i. 30.
Miscreating. iv 347, (No 34)
Misprision, i. 15, 233 ; ii. 12, 30 ; iii. 180.
Mistery, 219, 252, 265.
Mixt, i. 17 ; (See iv. 345, No. 15).
Module, iii. 13.
Moe, iv 242
Mon'ments, iii. 367, 484 (note 202.)
More, iv. 345, (No 18)
Mote, ii. 76 ; iii. 218.
Mouing, iii. 71.
Mountebanks, ii. 96.
Moyle, iv. 277
Muity, i. 89 ; iii. 309.
Munging, i. 261.
Murmur, iii. 328.
Murmure, i. 268.
Mussel-man, iii. 349.
Mutine, i. 121.
Mynde, iv. 347 ; (No 60.)

N.

Naught, i. 123 ; ii. 87.
Negars, i. 160.
Neighborless, ii. 42.
Neutralitie, iv. 111.
Nice, i. 86.
Nicenesse, ii. 28.
Nick't, i. 171.
Nimble i. 78, 104.

Not, iv. 369 (No 447
Nought, iv. 359 (No. 254).
Nurse-life, iii. 46.
Nurst, iv 363 (No. 355).

O.

Oare, ii. 118, 364 ; iv. 255, 355 (No. 189).
Odds, i. 230 ; iii. 331.
Officious, iii. 169.
Ominous, i. 127.
Omnious, iv. 14.
Or, iv. 361 ; (No 296).
Ore-peazes, i. 202.
O're-rack, i. 14.
Orizons, i. 110.
Ouer-built, i. 198, 270 ; ii. 20, 61, 118 ; iii. 216, 297.
Ouer-rake, iii. 394.
Overthrown, i. 335.
Overthwart, iii. 81, 122, 163.
Over-work, i. 263.
Owned, i. 241.

P.

Pædagogies, i. 170.
Pain and pains, i. 38, 67, 136, 181, 198.
Paine, ii. 103 ; iii. 72.
Painful, i. 85.
Painstaking, ii. 60.
Parallells, iii. 74.
Peaz'd, i. 10, 16, 30, 50, 54, 67, 113, 194, 230, 251 ; ii. 44 (not please), 90, 119 ; iii. 302, 469 (note 65), 470, (note 76) ; iv. 349 (No. 85).
Peece, i. 67, 193 ; iii. 44, 72, 175, 324 ; iv. 254.
Pensil, i. 83.

Pettie, iv. 383 (No. 643).
Phantasmes, ii. 11 ; iii. 390.
Phantom'd, iii. 252.
Pharos, iv. 383 (No. 670].
Phormios, iv. 153.
Policy, i. 230. ii. 72.
Polity, iv. 361 (No. 286).
Port, iii. 308.
Poyze, i. 38, 128; iii. 492 (note 310).
Practice, i. 109, 110, 195, 197, 229; iii. 351.
Practick, i. 72, 173.
Practise, ii, 20 ; iv. 123.
Preheminence, i. 119, 120; iv. 245, 297.
Preoccupately, ii. 10.
Preposterous, iii. 412.
Present's Time; iii. 299, 408, (note 47) ; iv. 384, No. 688.
President, iii. 201.
Prize, iv. 48.
Private, i. 153, 234.
Privateness, i. 181.
Probabile, ii. 22.
Prop-stage, iv. 357 (No. 220).
Puppy, iv. 67.
Pygmean, I. 11.
Pyramis, i. 9 ; iii. 249.

Q.

Quicke, iii. 268.

R.

Raines, i. 63, 230, 239 ; ii. 41, 106.
Ramas, iv. 118.
Ravening, i. 277 ; ii. 92.
Rauine, iii 229, 316.

Realm, ream, i. 70-71 99, 208.
Recorders, ii. 9
Reflect, iv. 365 (No. 391).
Regiment, iii. 161; iv. 189.
Regresse, ii. 34.
Remediless, i. 45 ; iii. 374.
Remission, i. 73.
Remorses, iv. 381 (No. 600).
Rendevous, iv. 37, 61.
Repercussions, i. 18.
Reservedness, iv. 25.
Reuenges, iii. 342.
Reyne, iii. 388.
Rightfulness, i 269.
Rites, iv. 345 (see iv. 344, No. 17 and No. 104).
Romanties, iv. 15.
Rome, iv. 179.
Rote, iv. 351 (No. 141).
Rounds, i. 28 ; ii 19
Roul'd, i 235.
Roytelets, iv. 96.
Rust iv. 303 (No. 642).
Ruth, iii. 324.

S.

Saws, ii. 46, 122; iii. 347, 350.
Satyr, ii. 113; iii. 478 (note 167)
Science, ii. 15.
Science-monger, ii. 16.
Scientiall, scientificall, ii. 14; Scientiall, iv. 365 (No 395).
Seate, ii. 297, 466 (note 22).
Seamarks, i. 102, 250; iii 51.
Seele, iii. 296; iii. 465 (note 6) 474 (note 139)
Scene, ii. 80.

Selfness i 9, 11, 52, 74, 96, 176 ; ii. 61, 72; iii. 319, 384
Sepulture, iv. 214.
Sergeant, ii. 105.
Seraglia, iii. 346 ; iv. 86.
Ser'd, iii. 241.
Serens, iii. 335, 475 (note 140.
Seruing-rooms, iii. 78.
Sharp'd, iii. 358.
She-David, iv 165.
Sillinesse, iii. 162.
Simplicitie, iii. 84.
Sinne, ii. 39.
Sinews, i. 105
Sinnowes, iii. 422.
Sire, iii. 349
Slack, i. 194
Slake iv. 357 (No. 256)
Slight, i. 10, 22; iii. 300, 468 (note 53.)
Sleights, iii. 232, 300, 320,
Sleeues, ii. 8; iv. 93. 330, 470, (note 77)
Smart, ii. 34.
Sometimes, iii 245.
Sonn, iii 8.
Sower-eyed, iv. 15.
Specious, i. 183
Spungie, iii. 209.
Stale, iii. 101, 304, 469 (note 68)
Standard, iv. 213.
Statuminate, iv. 9.
Stayed, I. v.
Starke, iii. 322.
Steepe, iii. 323.
Stepmother, iii. 330.
Still'd, i. 115.
Strifes, ii. 56.
Studious, ii. 86.

Stuff. i. 71, 156.
Subaltern, iii. 3, 388; iv. 16.
Subalternate, i. 127, 138, 231.
Subalterness, i. 129
Suffique, iv. 57.
Super-Jesuited, iv. 95.
Supersedeas, iv. 218
Sun-rising = heir, iii 306, 469, (note 69).
Swarue, ii. 57, 89.

T.

Table, iii. 416.
Taxe iii. 349.
Tedious, i 28
Thee, iv. 373 (No. 494).
Their, iv. 361 (No. 295).
Then, i. 53, 58, 78, 207 and frequently throughout.
Theorick, i. 86 ; ii. 50.
Thought-bound, iii. 69.
Thrall, ii. 60.
Throw, iii. 50.
Throws, i. 257.
Thus, iv. 363, (No. 327)
Tickle and tickely, iii. 169,
Time, ii. 45.
Tincture, ii. 70; iii. 315, 470 (note 71) ; iv. 8.
To, iv. 361 (No. 293).
Tones, iv. 365 (No. 390). 201.
Touch, iii. 320.
Toys, i. 141, 218; iii. 49, 100, 226, 385 ; iv. 145.
Traduced, ii. 21 ; iii. 359, 481 (note 189).
Trance, I. 209 (see iv. 359, No. 283).
Trancendence, i. 77.

Transcrib'd, i. 23.
Trauells, iii 48.
Travailetᴜ ,ii. 115.
Travel, i. 54, 262.
Traverses, iv. 19.
Treatie, ii. 5, 100.
Treits, iv. 21.
Tropheas, ii. 15, 126; iii. 364, 366, 397.
Truthless, i. 68.
Trypode, i. 26.
Tun, iv. 14

U.

Ubiquity, ii. 45.
Unactive, i. 21, 37, 49; iii, 103.
Unactiveness, i. 38.
Uncase, ii. 98,
Uncompetible, iii. 199.
Uncorrupt, i, 51.
Undermining, iii. 325.
Undependent, i. 25.
Undertaking, i. 230.
Undertakinge, iv. 77.
Unexperienced, i. 50.
Unglorious, iii. 266.
Uniform'd, iii. 432
Unjudicially, iv, 174.
Unmeasurable, iv 271
Unmiracled, iii. 388.
Unnaturiᴅg, ii, 74.
Unnobly, iii. 208.
Unoffending, i. 45.
Unordinate, ii. 86.
Unperfect, i. 18, 99; iii. 244 309.
Unpossible, ii. 106, 199.
Unproper, iv. 263.
Unremovable, iv. 245.
Unresolute, iii. 223.
Unvizarding, iv. 101.

Unwrest, i. 29; iv 347 (No. 33).
Us, iv. 367 (No. 431)
Unsensible, iv. 28.

V.

Vagabond, iii. 393
Varnish, i. 182.
Vayl'd, ii, 40.
Veil, i. 67,
Venime, ii. 120 ; iv. 245.
Vents, i. 61.
Vice-vicissitudes, i. 37.
Vilde, iii. 440, 490 note 279).

W .

Ware, i. 164.
Warre = ware, ii. 59 (remove , after it here)
Was, iii. 267.
Wast-coat, iv. 24.
Waving, i 46, 106, 126, 275; ii. 25, 128 ; iii. 397 ; iv 96, 2, 6
Weakenesse, ii. 41; cf. iv.
Weakeness, iv. 371 (No. 477).
Weld, i. 24, 77 ; iii. 297, 466 (note 25)
What, i. 245 ; ii. 73 ; iv. 363 (No. 328) ; iv. 357 (No. 428)
Wheeles, iii. 422.
Whit, iii. 218 (misprinted ' wit') .
Windows, iii. 160.

* Probably = eyes and so ways of escape, mediums for observation. G.

Winding-sheet, iii. 377.
Wisdome-monger, ii. 20.
W is, i. 25.

Wit and witty, i. 86, 188, 192, 196, 342, 244; ii. 8, 17; iii. 129, 348; iv. 8, 268.

Withall, ii. 17.

Woe. i. 27.

Wombed, i. 50.

Word, i. 182 ; ii. 40.

Worth v wrath, iii, 107; cf. iv.

Wrests, i. 20, 28, 108, 188, over i. 231 ; iii. 324, 472, (Note 95).

Y.

Yeomandry, iv. 189.

Yet, iv. 365 (No. 396).

Z.

Zecchins, iv. 212

C. TIPLADY & SON, PRINTERS, CHURCH STREET, BLACKBURN.

Errata

The Editor requests that the following 'escapes' be corrected : certain others of less moment are marked with an asterisk [*] in the Description of the MSS. at Warwick Castle, in the present Volume.

Vol. I.

Page 40th, st. 97th, line 1st, for ' While ' read ' Which '.
,, 42nd, st. 103d, line 4th, for ' blaze ' read ' burne '.
,, 70th, st. 180th, line 6th, for ' legal ' read ' regal '.
,, 95th, st. 248th, is inadvertently numbered ' 247 '.
,, 117th, st. 318th, line 2nd, for ' Some ' read ' Since '.
,, 134th, st. 369th, line 5th, for ' The ' read ' That '.
,, 150th, st. 415th, line 3rd, for ' induce ' read ' to induce '.
,, 205th, misprinted 250.
,, 226th, st. 638th, ' be ' inadvertently dropped before ' the '.
,, 233rd, st. 658th, line 1st, ' men ' vexatiously dropped out before ' fall '.
,, 254th, st. 44th, line 3rd, read ' newe .. thence' for ' poor..then '.
,, 277th, st. 111th, line 6th, read ' reserv'd ' for ' pre-serv'd '.

Vol. II.

,, 5th, st. 8th, mis-numbered ' 1 ', and st. 11th, mis-printed ' 81 '.
,, 37th, st. 84th, misprinted ' 85 ', and so to my great annoyance the numbers run on to 152—the more annoying to me in that it has happened while correcting a like mis-numbering of the folio at st. 90. There are 151 not 152 stanzas after all : but I (necessarily) adhere to our (mis)numbering in these Notes in their places.
,, 44th, st. 103rd, line 1st, for ' their instruments all ', read ' these instrumentall following '.

Vol. III.

., 32nd, line 2nd, for ' and ' read ' hee '.
,, 35th, line 1st, misprinted ' 53 '.
,, 42nd, line 10th, read ' him ' for ' his '.

„   44th, line 1st, read ' for ' not ' or '.
„   49th, line 6th, read ' to my Iuno '.
„   82nd, line 11th, of Sonnet lxx, read ' figures ' for
     ' shadowes ' an inexplicable substitution by us.
„   97th, line 6th, of Sonnet lxxvii, ' all ' mis-inserted.
„   410th, line 10th, read ' even' for ' then '.
„   414th, line 5th, read ' languish' for ' anguish'.

Vol. IV.

Any oversights, so far as noticed in a final revision,
are so trivial as not to be worth record, being self-
corrective, save ' shreeves ' misprinted ' sheeves ' = sheriffs,
page 353, No. 150.